Buy, Sell and Move House

Home Information Packs

The Housing Act 2004 will lead to major changes to the way we buy and sell houses. The Act introduces Home Information Packs (HIP's) which will become compulsory from 2007.

Which? campaigned for HIP's because we believe home-movers will benefit from more detailed information on the properties they buy and sell, and therefore prevent millions of pounds being wasted in failed transactions.

Home information packs will apply to most residential property sales of homes marketed for owner occupation and the pack is likely to contain documents and information such as the terms of sale; evidence of title; replies to standard searches and the home condition report – which reports on the physical condition of the property including an energy efficiency assessment. See page 144 for further details.

Acknowledgements

The publishers would like to thank the following for their help in the preparation of this edition: Charlotte Ali, Andrea Baron, Paul Butt, Teresa Fritz, Melanie Green, Michael Haley, Emma Harrison, Linsey Lewin, Mike Naylor, Janine Paterson.

Buy, Sell and Move House

Which? Books are commissioned by
Consumers' Association and published by
Which? Ltd, 2 Marylebone Road, London NW1 4DF
Email address: books@which.co.uk

Based on *Which? Way to Buy, Sell and Move House* (Consumers'
Association), first published in August 1987, text completely revised
and new material written by Alison Barr (1993). Diane Campbell is the
author of Chapter 13.

First edition October 1993
Seventh edition April 2004
Reprinted April 2005

Copyright © 1993, 1997, 1998, 1999, 2000, 2002, 2004 Which? Ltd

British Library Cataloguing-in-Publication Data
A catalogue record for *Buy, Sell and Move House* is available from the
British Library

ISBN 0 85202 975 6

Editorial and production: Alethea Doran, Robert Gray, Mary Sunderland
Index: Marie Lorimer
Original cover concept by Sarah Harmer
Cover photograph by Sarah Jones (Debut Art)/getty images

Typeset by Saxon Graphics Ltd, Derby
Printed in Great Britain by Creative Print and Design, Wales

Contents

	Introduction	7
1	A bird's-eye view of house-buying	9
2	Costs and expenses of moving	20
3	Finding a home	30
4	Agreeing terms	72
5	Carrying out work on your new house	97
6	The mortgage	113
7	Finding a buyer for your house	144
8	Countdown to the move	177
9	Moving house	196
10	Conveyancing	232
11	Doing your own conveyancing	258
12	Auctions	268
13	Buying and selling in Scotland	274
	Epilogue	294
	Glossary	295
	Addresses★	300
	Index	308

★ An asterisk next to the name of an organisation in the text indicates that the address can be found in this section

Introduction

After years of debates, consultations and some bad-tempered exchanges between the government and estate agents, a decision has been made which will change forever the way people buy and sell homes in England and Wales.

Home Information Packs (HIPs) will become mandatory in January 2007. From then on, nothing will be the same. No longer will buyers be in the position of having to make an offer on the most expensive purchase of their lives on the basis of no more than a cursory viewing, and then needing to embark on a tedious and expensive exercise to find out more about what they may be buying. No longer will an estimated million pounds go down the drain every day as one in three offers comes to nothing.

The government announced its intention to go ahead with the HIPs in February 2004, bolstered by research from Which?. This research found that 82 per cent of buyers would find HIPs very useful. Which?'s staunch support helped the government resist vociferous opposition from estate agents, some of the legal profession and some MPs.

Under the new rules, sellers will have to produce a package containing title documents, replies to standard enquiries, copies of all planning, listed building and Building Regulation consents, a draft contract, local authority searches and a standard Home Condition Report (HCR).

For leasehold flats, the pack will also contain a copy of the lease, the most recent service charge accounts and receipts, details of buildings insurance and information about the landlord/management company. For new properties, the pack will contain copies of warranties and guarantees. This and future editions of *Buy, Sell and Move House* will prepare readers for the forthcoming changes and their implications.

In the shorter term, following another Which? campaign, action to curb the worst practices of estate agents may be on the way. Voluntary regulation, in the form of the Ombudsman for Estate Agents scheme, is not working because only a third of agents are part of the scheme. The worst offenders tend not to belong and so cannot be controlled. Which? has campaigned for membership of the scheme to be made compulsory, and hopes that the Office of Fair Trading will make this a key recommendation of its report into estate agency, due at the time of writing.

This would be a welcome first step and, it is hoped, one that might lead to the robust training, monitoring and sanctions regimes that Which? recommends to ensure that the industry is adequately policed. However, at present the signs are that the OFT will steer clear of introducing firm consumer protection measures. Whatever the result, the Which? website *www.which.co.uk* contains a standard agency contract that will help readers avoid the pitfalls of contracts from rogue estate agents containing unfair terms and clauses.

HIPs and estate agent horror stories may, in the coming year, take over from house prices as the main topic of property-related chat, as stability in the housing market may at last have arrived. Not even the most pessimistic of analysts think that any kind of price crash is on the way, and the consensus is that prices will rise or fall by no more than low single figures over the next few years.

It is also agreed by most experts that prices in the north of England and Wales, which rose by around 20 per cent in 2003, will continue to grow faster than London prices, where, according to government statistics, they rose by less than 4 per cent last year. However, this is not really good news: it has caused the crisis for first-time buyers, and key workers in particular, to ripple out of London and the south-east, and this now affects half of all the UK's major towns.

Homes in 496 provincial centres are now unaffordable for nurses; 400 are too expensive for police officers, and 390 are out of reach for teachers. In 2003 alone, six regions from the Midlands southwards became unaffordable to key workers when average prices rose above four times average earnings.

The problems affect tens of thousands of young people, and the various much-heralded government initiatives are incapable of helping more than a tiny minority. Stable house prices for a decade may not be a sexy concept, but it is absolutely vital to all our futures.

Mira Bar-Hillel, Property and Planning correspondent, London *Evening Standard* (See *www.mirasmailbag.co.uk*)

February 2004

Chapter 1

A bird's-eye view of house-buying

It sounds simple: you live in one house, you decide to sell it and move to another. Easy. Just sign a few pieces of paper, book a van and away you go. Unfortunately, it is seldom like that.

Moving house, especially when a new mortgage is needed, is a highly stressful event, for several reasons:

- the sheer physical upheaval of packing, throwing out and making ready for the move, followed by the unpacking, rearranging – and regrets that so many things have had to be thrown out
- the emotional attachments that develop with the activity of house selection. People do fall in love with houses – and go through withdrawal symptoms if they are let down
- the legwork needed: dealing with estate agents, lenders, removal men, solicitors, not to mention all the public utilities and remembering to notify everyone in your address book of your move
- the stress of the legal process. Many attempts have been made to simplify it, so far to no avail.

And yet, it can be done. In reality, although the experience is rarely as traumatic as that of the Greens (see box overleaf), few people manage it as painlessly as Mr and Mrs White. None the less, the experiences of the Whites are far more common than those of the Greens.

You, the house-buyer, have much more control over the situation than you may believe. This book should help you to keep that control and avoid unnecessary expense.

Why move?

People may move because of a change of job or a re-location with the job. Or a change in family circumstances may bring a need for more space – or for less.

A home may have become too big after the family has grown up and left, or after the loss of a husband or wife. It may have become too expensive to run because financial circumstances have changed. When children are on the way or where the financial situation in a family has improved, a couple may decide to move into a better house to obtain more accommodation, to improve their standard of living or be near good schools. When the property market is buoyant, a house may also be regarded as an investment, but the experiences of the end of the 1980s and beginning of the 1990s have shown that property may decrease in value as well as increase. It is probably safer to regard a house as a home, rather than an investment.

Mr and Mrs Green decided to move to a larger house. They quickly found the house they wanted to buy and put in an offer, which was accepted. They also found a buyer for their own house. After they had been involved in the transaction for many weeks they were told by the seller that he had received an offer of £5,000 more for the house. He would be happy to sell to the Greens, but only if they matched the offer. Reluctantly, they agreed.

A few days later the Greens' own buyer was on the point of exchange of contracts when she informed the Greens that 'because of an adverse survey report' she would only proceed if they reduced their price by £5,000.

Later still, the Greens were told by their solicitor that their seller had now decided to call for a contract race and he would sell to the first person who signed the contract and deposited it with the seller's solicitors.

Unfortunately, the Greens were pipped at the post by a matter of only two hours, so they had to start house-hunting again.

Next time they were luckier, but their own buyer insisted on a further reduction in the price 'because of the delay'. However, contracts were eventually exchanged, with completion due to take place three weeks later.

Retirement, or the period just beforehand, is, of course, often the time to decide to move into accommodation suitable for older age – perhaps a flat or a bungalow. A move may be unavoidable for those living in 'tied' accommodation.

Whatever the reason for the move, it may provide the opportunity to make an additional change – by switching from town to country living, or *vice versa*. Before making the choice, any cost of living differences between one part of the country and another – for example, the higher cost of living in the Home Counties – should be considered, and also any climatic differences, particularly between south and north.

For many, the thought of living in the country may seem idyllic, but the seaside village that looked so idyllic during the summer holiday may resemble a bleak graveyard out of season. Some of the very things which lent charm – peace, quiet, lack of bustle – can also be disadvantages: the level of many services is much lower in the country than in the town.

Two days after exchange of contracts, the seller died. The contract was still valid, but completion was held up for several weeks while the technicalities were sorted out. In the meantime, the Greens' buyer made a claim for compensation for the delay in completing.

Feeling much older, and with numerous grey hairs, Mr and Mrs Green moved into their new house and prepared for their first relaxing moment in several weeks. Their peace was broken almost immediately by the postman, who was delivering a recorded delivery letter informing them that road-widening work was shortly to begin in their new front garden.

Mr Green picked up the telephone to get in touch with his solicitor . . . the number was unobtainable.

At the same time, in another part of the country, Mr and Mrs White had just waved goodbye to their removal men. They had moved into their new home just under two months after they had first decided to get a larger house.

Everything had gone smoothly from start to finish and the greatest problem they faced, as they looked out of the window of their new living-room, was that the lawn needed cutting.

Living in the country

There are reasons for and against living in the country.

For

- Environment: the natural beauty of the countryside; facilities for walking and other outdoor activities; fresher unpolluted air; no overcrowding; usually quieter than town living.
- Housing: often more land with the house; more garden space with safer play areas for children; the chance to grow your own food; often more bungalow housing available; suitable for retired people; insurance rates are lower for burglary cover, and for motor insurance; seldom problems over parking.
- Services: it is possible to use coal or wood as alternative heating fuel (there are seldom smoke-control restrictions), perhaps cheap wood supplies are available.
- Social life: the pace of living is slower than in town; more personal contact with neighbours; easy involvement in local activities.

Against

- Environment: areas may be inhospitable in winter – fog, wind, cold; roads are often not salted or cleared of snow quickly; smells from nearby farms are not always agreeable and can be unpleasant in hot weather; the country is not necessarily always quiet (aircraft flight paths?); holiday areas may attract an influx of summer visitors.
- Housing: not as wide a choice; free-standing houses in exposed positions are costly to heat; you may have to buy more land than you wanted; if in the 'green belt' area, planning permission may be restricted.
- Services: there may be no mains gas laid on (making it necessary to rely on electricity or oil); there may be no mains drainage but, instead, a septic tank or cesspool (emptying required); in many places, there is no (or poor) street lighting; public transport may be sparse (or non-existent) for getting to work, shops, schools; difficulties in wintry conditions; might need a second car for the family; the doctor, baby clinic, hospital, chemist may all be some distance away; health visitors or district nurses may be in short supply; schools may be limited in number and type, nursery schools few or non-existent; adult classes and library facilities may be far away; choice for shopping may be

poor, village shop(s) within walking distance, if any survive, may be expensive and have a small range of goods.

- Social life: lack of choice (you have to get on with neighbours and be prepared to join in local community activities); it may take time to get accepted in a village community; public entertainments and sports facilities are limited; there may be fewer neighbouring children for yours to play with; guests will need transport (yours or theirs) to visit.

Living in a town or city

For
- Housing: there is usually more choice of neighbourhoods and houses; more flats are available; some savings on heating costs may be possible (terraced or semi-detached houses and flats keep each other warm).
- Services: more public transport, health care and school facilities are available; shopping is more convenient, with more choice; there may be more facilities for older people (sheltered housing, local welfare and social clubs); visiting is easier.
- Social life: closer proximity of neighbours can be useful in times of emergency; children may benefit from nearby children to play with; more entertainments, sports and recreations will be available.

Against
- Environment: close proximity of neighbours may mean a lack of privacy – your house or garden may be overlooked; the pace of living is likely to be faster; the hustle and bustle and the pressure of people will be greater; there are traffic or factory noise and smells; your clothes and home are likely to need more cleaning because of traffic or industrial pollution; parking may be difficult and more expensive.
- Housing: prices are higher; you may have to accept a smaller house and a small (or no) garden; there may be no garage; play-space for children may be restricted or non-existent; insurance rates for burglary cover are more expensive (or unobtainable); motor insurance may be dearer.
- Services: health and welfare services may be overstretched, particularly in holiday or retirement resorts. Inner-city schools may have more discipline problems.

- Social life: it is easy to feel isolated in a large city; friends may not be immediate neighbours but may have to be made through your job or hobby, or school (school friends often bring parents together).

What kind of accommodation?

If you are considering living in a different kind of home, weigh up carefully the new factors involved. You may have been living in a rented flat and are to become the owner of a house, perhaps with a garden, for the first time. Or the change may be from a large house with its responsibilities into a small flat with lesser ones.

From flat to house

Moving to larger accommodation can mean additional expenditure for more furniture, carpets and curtains. Heating costs are likely to be higher. If there is a garden, there will be the expense of tools and plants, and the added cost and time required for its maintenance.

A householder changing from a flat to a house must be prepared to accept a greater degree of personal responsibility for the property and be prepared to devote a considerable amount of time to it: roof and gutters, fences and walls, plumbing and drains have to be kept in good repair. But you can choose when and how to get repairs done, and stagger the outlay.

In a flat, insurance for the building was probably not your personal responsibility but rather the responsibility of the landlord or management company (you would have paid a service or maintenance fee). In your own house, it is up to you to take out the insurance for damage to or destruction of the building (as well as any insurance you may want for the contents). If you have a mortgage, the building society or bank may arrange the insurance or, for a small administrative fee, you may be allowed to arrange your own, subject to their approval.

Having a house may mean having a garage for the first time, which can be a big advantage – not only for housing the car, but space for storage, e.g. for your freezer, tools or workbench.

Although a family may find that, with more space, they have better facilities, these will be on more than one floor and they may find this physically more demanding, particularly at first. Various household activities will have to be re-organised and housework re-planned to avoid unnecessary numbers of journeys up and down stairs. If there are small children, it may be less easy to keep an eye on them. Stairs can be a source of injury.

A house can give more privacy and, within reason, permit more noisy activities without the worry of disturbing close neighbours. A piano or a highly amplifying sound system may be possible for the first time – and so may a Great Dane or other large pet.

Changing in size or type

When moving into a bigger house you should budget for more expenses. Perhaps more or new furniture and appliances will be needed, more curtaining and floor coverings, followed by higher running costs in the future. If moving to a smaller place, there may be large items to dispose of and smaller (and perhaps more expensive) replacements to buy.

When considering a larger property, bear in mind that the buildings insurance is likely to be higher. You have to insure for the cost of re-building and this is calculated by taking a figure based on building costs per square foot and multiplying this by the area of the building. For a thatched house, the insurance premium may be as much as four times more (though some companies have special packages for this kind of house).

A bungalow is sensible for older people because there are no stairs to climb and it can be run easily and with less risk of accidents. But a bungalow has to be maintained – it may have a greater roof area, and often has a garden. And a lifetime of 'going up to bed' can inhibit some people from sleeping easily on the ground floor.

If the reason for moving is simply to gain more space, consider extending your present house. Moving is expensive and an extension may be less costly, though the cost of an extension is rarely fully reflected in the increased value of the house. If you are looking for less space, think of converting your house into two flats – or even taking in lodgers.

Changing style

Try to anticipate what changes the move may bring in the pattern of your daily life and outgoings, both immediately and in the long term.

Aspects that might be affected include:

- mortgage – monthly payments may be higher/lower (you may previously have been paying a weekly or monthly rent)
- life-insurance premiums – perhaps payable now on an endowment or mortgage protection life insurance policy
- council tax and water charges – may be higher if you move to a larger house or to a different authority's area
- house contents insurance – premiums will increase if you move to larger premises or to a more burglar-prone area
- fuel consumption and costs – may be different (you may spend more/less on electricity, more/less on gas; or use oil instead of solid fuel or *vice versa*)
- telephone bill – your bill may be higher/lower if more/fewer calls are within local range (it may be a big one for the period of the move, anyway)
- daily travel – there may be a change in the easiest method of getting to work/schools/social or cultural activities (more by car, less by public transport or *vice versa*)
- car – a second car (or none) may be needed; a garage may be needed; your insurance premium may be higher/lower
- daily timetable – you may get home earlier/later; or have to get up earlier (dark in winter); there may be more/less housework; opportunities may be expanded/restricted for part-time or voluntary work
- neighbours – adjustment to new neighbours (more or fewer, different ages) will be needed; your accessibility to friends and/or family may change, resulting in more or fewer visitors
- clothing – a different category of clothes and footwear may be required if moving from town to country or *vice versa*
- upkeep of property – there may be more maintenance and redecorating (higher ceilings, more woodwork, windows, doors to paint)
- garden (perhaps for the first time) – you may want to alter the layout and/or contents; bear in mind the cost of re-stocking, upkeep of a fence or hedge, walls or other boundaries; you may need to resurface paths or driveways; tree care may be an added job.

None of these items needs be a deterrent to moving to the place you want to go to. But you may have to adjust your priorities.

Finding a solicitor or licensed conveyancer

It is sensible to decide at an early stage who is to do the mechanics of the legal side of buying or selling. The choice between a solicitor and licensed conveyancer may be very much a matter of personal preference. Both should be able to provide a full house-buying service and carry out the basic legal work for you. The best ones will also give you guidance and support, and act as a forceful intermediary if things go wrong.

Licensed conveyancers are required to operate the same safeguards to protect the public as solicitors, and there may be little to choose on price, particularly as solicitors' charges were considerably reduced in the early 1990s. Licensed conveyancers are able to offer a highly specialised service but one which is limited to house-buying transactions. There are also far fewer licensed conveyancers than there are solicitors.

Coping with legal jargon

'WHEREAS the said Albert Jones is seised of the property hereinbefore described AND WHEREAS the parties hereto have hereunto agreed for the sale of the said property to the purchaser for an estate in fee simple subject as hereinafter mentioned but otherwise free from encumbrances NOW THIS DEED WITNESSETH as follows . . .'

The language of lawyers is seen by many as a quaint and at times irritating archaism. The truth of the matter is that lawyers, like most trained professionals, have their own technical language. The difference is that lawyers (as opposed to, say, mathematicians or scientists) have to communicate their thoughts to ordinary people who do not have legal training. It is widely felt that many lawyers are not very good at this. Chapter 10 looks at the legal side of buying and selling a house, and at the end of this book there is a glossary which will help to guide you through the maze.

What should you do if you are confronted with legal jargon you do not understand? The answer is that you should ask – and keep asking – till you have had it explained properly to you. Solicitors and licensed conveyancers have a duty to make sure that their clients understand fully the obligations they are taking on in house-buying or -selling. Do not hesitate to demand full explanations in plain English.

Organising your work

House-buying is the biggest financial commitment in most people's lives. Even if you are not attempting to sell the house or carry out the legal procedures yourself, there is a lot to remember. You will find that things go much better if you are well organised.

- Put everything in a file: you will generate a large amount of paper. (Solicitors attach correspondence to a green treasury tag, which automatically keeps it in date order.) The file will help you to keep control and will act as a permanent record of your house purchase or sale. File a copy of every letter you send. You should also make a note of the details of every conversation: '28 January – spoke to seller. Decided not to buy the house in Turner Road after all.'
- Record financial details: you will be dealing with (directly or indirectly) large sums of money. At the front of your file keep a note of all the money you spend.
- Give yourself enough time: you may need time off work, depending on the pressures and time available. You should not rush.
- Have access to typing/photocopying/telephone facilities: you will need to make photocopies and be available by telephone. If you need to be contacted at work, make sure you clear it with your employer. Sometimes a fax or email saves a lot of time. If you do not have access to a fax machine, make arrangements with a local fax bureau – both to send and receive faxes.
- Typed letters and documents give a more professional appearance.

Buy first or sell first?

Probably the most difficult question to resolve is the timing of the whole operation. The legal position is that you are not committed to going ahead with either a sale or a purchase until contracts are exchanged. None the less, you can waste a great deal of money and time if your efforts to sell or buy prove abortive.

If you are selling and buying at the same time, you will not want to risk being the owner of two houses at the same time – or even none.

Although bridging finance is available from a few lenders, if you want to conclude your purchase before your sale, it is not to be recommended if you are bearing the cost yourself. It is hardly ever advisable to take on what is known as an 'open-ended' bridging loan when you commit yourself to your new home without having exchanged contracts on the old. If houses are difficult to sell at the time, very few banks would be prepared to make you a loan in this situation.

The general rule is that, in a buyer's market, you should concentrate your efforts on selling your house first before looking too hard for a house to buy, though it costs nothing to get on estate agents' mailing lists and find out what is available. Once terms have been agreed to sell your house (or at least there is real interest in it from would-be buyers), you can start house-hunting in earnest.

In a seller's market (when prices seem to be going up almost by the day) you will know that your house should be easy to sell, and you must then move heaven and earth to find a house to buy at a price you can afford. Very rarely, the house market is balanced. In that situation, you should put equal effort into selling and finding a house to buy.

Chapter 2

Costs and expenses of moving

Before you start hunting for a new home, you need to work out how much you can afford to pay.

Financing the move

To give you an idea, add together:

- any money you have left over from selling your home and repaying your mortgage
- the maximum mortgage you can comfortably afford
- other capital or savings.

Then, deduct:

- the estimated expenses of moving, including the various fees and stamp duty plus the costs of any repairs, possible redecoration or improvements to your new home. In 2003 the average cost of moving from a £100,000 house to a £150,000 house (for solicitor and estate agent fees, Land Registry searches and stamp duty) was £4,300.

The result of this calculation will give you the approximate maximum price you can afford to pay for your new home.

Net proceeds from the sale of your present home

Estimate what price you think your present home will fetch. If you have had an estate agent's valuation, you can use this as a guide but you might get more, or less, depending on the state of the market. If houses in your area change hands frequently, you could ask neighbours and friends how much they bought or sold their house for. You could also look at property prices in local papers, local estate agents or on the Internet. You can then deduct from this the balance of any mortgage to be paid off on your present home and the estimated costs of selling it. For very rough budgeting purposes, you should allow 2 per cent of the sale price to cover these expenses.

If you need to sell quickly you may have to accept a lower price for your house.

Mortgage

Mortgages are covered in detail in Chapter 6. Briefly, a mortgage is a loan secured on a home – a way of raising the large sum of money you need to buy a house. If you already have a mortgage it may have to be repaid when you sell your home and a new mortgage taken out for the next home. However, you may be able to move your current mortgage to the new property. The new mortgage could be for the same, a greater or a lesser amount, depending on your circumstances.

Your savings

Work out how much you have available in:

- building societies, bank deposit accounts and other savings schemes
- investments, such as bonds, shares and unit trusts (take into account the cost of getting access to your money)
- a life insurance policy (if its current cash-in value will yield enough to make it worth using). You need to make sure you have sufficient life cover in place.

Remember that you should always have some savings that you can use in case of an emergency quite unconnected with house purchase. And you may want to keep some additional money aside to help pay for such items as new carpets and curtains, or for redecorating your new home.

Money for the deposit

You will be asked for a deposit of up to 10 per cent of the purchase price to put down on the house you are buying when you exchange contracts. In some areas of the country, you may be able to use the deposit which your solicitor or agent may be holding in respect of the property you are selling, but in other areas this is not possible.

If you do not have the necessary deposit, you may be able to get a **bridging loan** from your bank (this can be expensive and you should allow for the extra cost), to be repaid on completion of the sale of your present house (see page 178 for details).

Selling costs

A major cost is the **solicitor's fee**.

Solicitors and licensed conveyancers can charge what they choose. However, the Law Society★ recommends that solicitors' fees should be 'fair and reasonable' based on a number of factors. For a house sale these would include the value of the house; how complicated the transaction is; how much time is spent; how much skill is involved; the number of documents involved; the place and circumstances of the conveyancing; and whether the land is registered or unregistered.

It is worth getting estimates from more than one solicitor/ conveyancer before choosing. Your estate agent, mortgage lender or financial adviser may be able to recommend one or you could use one recommended by a friend or relative. There are also online conveyancers to think about. Many solicitors will charge a fixed fee for all the work involved. A solicitor who has given a written quotation cannot exceed the quote unless he or she has reserved the right to do so.

Allow for from 0.5 per cent up to 1 per cent of the price (+ VAT); or a flat fee.

Other fees

Other fees you will have to consider are:

- the estate agent's fee – allow 1.5 to 2.5 per cent of the price (+ VAT). It may be more in certain areas – contact a few to compare costs and contracts
- or, your own advertising costs if you decide to do it yourself
- the mortgage redemption penalty on your existing mortgage: if you are repaying it within a short period (say, less than five years) this may be up to six months' interest or up to 5 per cent of the outstanding mortgage and/or administration or legal fees (redemption penalties are especially common with fixed- and

discounted-rate mortgages). You should check with your mortgage lender.

Buying costs

Allow for the **solicitor's/conveyancer's fee**: not based on a set scale. It will cost about the same as for the sale. See 'Selling costs ' for more details about the likely costs.

The following are statutory fees applicable to the majority of sales.

Stamp duty land tax This is a tax payable on the total purchase price of houses costing above certain amounts:

- Up to £60,000   nil
- £60,001 – £250,000   1%
- 250,001 – £500,000   3%
- £500,001 upwards   4%

From November 2001, stamp duty exemption has applied to properties valued at less than £150,000 in certain disadvantaged areas. For a list of the qualifying locations, check out the Inland Revenue website at *www.inlandrevenue.gov.uk* (you can make a post code search online) or call the helpline on (0845) 603 0135.

Land Registry fee This has to be paid on all purchases and varies depending on the purchase price.

Price of house		Land Registry fee
£0 –	£50,000	£40
£50,001 –	£80,000	£60
£80,001 –	£100,000	£100
£100,001 –	£200,000	£150
£200,001 –	£500,000	£250
£500,001 –	£1,000,000	£450
£1,000,001 upwards		£750

As at August 2003

Local authority searches Fees payable to local authority for information about planning in the area and suchlike (allow at least £60 – more in London boroughs); there is a nominal fee in Scotland.

Other search fees and disbursements These include index map, commons, the coal authority, land charge, company searches, bank transfer fees. Not all are applicable to every transaction, but allow around £70 to cover an average house purchase.

Lender's legal fee Usually, your solicitor will act for the lender as well as for you. The solicitor's fee for the purchase will include all the work on the mortgage. However, you should check this with your solicitor, as a few lenders require their own solicitors to act for them. In this case you have to pay their fees in addition to your own solicitor's fees for acting on your side of the mortgage (if these are not included in the fee quoted for the purchase). There is no statutory scale of charges for the lender's legal costs, either for work carried out by your conveyancer or, if a separate firm is used, by the lender's own conveyancer.

Valuation fee (for lender's surveyor's valuation) This fee is based on the price of the house (+ VAT); it varies according to the lender's arrangements with the valuers. For instance, allow around £125 for a £50,000 house, £200 for a £100,000 house. Ask your lender. See page 84 on structural surveys.

Top-up loan This may be needed to cover valuation and legal fees.

Mortgage indemnity guarantee or high-lending fee (if required). This is charged by some mortgage lenders if you are borrowing above a given percentage of the value of the property – usually 75 or 80 per cent. If you are borrowing 90 per cent of the value of the property the one-off payment will be between 6 and 9 per cent of the amount above the threshold. The one-off payment is payable to the lender who organises the policy – see Chapter 6. It is important to note that the policy protects the lender, not you.

Mortgage arrangement fee This is payable on practically all fixed-rate and capped mortgages – expect to pay £50 to £400.

Bridging loan If required, the interest will be charged between 2 and 7 per cent above the current bank base rate; plus the bank's charge for arranging the loan (between £75 and £300 or 1 per cent of the loan).

Structural survey (allow for the cost of more than one survey during house-hunting). If you are getting a mortgage, you have the choice of a valuation, a house-buyers' report or a full survey. It is wise to have at least a house-buyers' report, which should throw up major defects in the property. Your lender will offer you a valuation; it is advisable to approach an independent surveyor for a structural survey.

For the surveyor's fee for a full survey, allow £250 to £1,000 + VAT (get a quotation before instructing the surveyor). There could be a reduction if it is combined with a building society valuation. If you are buying an old property, budget for extra charges if tests by specialist firms are needed (e.g. drains, electrical, central heating). For a surveyor's intermediate or house-buyers' report which is less detailed than a full survey, the fee is linked to the price of the house: allow, for example, £400 for a £100,000 house.

House-hunting expenses

Travel and subsistence: allow for meals, telephone calls, travel costs and overnight accommodation if necessary.

Insurance

Buildings insurance: the first premium is payable in advance (the amount payable depends on the sum insured and on the area). You should shop around for this and shouldn't just accept the mortgage lender's insurance policy.

Removal expenses

You should be prepared for the cost of using a professional firm. It is best to get several quotations.

If you decide to do it yourself, budget for packing materials, the cost of hiring a self-drive van (+ VAT and insurance) plus petrol. You need to make sure your belongings are insured during the move under your household contents policy.

Services

- Gas: will there be disconnection and reconnection charges?
- Electricity: costs may be incurred for inspections and tests, or for installing additional circuits, e.g. for the cooker at your new house.
- Telephone: you may have to pay for the installation of a telephone at your new home or for taking over the existing telephone if the line is disconnected at all, even for a day. There is no connection charge if a line is unbroken between owners.
- Redirection of letters: £6.45 (one month), £14.05 (three months), £21.60 (six months), £32.40 (one year) – per surname.

- Plumber: perhaps needed for disconnecting and reconnecting the automatic washing machine and/or dishwasher.

Incidentals

- Notifying change of address to friends and family and companies: cost of cards and postage.
- Rubbish disposal – for tidying up your old or new house.
- New locks and/or security devices in your new house.
- Kennelling for pets during the move.
- Thank-you presents for helpers. Remember child minders, friends who heaved furniture and cases and others who helped with your move.

As well as the expenses of moving, also take into account the cost of any immediate repairs (such as rewiring), improvements or redecoration which might be required in the old and/or new house. Also for buying new furniture or kitchen equipment, for example.

Contingency fund

You should allow for the costs of purchases (or sales) which fall through, and for any one-off expenses.

The contingency fund should allow for paying for repairs to any items you have taken over from the previous owners and for buying replacements for fittings you expected to inherit (or believed were included in the price) which the previous owner has taken.

It is not possible to do more than set an arbitrary figure for contingencies – say, 3 per cent of the total of the purchase price plus all other expenses.

If you are moving to a smaller house, you could raise additional money by selling surplus furniture – in which case your contingency fund can be marginally reduced.

Help with the expenses of moving

If you are offered a new job and have to move, you may be able to make it a condition of acceptance that you will get help with removal expenses from the new company.

For some employees, such as civil servants, doctors and members of the armed forces, the moving allowances are laid down. Some private employers will bear the costs of moving when they transfer any of their staff from one branch to another, or if the firm itself moves its premises from one area to another.

Be sure to find out beforehand what the employer means by 'costs of moving' and whether this will include:

- all solicitors' fees
- other fees, such as Land Registry fee, stamp duty, search fees
- any surveyors' fees
- estate agent's fee (for selling)
- removal firm's charges
- temporary storage of furniture
- temporary rented accommodation while you house-hunt or wait to move in
- transport costs
- overnight hotel expenses.

If you find you need a bridging loan because of the timing of your buying and selling, it is worth approaching your employers to see whether they will advance you this, perhaps interest-free or at a low rate of interest. If the move is at their request, the onus is on them to help you with it.

If it is your employers (or the state) who will be paying, keep receipts for everything.

Basic checklist of expenses

	Estimated £	Actual £
Maximum possible price to pay for house	_____	_____
Solicitor's/conveyancer's fee	_____	_____
Estate agent's fee (if agent used for selling house)	_____	_____
Advertisements (if selling house yourself)	_____	_____
Land Registry fee	_____	_____
Stamp duty land tax	_____	_____
Fee for local searches	_____	_____
Other searches and disbursements	_____	_____

Mortgage

• lender's solicitor's fee	_____	_____
• own solicitor's fees	_____	_____
• lender's valuer's fee	_____	_____
• top-up loan: charges	_____	_____
• mortgage indemnity policy	_____	_____

Structural survey

• surveyor's fee	_____	_____
• fees for specialist tests	_____	_____

Insurance

• buildings insurance premiums	_____	_____
• removals insurance premium	_____	_____

Bridging loan

• bank's fee	_____	_____
• interest	_____	_____

House-hunting expenses

- transport   _____   _____

- accommodation   _____   _____

- time off   _____   _____

- other   _____   _____

Removal expenses

- removal firm   _____   _____

- cost of hiring van   _____   _____

- other   _____   _____

Services

- disconnection of utilities   _____   _____

- reconnection of utilities   _____   _____

- installation of new equipment   _____   _____

- carpet laying   _____   _____

- mail redirection   _____   _____

Incidentals

- change of address   _____   _____

- boarding animals   _____   _____

- meals out   _____   _____

- rewarding helpers   _____   _____

- telephone calls   _____   _____

- tips   _____   _____

- other   _____   _____

Contingency fund (percentage of total)   _____   _____

FINAL TOTAL   _____   _____

Chapter 3

Finding a home

This chapter looks first at buying a brand-new property, perhaps on an estate, then at house-hunting in general and what to look for, then at special types of purchase such as buying from a local authority or housing association, or as a leaseholder. When you have found somewhere that appeals, consider the issues raised in the last 10 pages of the chapter, so that you are aware of potential problems before it is too late to walk away.

Buying a newly built house

Many buyers prefer a new house to an old one. This could be a house designed and built to your specifications on your land. For most people, however, buying a newly built house means one being built (or just completed) by a developer, often on a new estate. A house may be advertised before it has been built. The developer or estate agent can show you the site or the plans of the house, with perhaps a glossy brochure, or there may be a show house for you to look at before you choose a site.

If you need a mortgage for buying a newly built house, you will find that lenders such as building societies normally lend only on new houses built under the supervision of an architect or surveyor employed solely by the buyer, or which are built by an NHBC-registered builder or under the Zurich Insurance scheme (see page 32).

NHBC

NHBC* (formerly known as the National House Building Council) is a non-profit-distributing body with a register of some 18,000 builders and developers who undertake to build houses to a set of standards drawn up by the NHBC. Around 85 per cent of new homes in the UK are registered with NHBC. Each house is covered by the NHBC's ten-year Buildmark warranty. The scheme is not a guarantee for putting right all faults that may occur in that period. It is an undertaking to repair faulty work within the first two years after completion of the property, followed by a further eight-year insurance cover in case major structural faults develop. The Buildmark scheme applies to flats and maisonettes as well as houses and bungalows. It does not, however, apply to self-build projects. For information on products for this type of building, contact NHBC.

- If the builder goes bankrupt before the house is completed, NHBC will either refund the buyer's lost deposit or pay the cost of completion (up to a maximum of £10,000 or 10 per cent of the purchase price, whichever is the greater).
- During the first two years (the Buildmark cover period) after the house has been completed, any defect resulting from a failure to comply with NHBC technical requirements must be put right by the builder at no cost to the buyer.
- During the following eight years, insurance cover is provided for damage caused by defects in specified parts of the building which cost more than £500 (indexed) to put right. This includes, for example, major settlement or subsidence, collapse or serious distortion of joists or roof structure, dry (but not wet) rot.

The builder registers the house just before he starts to build. The buyer's solicitor is given an 'offer of cover' form by the builder, together with a Buildmark booklet giving full details of the scheme. He completes the acceptance form on behalf of the buyer and sends it to NHBC. NHBC inspectors carry out key stage inspections on registered buildings under construction. For built-to-contract properties, when financial completion of the purchase takes place, and the inspector is satisfied that a house has been built substantially in accordance with NHBC's requirements, an insurance certificate is issued. NHBC sends a copy of the certificate to the buyer's solicitor or licensed conveyancer for the buyer (to be kept with the booklet and handed on to the new owner if the house is sold within the ten-year period), and another copy goes to the buyer's lender.

In addition to the Buildmark policy, home owners receive a *Guide to Your New Home*, giving advice on running in and taking care of the new home, and also explaining further what can and cannot be claimed from the Buildmark scheme, what the payment limits are, and how to appeal to NHBC's resolution and arbitration procedures should a dispute arise over rectifying defects.

Zurich Insurance Building Warranty

The Zurich '10' warranty policy provides similar cover to the NHBC scheme. Sites are registered by the developer prior to construction. Zurich Insurance* surveyors carry out key stage 'risk management' inspections.

First-stage warranty cover, needed at exchange of contracts, is provided by the building period certificate. If the developer goes out of business during the course of construction, the deposit paid by the buyer to the developer will be refunded (up to 10 per cent of the purchase price). At exchange of contracts Zurich also provides a *Home Owner's Guide*, a letter explaining the 90-day offer of additional cover and, most importantly, the '10' policy document.

The insurance certificate indicating that full warranty cover is in place is provided once all of the risk management inspections have been completed. Contract completion should not occur without this document. Either this or the cover note issued on site is required by mortgage lenders in order to draw down funds.

During the first two years (or one year for conversions) after the house is completed – the Developer's Warranty Period – the developer will put right damage or defects if these arise from a failure to meet the necessary standards of construction. If the developer fails to do so, the insurers will step in.

After the Developer's Warranty has expired, the policy covers damage affecting the structural stability of the property for eight years in newly built homes and nine years in conversions. Holders of a Zurich '10' warranty policy may have been provided with additional cover (extending the warranty period or the level of cover) by their developer, but will also have the option to take this up for themselves in the first three months if they so wish. The developer may also have provided Environmental Impairment Cover as protection against the homeowner being served with clean-up notices, but this is not always a requirement. Always examine your schedule of cover and get it checked by your solicitor to be sure you have the cover you need.

Choice of scheme

The builder/developer will choose the scheme. The buyer will have no choice – though he/she should always insist on some form of cover. Mortgages and later sales of the house within ten years might be difficult or impossible if one of the schemes is not in force.

With 'one-off' houses or very small developments, an alternative to the NHBC or Zurich Insurance schemes might be the supervision of the works by an architect or surveyor, who will have made interim inspections and a final inspection and issued certificates for these. This is acceptable to most (but not all) building societies and banks, who normally require full details of the architect's or surveyor's professional negligence insurance. From a buyer's point of view this is less satisfactory than either the NHBC or Zurich Insurance schemes. In order to get defects put right it will be necessary to show that the builder or the architect or surveyor has been negligent. There is no protection against the bankruptcy of the builder.

The advantages of a newly built house
- Major repairs and redecoration should be unnecessary for the first few years (although you will probably need to decorate initially).
- If, as is probable, the property is registered with the NHBC, it will come with its ten-year warranty and protection scheme.
- If the house is not yet built or not yet completed, you may be able to get some features changed to suit your requirements – the position of a door, sockets, kitchen work surfaces, cupboards, for instance. But you will have to pay extra for this (and the builder may not agree to undertake any variations until after contracts are exchanged).
- The deposit required may be small.
- It may be easier to get a mortgage on a new house than an old one. Many builders arrange mortgage facilities for a whole estate in advance. There is often a link between the property developer and a particular building society, which makes it possible for a loan of a high percentage of the purchase price (sometimes as much as 100 per cent) to be given.

The disadvantages of a newly built house
- The house may not be finished for some time.
- There may be no more than the site and a plan to show to the solicitor and building society or other mortgagee.

- Most building societies or other lenders will not release the final loan until all the work is completed – down to the last coat of paint.
- You generally have to put in fittings, such as cupboards, which previous owners would already have installed in an inhabited house.
- There are often teething troubles – plaster drying out producing cracks, for example.
- The roads on an estate may not have been finished (this may cause problems with a building society's loan – and muddy floors in the house).
- The garden may have to be laid and planted and there may be restrictions on what you can do to the front garden (front gardens on an estate are often landscaped by the developers).
- Even in a rising property market you may not get your money back if you have to sell within one or two years (particularly if the newly built price was a package including 'free' extras, such as fixtures and fittings which depreciate; general inflation takes care of longer periods).
- You may be required to pay for the new home by stage payments (instalments) and therefore find yourself borrowing to pay for two houses at once.

A crucial disadvantage is that the date you are first given for the house to be ready is unlikely to be met. This could lead to delay and difficulties over the sale of your present house and extra expenses with your removal arrangements – and wear and tear on you. If possible, you should try to get the builder to agree a 'long stop' completion date, so that if he does not finish the work by that date, he will be in breach of contract and liable to pay you compensation – though not many builders will agree to this. Ask your solicitor to advise.

The builder could go bankrupt and so be unable to complete the building or not be available to carry out any work to remedy defects. This possibility is covered under the NHBC or Zurich Insurance schemes, but you could still suffer a lot of inconvenience.

Looking for a newly built house

When touring an area, look out for signs of building works, either single houses or estates. Advertising boards may have been put up by:

- a national firm which has its own sales organisation
- a large building firm working in the district

- an estate agent working in conjunction with a building firm
- a local builder.

It is worth asking local builders, or a national firm, whether they have any future plans for putting up houses in the area. Ask local estate agents not only for details of houses being built or just completed but also about any plans for future estates. They may recently have sold land to a builder or developer for this purpose.

A builder who is not on the NHBC register or registered under the Zurich Insurance scheme may be an excellent builder with a good local reputation but he may be just a good jobbing builder with no experience of house-building – or he may be one who has been expelled from the NHBC or Zurich Insurance schemes. In either case, you will have difficulty getting a mortgage; you may have difficulty also when you come to sell if your prospective buyer cannot get a mortgage.

Advertisements

Monthly magazines such as *What House?* and *The Property Magazine* contain much useful information on new estates being built, and have regular articles on different areas of the country, with plenty of information about new developments, a round-up of mortgage prospects, and frequent supplements on specific aspects of new-house building and buying. From specialist magazines, you can get the names of large developers and the areas in which they operate, so that you can apply to them for details in the area of your choice and in your price range.

The local paper will almost certainly carry notices with details of property developments, and advertisements of recently granted planning permissions may appear with the names of builders and developers. The local authority planning officer and the building control officer know about ongoing and projected developments, and may be prepared to give you information.

Timber-frame houses

If you want to buy a timber-frame house (constructed with prefabricated timber panels as opposed to a house of masonry construction) the UK Timber Frame Association (UKTFA)★ can supply the names of quality assured suppliers. Further details of timber-frame construction, as well as a plot-search facility and a supplier-search facility, are available on the UKTFA website. A brochure entitled *Timber Frame – The Choice is Yours* is also available from the UKTFA free of charge.

Finding out about the house and the estate

Find out as much as you can about the reputation of individual builders or developers. If possible, talk to people who live in their houses; if an estate is still being built, talk to someone who has already moved in. Ask:

- have there been many problems with the houses?
- has the builder put them right quickly?
- does he keep his promises?

Ask if there is a show house on the estate. Some developers complete one house and furnish it as a demonstration model. (But remember that the show house may have a number of optional extras fitted as if they were standard.) A small building firm may have put up a similar house in the district which you could arrange to look at.

Where you have a drawing rather than a finished house to consider, check at the actual site or compare the drawing with the Ordnance Survey map in the local authority planning office. A site plan may be accurate as to what it does show, but may fail to reveal the proximity of railway lines, sewage works, quarries, factory estates and other unsuspected horrors. For the inside of the house, get confirmation of actual dimensions of rooms and stairways.

Some builders fully equip a house and then sell it on its merits. Others provide a basic shell and offer a long list of options – types of doors, floor finishes, kitchen equipment, bathroom suites – to suit the taste and pocket of prospective buyers. There are all sorts of permutations. It is vital to study the detailed specification if the house is not already finished and available to be seen.

The developer's or agent's particulars are sometimes not as detailed as they might be – perhaps because the builder is wary of naming specific materials or fittings, in case at a later date these become unobtainable. The quality of fittings tends to vary, so try to get what you want written into the specification as part of the contract for your house. Be sure to confirm all variations in writing and obtain a written acknowledgement. Insist that all quotations (for additional work or substitutions) are in writing.

Take special care to check exactly what you are paying for. Is the garage an optional extra, for instance (or obligatory even if you do not want one)? Is there planning permission for a double garage if you need one? Find out what type of heating is to be installed and be sure not only that you like the type but can afford the fuel. Some estates are all-electric with no gas laid on – you may feel strongly about cooking or heating with one fuel rather than another.

Roads

On a new estate, the cost of building the roads and laying the drains should be included in the purchase price of the house. The water authority becomes responsible for the drains, the local authority (county council or equivalent) for the roads, cleansing and lighting.

Most local authorities insist on the base of the road and kerbs being laid before building work starts. Later, when the top surfacing has been completed to their standard, the roads are adopted and maintained by the authority. There can be delays since the final making up of the roads is done at the end of all the construction work.

A building society may withhold some of the mortgage money until the roads are completed, unless there is an agreement between the authority and the builder (a Section 38 agreement). This is backed by a bond so that if the builder fails to complete the road or goes bankrupt before doing so sufficient money will be paid under the bond to complete the road to the authority's satisfaction.

The roads will not be adopted by the local authority unless they are satisfactorily completed. Even then, it may be some time before the local authority passes the necessary resolution to adopt and there may be no street cleansing until formal adoption is finalised.

Drains

In a similar way, the construction of the sewers may be covered by an agreement between the water authority and the builder secured by a bond (a Section 18 agreement). The house may be connected directly to the main sewer or may be served by a private drain serving a number of houses. This then connects to the main sewer. You will probably be asked to be responsible for sharing the cost of any maintenance of the private drain.

While the house is being built

A prospective buyer who has chosen a specific house should, if possible, make regular visits to see what is going on and check regularly whether the target date is likely to be met and that the construction is being carried out in accordance with the plans and specification. Builders can and often do make changes to methods and materials. These may not affect the value but they may not be precisely what you contracted for. If mistakes are found (a yellow bathroom suite where blue was ordered, for instance), the earlier the builder is warned the better.

A survey towards the end of the work might be advisable to check, for example, that the agreed boundaries have not been altered.

The price

A builder may quote for a house that has yet to be built a price which he undertakes to hold for a specified period. Once contracts are exchanged, he will have to keep to that price unless the contract specifically provides for price fluctuations. You may be asked to pay a small deposit for the offer to be kept open.

The price of a newly built house is seldom negotiable, especially if it is part of an estate. National firms fix their asking prices and are not likely to reduce them. A smaller firm which finds one or more houses on a particular site remaining unsold may (particularly if interest rates are high or money is tight at the time) make some reduction in order to complete the scheme and so release funds to finance the next development.

Incentives to buy

Depending on the state of the market, builders may provide financial incentives to persuade you to buy. Amongst them is a reduction in price if you exchange contracts within a specified number of weeks. If you do not meet the date, you may lose the house at that price.

The builder may offer to buy your present house in part-exchange for the new one. This avoids the risk of a chain but you may find that the builder's trade-in price is lower than the open market price for your house. Or the builder may pay the estate agent's and solicitor's fees and even the stamp duty and Land Registry fees.

Some builders have their own 'pet' solicitors whom they will encourage you to use. But you are free to use the solicitor or conveyancer of your choice. Note that the same firm of solicitors is not allowed to act for both you and the developer.

Another incentive is for the builder to arrange a mortgage of 100 per cent and/or to offer a mortgage subsidy for a year in the form of a reduction in mortgage rate or refund. All incentives have to be reported to your building society if it does not already know about them. Remember that if the builder gets into financial difficulties he may not be able to honour the obligation to subsidise interest rates.

Paying for a new house

Some builders insist on being paid by instalments and they will put the price up if you do not want to pay for the home in full until it is finished. This is more likely to happen when the house market is buoyant or where you own the plot and employ a builder to build a house for you.

If you are obtaining a mortgage and want to have stage payments as the work progresses, at the various stages the lender's surveyor will have to inspect (and be paid a fee).

It is important to tell your building society when you apply for a mortgage that you will need instalment payments. Building societies are generally quite happy to release a mortgage advance by instalments, as long as the value of the work done at any stage covers the amount they have advanced, and as long as the stages in construction tie in with their own requirements.

The society will issue an offer which spells out the stages at which money will be released. Generally, these are as follows:

(1) roof plate level
(2) roofed in
(3) plastered out
(4) final completion.

Make sure that the payment stages in the builder's contract are the same as in the mortgage offer. If there is a discrepancy, you may find it easier to get the builder to change than the building society. Get your solicitor to send a copy of the mortgage offer to the builder with a request that the building society payments are accepted instead.

Even though the lender's surveyor will inspect the house at the end of the construction work before paying out, you yourself should check on doors and window finishes and decorations, whether all the services are connected and working and whether any extras you ordered have all been provided.

Look for details:

- have all the walls been painted with the right number of coats of paint?
- do the doors shut properly?
- are any items missing?
- has the builder included everything that was in the original specification?

Unless everything is in order, you would be wise not to complete, but the contract may specify that you cannot refuse to complete if the outstanding items are of a minor nature. At the very least, you should be given an undertaking that the outstanding work will be carried out – and perhaps hold back part of the money till it is done.

It is unlikely that the builder will let you in before he is paid, so if the building society will not advance the money until the house is completed to the surveyor's satisfaction, there may be a critical and frustrating period when the house is to all intents and purposes finished but cannot be occupied. The contract will probably say that legal completion is to be 14 days after notice being given that the house is physically completed. Try to get the buyer of your own house to agree to a completion date based on the same arrangement.

If you have to agree a fixed date with your buyer in order not to lose the sale, you may need to arrange some temporary accommodation.

If the date of moving in is vital (and earlier than the completion of your sale), you may have to get a bridging loan from the bank.

House-hunting

It is sensible to use all methods of looking for a new home: estate agents, advertisements, searching the area, word of mouth and the Internet. Let it be known to as many people as possible that you are looking – friends, neighbours, colleagues, solicitor, postman, landlord of the pub.

Look out for 'House for Sale' signs. These may have been put up by the owners themselves but more commonly they are notices erected by estate agents on behalf of a seller. Unless the board says that viewing is 'by appointment only' or 'no callers at the house', there is no reason why you should not approach the owner direct. The board may even say 'apply within'.

If the owner is selling direct and you are interested in viewing, you can either call and ask if it is convenient to look around immediately or make an appointment to see it later. But, if it is in the hands of an estate agent, you will usually have to see him or her first. Although the board may be that of one agent, the house may be on the list of other estate agents as well.

At times when there is a seller's market (that is, few houses for sale in relation to the number of buyers), property may be bought up so quickly that agents do not need or have time to get their boards up. There is little point then in searching a district for boards: go straight to the agents' offices and register your name and requirements with them so that they can send you details of any likely properties.

In London and many other areas, there are 'property shops' where details of houses and flats, including a photograph, are displayed. You can get particulars there of any property you think looks suitable and make arrangements directly with the vendor to view it. Some property shops or centres, in particular those set up by solicitors, offer a package deal, including the conveyancing. Some firms of solicitors have established a specialist estate agency department within the firm and are directly involved in the practical and financial aspects of buying and selling property as well as handling the legal side.

Estate agents

To find the names and addresses of local estate agents, start by looking for the names of firms advertising property in the local paper. Property websites (see page 312) may include listings of estate agents by area. Also look in the *Yellow Pages* or other business directory.

Most of the estate agents in England and Wales have principals or senior partners who are members of professional associations (such as the National Association of Estate Agents (NAEA)★ and the Royal Institution of Chartered Surveyors★) and are bound by their codes of professional conduct. You could ask if agents are members of these schemes when approaching them. An Ombudsman for Estate Agents★ was appointed in 1992 and in 2003 published a Code of Practice for estate agents (see page 163).

A country-wide list of members is available from the head offices and professional estate agents will normally have a list of their fellow members.

When you have located the offices of estate agents, study any advertisements outside. Most agents have window fronts in which they display particulars of properties they sell, usually accompanied by a photograph. These can give you a rough guide to prices and types of property in the area handled by that agent. Only a small proportion of an agent's properties will be displayed in the window so it is advisable to go into the office to talk to the agents. Agents advertise not only in order to sell a particular property, but also to establish their identity in the market: 'I have this type of property for sale. I operate in this area. Entrust me with the sale of your house and I'll handle it like this'- this is what estate agents are trying to put over.

Call on agents who seem to advertise the kind of property you are looking for. If you are restricted to weekend viewing, check which agents are shut on Saturdays and/or Sundays.

Buying the right house is so important that you should certainly not restrict yourself to what is on offer from just one agent. Enquire of all the agents in a locality. The least flamboyant agent may have just the house you are looking for.

The agents you visit will want a fairly exact idea of what kind of accommodation you require. So, decide beforehand what is important to you: how many living rooms, bedrooms and bathrooms are the minimum you need, whether with or without a garage or garden and, most importantly, how much you are prepared to pay. Unless you feel very strongly about alternatives such as detached *versus* semi-detached, house *versus* bungalow, keep an open mind and let the agent know you are doing so.

The agent will ask for your name, address, home and work telephone numbers so that he or she can put you on a register and mailing list.

Be prepared to receive details of properties you may think you do not want. Curiously, estate agents find quite regularly that a lot of people buy types of property which they had initially ruled out.

You, as buyer, are not charged by the estate agent and you are under no obligation to him or her. Estate agents are in business to arrange the sale of a property on behalf of their client – the seller. They act as negotiators between seller and buyer but, since they make their living out of the commission they charge the seller, their duty is to him or her and not to you, the buyer.

To get an indication of the kind of buyer you would make, agents may ask you whether you will be a cash buyer or need a mortgage. They will do all they can to make it easy for you to buy (it is in their interest, too), and will possibly offer advice about mortgage, survey, solicitor and so on. If they do provide this service, check whether the advice is independent. Consider going elsewhere if it is not.

The more contact you have with an agent, the more likely he or she is to think of you and get in touch with you specifically when a suitable house is available. Be prepared to spend time initially calling in or ringing up regularly in order to establish a good relationship with the agent. For more on using an estate agent, see pages 161–9.

The Internet

The Internet is a growing source of information and is gradually becoming an important marketplace for property. It has great potential for direct sales. It is now possible to find out large amounts of mortgage information online (see page 134). Many estate agents now have their own websites.

In a new area

It is not easy to house-hunt at a distance. You are unlikely to know the area well enough to be able to assess advertisements or agents' descriptions: sometimes two streets, although adjacent, can be quite different in style and standard, as can opposite sides of the same street.

Estate agents in the locality may send you details of houses but some of these may no longer be available by the time the information reaches you: someone who lives in the area may beat you to it.

If you are not able to go to the area, you can call on an agent in your home town and ask if he or she has any contact with fellow agents in the other area. The agent may take the professional journal *Estates Gazette*, which publishes a monthly regional directory of agents. Internet sites can help you house-hunt at a distance

A national Homelink service is operated by members of the NAEA to provide a referral service for anyone moving from one area to another. The Homelink member in your present locality will contact another Homelink member in the area to which you are moving, giving details of your requirements, and the agents 'on the spot' will send you details of likely properties. The names and addresses of Homelink agents in any area can be obtained from the NAEA.

Some agents are linked to a regional or national multi-list computer system. Having registered your requirements with one agent, you will be sent details of properties that match your specifications currently on the books of all the others.

If the area to which you will be moving is some distance away, the costs of travelling to look at houses can be quite considerable. A good estate agent can save you making unnecessary journeys. He or she should know each property thoroughly and a telephone call for more details or an opinion may help you decide whether a potentially interesting house is worth a journey. The agent can also arrange appointments to see several houses during one visit. Ask the agent to email you details if you are a distance buyer.

It can be profitable to take time off to go and stay for a few days in the prospective new area so that you can assess the place for yourself and make a few personal contacts. Arm yourself with a large-scale map or street guide to make looking easier and quicker. (Many estate agents provide a free map or guide.) Start touring the area to get the feel of different streets or districts and mark on your map the ones you like.

Relocation agents

A number of agencies, which may be called 'homefinders' or 'home search agents', offer a country-wide relocation service. (Some smaller firms operate in specific areas.) They act solely on behalf of buyers – or, sometimes, people looking for rental properties – and set out to help them find the type of property they want in the area they want. Originally, such agencies were used mostly by firms for the relocation of staff being moved because of their job. Nowadays, many more agencies deal with individuals moving who do not have the time, opportunity or inclination to undertake the tracking down of potentially acceptable properties, particularly in an unfamiliar area of the country.

Relocation agencies vary from the individual consultant to fairly large organisations offering a full range of relocation-related services in the UK and abroad. They advertise in the national press, and many agencies are members of the Association of Relocation Agents (ARA)*. The ARA can supply a region-by-region directory of its members (also available on its website), which sets out the organisation's rules of conduct. All members are required to have professional indemnity insurance.

An agent's knowledge of the local property market should enable him or her to offer advice on the suitability of property and location according to a client's requirements. The agent should advise on a particular property's general value and condition, on planning considerations and resale possibilities. One advantage of using a relocation agent is that he or she is working for you, the buyer, and will get details of properties, view on your behalf and sift and select property within your specifications, so that you do not waste time on unsuitable places. An agent will negotiate terms for a client, if required, and can also be asked to oversee the sale of the present home.

Relocation services can include as little or as much as the individual client requests, including introductions to legal and financial advisers and to surveyors, making all the removal arrangements, organising storage of possessions, the cleaning and preparation of both the new and the old home, and providing information about the new area and facilities.

It is usual to pay a 'retainer' or registration fee (anything between £200 and £500) for the initial work of researching and selecting suitable property; when a purchase goes through, a further fee (perhaps 1½ to 2 per cent of the price) is payable on exchange of contracts. Any additional work the relocation agent is asked to do will be subject to negotiation.

Estate agents' particulars

Whether you call in person, telephone or write, the agent will supply 'particulars' – details of properties available which he or she thinks may be of interest. The information may be in the form of a list or even a glossy brochure or individual sheets for each property. You may be sent particulars at frequent intervals until you tell the agent to stop, or, if you do not follow any properties up, the agent tires of sending them.

One of the hazards of the house-hunting game is that by the time the list has reached you, you may find that the house which you like the sound of has already been snapped up and is 'under offer'. This is a good reason to make contact with agents and ask that they telephone rather than write to you.

An agent's particulars are part of the service of marketing the house for the seller, who would not thank the agent if a description were so worded as to deter potential buyers. It is intended to act as an inducement for the buyer to inspect: the assumption is that no one buys a house on the strength of particulars only. However, the facts given in the description of a property must be accurate – about, for instance, the number of floors or size of rooms. But you may find that because a room is on an upper floor it is counted and described as a bedroom when it may not really be big enough to hold a bed. So, check the room measurements if they are given, and beware if none is quoted.

Measurements are usually straightforward: reception room 16ft 6in × 20ft. 'Maximum' dimensions may mean that the room is not square: it may be L-shaped or have an alcove.

You have to learn to notice what is *not* said and extract the details from the traditional estate agents' descriptive style, which uses such terms as 'exceptional' or 'beautifully proportioned'. Beware of 'immaculate décor' or 'tastefully decorated' which has to be a matter of opinion – usually only the owner's and possibly only the agent's.

The Property Misdescriptions Act 1991 which came into force at the beginning of 1993 should have put an end to some of the more bizarre descriptions by estate agents. A similar set of rules to the Trade Descriptions Act is applied to estate agents' particulars. It is now a criminal offence to make a false or misleading statement about a property in the course of an estate agency business. Time will tell whether this will curb their more extravagant purple prose.

The particulars may also give the amounts of council tax payable, whether it is freehold, or, if it is leasehold, the length of the lease, the amount of the ground rent and sometimes the maintenance charge, and, finally, the asking price. The letters 'o.n.o.' (or near offer) after the price are an indication that the price is set high and the seller might be prepared to come down.

An estate agent must, by law, inform you whether he or she has a personal interest in a property (such as a house being owned by a colleague or employee). Such a 'personal interest' statement may appear on the particulars.

Photographs of houses serve as a rough guide to the kind of property involved but can be misleading – for instance, they may have been trimmed of their less attractive surroundings – and should be regarded

Estate agents' euphemisms

suitable for conversion: in need of a lot of repair and redecoration

bijou: can't swing even a cat

cottage: anything old and small

town house: front entrance through the garage

easy to manage: pokey

spacious: too big for most people to decorate or heat

exceptionally spacious: cold and draughty

full central heating: four storage heaters

conservatory: porch 18in x 3ft

full double glazing: constant traffic noise

interesting: only if you're selling it

individual décor: paper peeling off walls

convenient motorway/railway: runs at back of garden

convenient buses: bus tickets fall into your front garden

convenient school: children fall into your front garden

quiet cul-de-sac: children's playground early Sunday mornings and school holidays

secluded: the shops are a long way away

rural views: views of allotments, cabbage fields, pig sties, or all three

open views: faces league football ground

reasonably priced: overpriced

reduced for quick sale: still overpriced

potential garage space: if only there were access

potential: anything, if only money/time were available (we would have done some work but are moving instead)

full of character: full of woodworm, dry rot, damp

exposed beams: on which to hit exposed heads

light and airy: expensive to curtain

deceptively spacious: too many small rooms

potential for extension: cramped

garage space and driveway: no parking

neat garden: minute yard

garden laid to lawn: grass patch

mature garden: overgrown wilderness

sea view: if standing on seat in WC

merits further improvement: can only get better

suitable for d-i-y enthusiast: present owners did nothing

ideal for modernising: quick, before it falls down

with caution. Remember that the agent is being paid to sell the house and must therefore present it in the most favourable light, without deliberately misleading or blatantly misrepresenting it or its size or position.

Advertisements

Estate agents often advertise the properties they handle in the local and national press. Although in a buoyant market these may well have been sold by the time the advertisement is published, it is well worth studying advertisements to get an idea of prices and of agents and because advertising is a useful pointer to the current state of the market.

Owners who wish to sell privately often advertise in the 'Property For Sale' columns of newspapers and magazines. Do not be put off buying a house which is advertised privately rather than through an agent. (An agent gives no guarantee of the quality of the house being sold – and remember, he or she is acting for the seller and not the buyer.)

If you are unfamiliar with the area, ask at the local reference library which papers cover the district. It is important to find out on which day property advertisements appear, and get your copy immediately.

Advertisements in the national dailies, Sunday papers and glossy magazines are likely to be for houses at the upper end of the market; local morning and evening papers and weeklies will give a wider choice. Publications worth consulting include *Exchange & Mart*, *Loot* and *Dalton's Weekly*. Top-of-the-market property is advertised in such magazines as *Tatler*, *The Field*, *Vogue*, *Harpers and Queen* and *Country Life*; often these are houses which are to be sold by auction.

Property is also advertised on the Internet, either on estate agents' websites or property websites. See the end of the Addresses section.

House-hunter's advertisement

You can yourself put an advertisement in the 'Wanted' column of a local or national newspaper. Specify what you want: house/bungalow; location/position; size/number of rooms; garden?; garage?; price (approximate); and why you would be a good buyer, such as 'no chain' or 'mortgage arranged', 'cash purchaser' or 'bank employee'.

Local newspapers are likely to be more useful and less expensive. Most newspapers offer reductions for repeated inserts; take their advice about which days are the best to place the advertisement. If you are lucky enough to find a house in this way, you can ask the seller to reduce the price since he or she will not be paying an agent's commission.

Buying an old house to do up

If you want to buy an old house to renovate and improve, you must be prepared for the work to take a long time. You must also ensure that you have the financial resources to carry out the necessary repairs and improvements. There have been changes to the legislation under which there was a statutory right to a house renovation grant where the property was judged by the local housing authority to be unfit for human habitation. All grants for repair and improvement are now discretionary and, in most cases, the grant applicant must have lived in the house and had an owner's interest for three years prior to making the application. Applying to the local authority for and receiving planning permission could take anything from two to 12 months or longer, plus a further six months or more for the building work to be carried out. In some cases, it may not be practical to live in the house while the work is being done. If you are eligible for a renovation grant towards the cost of the works, the local authority may take up to six months to decide the application and any works commenced before the grant is approved will not be eligible for grant.

Before you buy the house, find out what, if any, planning permission you need for the work you would like to do and the possibility of getting a grant. Go to the planning department and the environmental health department of the appropriate local authority and ask what the position is likely to be in your case. The more accurate and realistic the details you are able to provide, the better.

Conservation officers working for district or county councils can sometimes offer general advice.

House improvement grants

Local authorities administer and give grants (towards which the government contributes the greater part) for improving or renovating property. All are discretionary and a three-year prior residence and ownership qualification will apply in most cases. Contact your local authority for details of grants that may be applicable to you.

- **House Renovation Grant** This is roughly equivalent to what used to be known as an improvement grant. It does not cover second homes, homes built or converted less than ten years ago (unless the application is for disabled facilities), non-essential works, council tenancies or works under the Housing Defects legislation.

- **Common Parts Grant** This covers the cost of repairs or improvements to the common parts of buildings containing one or more flats. The landlord, or all the tenants, can apply.
- **HMO Grant** This grant is for houses in multiple occupation. Only the landlord may apply for this grant.
- **Disabled Facilities Grant** This is designed to help to make the home of a disabled person more suitable for him or her to live in. Anyone registered (or registrable) as disabled can apply, whether owner or tenant. For more information see the leaflet *Disabled Facilities Grants* from the Publications Centre★ which represents the Office of the Deputy Prime Minister (ODPM).

Note that grants are now means-tested. The applicant's finances will be taken into consideration in deciding whether to make a grant or how much grant to give. You should be able to obtain statements of local grant policy and application forms from your local authority. It is important not to start work until the grant is approved and you get the go-ahead from the local authority.

The grant you can get is a percentage of an amount called the eligible expense of the cost of the improvement plus some repair work. A local authority can make it a condition of a grant that you carry out certain repairs – for which you may not get a grant. Thus, you might finish up getting only 25 per cent of your total expenditure, even though a 50 per cent grant was promised.

Planning permission

You do not need to be the owner of the property to apply for planning permission (but you must inform the owner). Planning permission is required for many alterations and extensions to a building, particularly if they affect the external aspect and appearance, and for changing the use of a building. The permission has to be obtained from the local planning authority.

Permission is not required for what is specified as permitted development – for example, extending the house within certain limits. But the rules are very complicated and you would be well advised to contact the planning department of your local authority for informal advice from a planning officer. Sometimes, the permitted development provisions do not apply to certain areas, such as conservation areas.

Whether planning permission is needed or not, building regulations will apply to the materials and method of building. The local authority's building control officer should be consulted about getting building regulations approval (in Scotland, building control consent). A fee is payable when you apply for approval.

Listed buildings and conservation areas

Under the town and country planning legislation, the DTLR compiles lists of buildings of special architectural or historic interest. A listed building must not be altered or extended in any way which would affect its character without authorisation from the local planning authority. This is a separate issue from planning permission, but getting listed buildings consent can be dealt with at the same time. Depending on the grade of the listing, the listing can extend to the whole of the building, inside and out, and sometimes the whole site, even though only part may be 'of interest'.

A conservation order can apply to a whole town or village, or a square, a street or even part of a street.

No part of a property in either of these categories may be demolished without consent and all trees within a conservation area are automatically subject to preservation orders. The rules are strict and cover outbuildings and boundary walls. Breach of the regulations is a criminal offence.

You can check whether a house is in a conservation area or is a listed building by going to the local authority offices to inspect the list. Do this before buying a house if you have ideas of making alterations or extensions to it at any time. Not only very old houses are listed – a building may be listed that is only 30 or so years old if it is of outstanding quality or design. The local authority search made by your solicitor will show whether or not the house is a listed building or in a conservation area.

Certain grants may be available from the local authority in respect of essential structural repairs to a listed building, and to repair or retain aspects of architectural interest; ask about this possibility at the local planning authority. Grants may also be made by English Heritage for buildings of outstanding interest. Notes for guidance and an application form are available from English Heritage*.

Ancient or unusual properties

For those prepared to buy a decayed or historic building, the Society for the Protection of Ancient Buildings (SPAB)* compiles a quarterly list of historic buildings for sale which are in need of sympathetic owners to repair and maintain them. It also runs courses for homeowners on how to care for old buildings.

Some people prefer the challenge of finding a building not originally designed as a home, and converting it themselves. If you would like to know whether there are any redundant properties available in your chosen area or happen to see a disused or unoccupied one, the organisations to get in touch with are:

- for a redundant church, rectory or other church building: apply to the diocesan office or registry (address in the local telephone directory) or ask the vicar
- for disused railway property: contact Spacia★ (Network Rail's property arm) for the names of regional estate surveyors and managers to apply to in Birmingham, Bristol, Glasgow, London, Manchester and York
- for buildings in the forest: the Forestry Commission★ sells some of its property by auction or by tender through regional offices
- for an unoccupied warehouse or other derelict property: trace the ownership by contacting the local authority for the name and address of whoever is responsible for the rates on the property
- for a redundant schoolhouse: ask the local education authority
- for a redundant pub: ask the estate manager of the brewery.

Other types of purchase

Other ways to buy properties depend on special circumstances. Some are listed below. All need very detailed consideration and specialist advice.

Buying from a local authority

Secure tenants who have lived in a council house for two years or more (this will be raised to five years in the 2004 Housing Act) or in another state-owned 'right to buy' property may buy it at a substantial discount (up to 60 per cent of its value). The discount is calculated on the number of years as a council tenant (maximum 30 years), and is based on where you live – for example, the maximum discount for Wales at the time of writing is £16,000, in the West Midlands it is £26,000 and in the south-east the figure is £38,000. You do not have to have lived in the same council house over that period.

Similar rights to buy are granted to tenants of property owned by various other public bodies. A leaflet, *Your Right to Buy Your Home,* is available from the Publications Centre★ of the Office of the Deputy Prime Minister.

The procedure is triggered by sending a form (RTB1, obtainable from the authority) to the local authority. It will respond by telling you its view of the valuation, and you may appeal to the District Valuer if you think it is too high.

Ownership is exactly the same as for any other house, except that if you sell within three years (five years from 2004) you have to refund a proportion of the discounted price. There may be certain restrictions on the sale if the property is in a rural area or has been specially adapted for use by the elderly.

Right to buy companies

In 2003, a government report was published concerning the involvement of (and possible exploitation by) companies in the right to buy scheme. There are two types of company in operation: right to buy service companies and right to buy incentive companies.

A service company helps those who wish to exercise their right to purchase their homes by providing advice, help with filling out forms, arranging finance and contacting solicitors. The usual cost of the total package provided (including legal fees) is over £2,000. Although this type of assistance is useful, these companies are viewed with suspicion by local authorities. It is claimed that some companies engage in sharp marketing practices targeted at people who cannot afford to buy their homes, and that they often provide inaccurate advice and information to the purchaser. These companies usually work one housing estate at a time and as result, the work of the local authority dramatically increases dealing with the new applications. Much of this work is fruitless, however, as a high proportion of applications are subsequently withdrawn.

An incentive company is a very different creature, and deals with people who would not otherwise wish to buy their homes or who cannot raise the necessary finance (for example because they have county court judgments entered against them, or their property is not mortgageable on the High Street because it is a high-rise flat). These companies provide the tenant with the money to purchase the house. At the same time, the tenant agrees to sell the property to the company in three years' time at less than the market value. In the meantime, the company might be granted a lease of the property. On exercising the right to buy, the tenant immediately moves out of the property in return for a cash payment (usually ranging between £5,000 and £26,000) made by the company. This cash payment is normally less than a quarter of the discount that the tenant would otherwise have been entitled to. This practice is perfectly lawful and has so far affected thousands of properties, primarily in Inner London. It offers the company a cheap way of building up a portfolio of properties to rent, and the tenant leaves financially enriched by the experience. The potential for exploitation of the right to buy scheme by incentive companies is one reason why the government has reduced the maximum discount available to tenants to 60 per cent (it was formerly 70 per cent).

Buying from a housing association

Housing associations (legally known as 'registered social landlords') are local organisations regulated by the Housing Corporation*, a government agency. The Housing Corporation part-funds several schemes for housing associations to develop. These aim to help people on lower incomes become homeowners, and to help some housing association tenants to purchase the homes that they are currently renting.

- The **Shared Ownership scheme** enables you to buy a share of the housing association property and pay a rent on the remaining share you do not own.
- The **Homebuy scheme** helps people to buy a home on the open market.
- The **Right to Acquire scheme** gives eligible tenants of registered social landlords the legal right to buy the home they currently rent.
- Under the **Voluntary Purchase scheme**, tenants of housing associations may be able to apply to buy the home they rent at a discount.
- The **Starter Home Initiative (SHI)**, introduced in 2001, aims to help key workers buy homes in urban and rural areas where high prices would otherwise prevent them from living in or near to the communities they serve. The list of eligible key workers for 2004/05 and 2005/06 comprises: nurses/healthworkers, police, police civilians, social workers, teachers, occupational therapists, prison staff, probation service staff and planners.

The Housing Corporation does not process applications for housing, or manage the waiting list. To make an application you need to contact your local housing association. Full guidance on how to access these schemes is available in the Your Home section of the Housing Corporation's website or from its publications department.

A leaseholder's right to buy

If you own a leasehold interest (see page 72) in a house – not a flat – and the lease is running out, you may have a right to acquire the freehold or a lease for a further 50 years. The lease must originally have been granted for more than 21 years in order to qualify. The requirements are complex and are likely to be costly, but nevertheless provide a measure of protection to those whose long leases are running out. The right is available only to tenants who have lived in the property for the preceding two years (or two of the past ten years).

The procedure is triggered by a tenant serving the appropriate notice on the landlord before the lease expires. The landlord can refuse to give a new lease, or to sell the freehold, only on very narrow grounds (such as showing a greater need for the house than the tenant). The property then has to be valued according to the procedure. If the price is too high the tenant has a month to back out.

The Commonhold and Leasehold Reform Act 2002 has made the process of acquiring the freehold, or extending the lease, easier for leaseholders of houses. It is no longer necessary for a tenant to occupy a house as his or her only or main residence. The qualifying period has also been reduced from three to two years (see above). In addition, the personal representatives of a deceased tenant can now exercise the right on behalf of the deceased's estate. The bill will also allow leaseholders of houses who have previously extended their lease the right to buy the freehold of their property.

Buying a mobile home

Mobile homes do not fall easily into normal categories of home ownership. Even though they are difficult to move, they are none the less considered not to be permanent structures and have the same legal status as caravans.

For many years owners of mobile homes had very little protection from the law. Since the Mobile Homes Act 1983 the position has improved.

If the site is licensed by the local authority and the home is used by the occupier as a sole or main home, the occupancy may only be terminated by an order of the County Court. Grounds for termination are limited, such as breaches of the agreement or failure to repair the home.

The owner of a licensed site must (within three months) let the occupier have a written statement giving details of the right to occupy the site.

It is possible for ownership to be transferred, but the site owner retains some control over the situation and can demand commission or around 10 per cent of the price as a precondition of agreeing to an ownership change.

Mobile homes cost substantially less than conventional houses. If you are considering buying a mobile home, you should insist on studying (and taking advice on) the agreement between the mobile home owner and the owner of the site. Give attention to the site regulations, the services available on the site and its general condition, and the transfer provisions in the agreement (in case you should want to sell on).

Buying a repossessed house

A house which has been repossessed by a lender could be in practically any of the categories which have been considered in this chapter; money is lent on the security of virtually any kind of property. If the borrowers do not keep up with payments, the home will be repossessed.

If you are buying from a lender, the quality of your ownership will still be the same: a lender in possession has the right to transfer absolute ownership. This is true even if there is a succession of loans on the same property. Lenders have to comply with strict rules about any surplus money which they hold. But that need not concern a buyer. It is something which you should leave for your solicitor or conveyancer to sort out.

A lender who sells a property will not have the same level of knowledge as a normal owner. There will be little point in asking where the boundaries lie, or whether the house is connected to mains drainage or a septic tank. It is also unlikely that a lender will know whether there have been any difficulties or disputes with neighbours.

It is also possible that a house which has been repossessed may not have been maintained as well as one which is being sold by a proud and caring owner. If there has been a forced repossession, damage might have been done to doors or windows. Make sure you insist that it is put right. It is also especially important that you ensure that the locks have been changed.

Should you buy a repossessed house?

There is no reason why you should not buy a house which has been repossessed, but you should exercise extra care in your investigations and enquiries. A survey would be virtually essential. There will be very little comeback against the seller if problems are found.

You may also find it harder with a lender. Lenders are required to obtain the best price reasonably available (having regard to the market conditions and the increasing indebtedness of the borrower). Sometimes they do this by selling at auction; sometimes by insisting on tender documents. You may also be asked to enter into a contract race (see page 92). With regards to mortgages regulated by the Financial Services Authority (FSA), the lender will have to market the house as soon as possible

The risk is that you could spend a lot of money on investigations, only to find that you have been pipped to the post by someone else.

On the other hand, there may be advantages: the price can sometimes be low, and the lender might be prepared to offer you a loan on favourable terms if you decide to buy.

How to view

When you have spotted a house or been sent details of one you wish to look at, you should make an appointment to view immediately. If you are the first person to view, you stand a better chance of getting the house should you decide it is the one you want.

If the property is with estate agents, they will make the appointment on your behalf. Sometimes they will accompany you; this can save time. If the owner is out, or the property is vacant but still furnished, and the agents have the key, they will want to go with you since responsibility for the house is theirs. If it is empty, you may be allowed to borrow the key to look round on your own.

If you cannot keep your appointment, you should let the owner or agent know. If, when you get to the outside of the house, you decide without even going in that it is not what you want, it is common courtesy to cancel your appointment there and then by knocking on the door and saying 'sorry, but no'.

Always take a pen, paper or a notebook and a measuring rule with you, and the agent's particulars, so that you can check dimensions, particularly where measurements are quoted as 'max.' or 'overall' or 'approx.'. Ideally, both partners should view together, but if this is not possible it will help in later discussions if there are notes or plans to refer to.

It is no bad thing to make up a short checklist. Write down on the left-hand side, line by line, all the factors you can think of – rooms, situation, all the merits you want and any demerits you do not want – with a few spare lines for points occurring as you go along. Draw vertical columns to the right of these headings, put the address of the house (and succeeding houses) at the top of the column and then tick off 'yes' or 'no', or '3', say, opposite 'bedrooms', or 'good' or 'bad', and so on, so that you have a ready reminder of the comparative merits of possible houses.

It makes sense to view a property more than once before making a firm offer. Try to view it at different times of the day and preferably on different days of the week, including at the weekend. Consider how far the nearest source of public transport is. If you will be using the bus or train on a regular basis, try walking the route home at night from the station or bus stop. Also check out the distance to the nearest shops, the level of traffic noise and the neighbours. These factors are covered in depth later in this chapter.

First look at the property

It can be distracting to assess a house when it is decorated or furnished to another's taste, or is in need of redecoration. Try not to be influenced by 'wrong' colours and furniture – or none at all – but concentrate on absorbing a general impression and imagine yourself and your family in it. You are equally likely to be misled by a beautifully furnished and newly decorated home – you can fall for it as it looks, forgetting to think: 'How will it look with my possessions in it?'

A strange house on several floors can be confusing at first sight: it may help to make a floor-by-floor plan as you go. But do not waste too much time on this. It is better to go back and do a second tour.

Do not let yourself be rushed or pressurised by the estate agent who accompanies you, or embarrassed by the presence of the owner.

As you go over the house, concentrate on the layout of each floor and each room. Do not forget to look at the windows. An empty house without curtains gives an impression of light rooms, but can appear dark and dismal when curtained and furnished.

The height of the ceilings is something to note from the point of view of heating and redecorating and how your furniture will fit. An open-plan house (where the dining and sitting area and kitchen lead into each other, without dividing walls or doors), will need a powerful heating system and good insulation. A parent working in the kitchen will be glad of being able to keep an eye on a small child playing in the adjacent living area, but privacy could be a problem, and difficulties could arise when children reach school age and need a quiet place to study or play on their own or as teenagers to entertain their friends.

If the house seems to provide what you need in the way of basic accommodation – sufficient bedrooms, living rooms and so on – and if your first impression of it as a possible home is a favourable one, you should consider it in more detail.

Looking in more detail

No single house will provide all you want. It is up to you to decide what points are most important and which – because others are so satisfactorily provided – you are prepared to forgo.

Think also how permanent you expect your stay to be in the new home. If you are likely to resell shortly, consider whether any aspect of the property may affect your chances of finding a buyer when it is your turn to sell.

Here are some points to weigh up carefully. If the answers to the majority are not positive, the house is probably not suitable for you. The answer to some of the questions may be 'no, but could be arranged'. But take into account that alterations or improvements will put up the cost.

Points to be considered include:

- is the accommodation what you want?
- is the layout suitable?
- is the situation of the house right?
- what are the facts about the heating, lighting and other services?

- what is the condition of the structure?
- what is the state of the decorations – inside and out?
- what about the garden?
- what about any garage, drive and roadway?
- when will the house be available?
- what is included in the price?

Accommodation and layout
Entrance (hall)
- is there an outer porch (as protection against weather, for delivery of parcels)?
- is there space for parking a pram, pushchair, bicycle, shopping trolley?
- is there anywhere to hang coats, store wellington boots, gardening shoes, umbrellas?
- is it well lit?
- which direction does the front door face?

Living-room(s)
- are they adequate in size? (in an irregular-shaped room or one with a bay window, take the exact measurements)
- is the dining-room or dining area convenient for the kitchen? are there steps up or down from the kitchen? (making a trolley impracticable, carrying trays hazardous)
- is there space for the children to play?
- is there space for the piano? (preferably not against a neighbour's adjoining wall)
- is there space for your furniture (large sofas can cause problems if access is restricted)?
- are the windows in convenient places?
- where are the electrical sockets and are there enough of them?
- where are the lights and switches?

Kitchen
- is it large enough, particularly if you want to be able to eat in it or work in it?
- does it lead off the hall/living-room/dining-room? how convenient is it for carrying food and shopping to, rubbish from?
- is there an outside door into the garden, for access to the garage or dustbin?

- is there a back porch?
- what does the window look on to? which way does it face? (if south or west, it may get too hot); could you keep an eye on a child in the garden?
- is the window easy to open? is there an air extractor system?
- does the layout of the worktop and sink area suit your way of working?
- is it well lit?
- what storage is there for food? is there a larder? is there space for your refrigerator? for your freezer? for your dishwasher?
- will your existing equipment fit?
- is there enough cupboard space, drawers, shelves? a tall cupboard for the vacuum cleaner, brooms?
- is the floor covering in good condition? comfortable to stand on? likely to be easy to clean?
- is gas laid on? (check particularly whether the present owner has an electric cooker)
- where and how many electric sockets are there? is there one for a cooker?

Utility room
- is there one? or what facilities are there for laundry?

indoors: is there space for a washing machine/tumble dryer? ironing area?

outdoors: is there space for hanging clothes to dry? are there any restrictions on hanging washing outside?

Staircase
- is it easy to climb (for small children or elderly people)? are the treads wide enough? risers not too steep? are there awkward curves or bends? are there handrails? is it well lit (top and bottom)? will you be able to get your furniture upstairs?

Bedrooms
- how many?
- are they large enough? for double bed/twin beds/four-poster/bunk beds?
- will other furniture (chest of drawers, wardrobe, for instance) fit in? (measure, do not guess)

- is there built-in furniture?
- is there a washbasin? (if so, fill it up and let it drain, and do the same with any others – they can be noisy and react to the plumbing elsewhere in the house)
- are the rooms convertible to nursery/playroom/study/bedrooms? (consider future needs as well as current ones)
- do they face a noisy road or a bright street light?
- how soundproof are the walls between rooms?

Bathroom(s)
- how many?
- is it large enough?
- is there a separate WC?
- plumbing: can another bathroom/extra basin/shower/WC be installed easily? (check where the water supply and waste piping run in the building)
- does everything work?
- is there an airing cupboard/linen cupboard or space to make one?

Other
- is there an extra room which you could use as a spare bedroom/study/sewing room/boxroom for storage/playroom/workshop?
- is there a loft? could it be used for storage or converted into a room?
- cupboards: are there any built in? or space to put some in?

Situation and location
You probably already know or, if you do not, you should decide now, how much it matters to you to have a sunny living-room, kitchen or bedroom. A kitchen or living-room which never gets any sun can be very dark and gloomy in winter – so, check which rooms are north-facing (cold and dark), which are east-facing (morning sun, best for waking up/breakfasting), which are south- or west-facing (warm and sunny for most of the day). This is especially important if you are viewing on a dull day or a winter evening. If you cannot work it out for yourself, ask the owner or agent and mark the direction of the rooms on your plan. Similar houses on opposite sides of a road may be quite different inside with regard to the light and warmth – and may be different in price, too, on this account.

Work out whether the garden gets the sun all day or only part of the day, or is always shaded. Consider how important this is to you – as a sun-lover or as a gardener. Look to see whether any trees, foliage or adjacent buildings take away light from any room. If you are viewing in winter, be observant and allow for trees in leaf during the summer. Do any houses nearby look into the windows or garden? If you are viewing in summer, study whether the trees obscure some overlooking building. Also, trees in leaf are a good barrier to traffic noise, so it may be much noisier in winter.

Think about any possible winter hazards: if the district is hilly or the approach to the house is steep, icy conditions might make access difficult or impossible. Draughts coming through front or back doors and along passages may be fierce in winter – but absent on the gentle summer's day when you are viewing.

- Is the property near the coast (risk of flooding from the sea, coastal erosion)?
- Is there a river or any streams close by which could cause flooding? (this may affect insurance cover)
- The exterior of a house in an exposed position, on high ground or by the seaside may need more attention in the way of upkeep and insulation. If there is industry nearby, note whether the prevailing wind would send any dirt, smoke or smell towards the house rather than away from it. Will there be any noise?
- What about the siting of the house – the immediately adjacent vicinity (neighbours), the general location and the effect on your journey to work?

If you are interested in the house, it is essential to go back again to see it at a different time of the day, on a different day of the week, and in different weather conditions. Check out the following points.

- distance from the railway station (are there parking facilities there?), bus stop and bus routes (and underground), post office, bank, library, shops, launderette, health centre (will you be carrying home heavy shopping or pushing a pram uphill?), schools (how safe is the route?) or college, church or chapel
- access to the countryside/sea, park or recreation ground, cultural and leisure activities
- neighbours: how secluded is the house? are neighbours likely to be a nuisance (children or pets) or *vice versa*? in a terraced or semi-

63

detached house, which rooms have the party walls? what is the division between gardens? is the next-door garage near your boundary? (late/early car starting); are nearby buildings (restaurant, pub, club, fish-and-chip shop or take-away) likely to cause parking problems, noise at night, cooking smells, or piles of rubbish? a factory can produce smoke, noise or smells; a farm may give rise to smells or flies or straying animals); on a new estate, could further building work or future buildings obscure a pleasant view?

Problems waiting to happen

Neighbour disputes tend to focus on things which are shared: gateways, drives, drains, hedges. If there are any shared facilities will you be troubled by constant use from the people next door? The kindly old couple who may live there now could sell to a family with a much more intrusive lifestyle. Imagine the worst that could happen. Could you live with it? Sellers must disclose any neighbour disputes in preliminary enquiries (see page 248).

Other factors that you could find either a nuisance or an advantage (if next-door or nearby) might be a school, a police station, fire station, hospital, church, garage or repairer, kennels, swimming-pool or sports ground.

If the next-door property is uninhabited (particularly if it is derelict) find out who owns it and what is likely to be happening.

If you are viewing on a weekday, try to find out whether things change at weekends. Or if you are there at a weekend, consider the other days of the week. In a market town, make at least one visit on market day.

Watch and listen for traffic noise and inconvenience:

- are there heavy lorries going by on weekdays? (none at weekends)
- are there traffic lights/a junction/hill/bend close by? (constant stopping/starting/gear noises)
- is it a favourite route for L-drivers?
- do commuters or shoppers pass or park on weekdays?
- do tourists pass or park at weekends or in summer?
- do nearby sports grounds cause parking problems and noise at weekends/evenings?
- do trains pass within hearing distance?
- is there a motorway or by-pass near enough to be noisy? or are there plans to build one?

- is there an airport or airfield near and is the house under the flight path?
- are there any nasty but short-lived noises such as a milk depot loading crates at 4 a.m. for two hours every day?

If you can find out about the ownership of the adjacent land or buildings, try to discover whether further developments are planned. Knowledge of the district if you live there already will obviously be a help. Local papers and local gossip are other sources of information. It is unlikely that the seller will tell you that he or she is putting the house on the market because a new pig farm is to be set up in the field opposite.

Heating and other services

How is the house heated? Is all or only part of it centrally heated? (Look for radiators in all rooms; a note on a plan can help later when working out the arrangement of furniture.) When was the system installed?

Is electricity the only laid-on fuel? Or is there a gas supply, even if not currently in use? (when was it last used?)

Is there an alternative to fall back on if the electricity is cut off or the central heating supply fails, such as an open fire or a stove? Are there working fireplaces and what can you burn (is it a smoke control area)?

If you view during cold weather, you should be able to tell straight away whether the heating system works effectively. If you view in summer, ask for the system to be switched on, if practicable. You should get it tested as part of the survey.

Ask the owners what the past year's fuel consumption and heating costs (including maintenance) have been – if they are able to tell you. When assessing any figures, remember to allow for differences in your ways of life – whether out all day, with or without children or of different ages, elderly people in the household.

- If oil-fired: where is the storage tank (and its vent pipe)? is it unobtrusively sited and what is its capacity? where is the boiler?
- If solid fuel: do you mind having to stoke a boiler? carry fuel? clean out ashes? what type of fuel has to be used? where is the fuel stored – is it convenient for the house/for delivery?

- If gas-fired: where is the boiler? How old is it?
- If off-peak electricity: electric storage heaters – how many and where, what capacity? how old and run on what tariff? underfloor or ceiling heating, in which rooms? warm air ducting? where are the vents/grills?
- Loft insulation: is there any, and, if so, of what type and thickness?
- Water supply: is it on direct mains water? If not, what water supply is there? Is the supply under anyone else's control (e.g. the pipe runs across a farmer's land from his supply)? What are the water charges per year? Is there a meter? How is the water heated? Is the cylinder likely to be large enough for your needs? Where do the pipes run?
- Electricity: ask how old the wiring is and whether the property has ever been re-wired (if so, professionally or d-i-y)? Are there plenty of sockets? Does the consumer unit have old-fashioned fuses or modern circuit-breakers? If you want to cook by electricity, is there a separate circuit (30-amp, at least) for the cooker?
- Gas: if there are gas fires, how old are they (older types may be neither legal nor efficient)?
- Drainage: is the house connected to a main drainage system? or is there a septic tank or cesspool? If so, what are the costs of maintenance and arrangements for emptying? Note where any manholes or access points are: if on your premises, you may be independent in case of trouble; if on someone else's land, there may be delay in getting a stoppage cleared. (On the other hand, if the communal manholes are on your site, you may be inconvenienced by calls to get obstructions cleared.)
- TV aerial: is there one? If you see a lot of fancy aerials on nearby houses, it is likely that reception is poor; if the house is under a cliff or hillside, it may be inaccessible to radio signals. If there is a satellite dish, does it comply with local authority requirements?

The structure of the building

Even if you will be having a professional survey of the house or flat done by a qualified surveyor, try, during a preliminary visit, to get as good an impression as you can of the structural condition of the building. If it looks to you to have a lot of faults, you could save yourself the cost of a survey by deciding there and then that the cost of repairs would not justify the cost of the house – or that the repairs would not be possible on your budget. Ask the owner what structural work has been carried out recently, when and why.

An owner is under no obligation to tell you of any faults: it is up to you or your surveyor to discover them. On the other hand, he or she is under an obligation to give honest answers to direct questions: for example, whether there have ever been any problems with dry rot or an insurance claim for flooding. If he or she does not answer truthfully and you can show that you relied on those answers, you can sue the owner later. On the other hand, if you discover the problems at an early stage you will save yourself a lot of distress.

Inside

From a structural point of view, the main things to look at inside are the walls and ceilings.

Ceilings

- are there stained patches? (tell-tale signs of leaks)
- are ceilings sagging or cracked? (cracked plaster ceilings in an older house may just need filling and painting over, but if cracks look to you to be alarmingly wide or run into corners or over window lintels, there may be a problem).

Walls

- are there stains on walls around the skirting, and crumbling plaster? (signs of rising damp)
- are there any long, diagonal cracks in walls which look as if they have been repaired but have re-cracked? (this may be a sign of settlement)
- is the existing paper or paint shabby, dirty or damaged? (note to what extent redecorating would be immediately necessary and include this in your budget)
- if the house is newly painted inside, ask yourself why? are they just house-proud – or covering up?

Woodwork and floors

- is woodwork showing cracks or shrinkage (going crinkly), especially skirtings? (a possible sign of woodworm or rot)
- if floors are springy, they or the joists underneath may be rotten (on the ground floor) or wormy (anywhere)

- ask what the floor surface is under a fitted carpet, vinyl or lino covering
- are any floor tiles cracked or wood blocks loose or bulging?
- are any floor coverings worn in places that take a lot of traffic? would any need replacing?

Outside

Go outside and study the building from top to bottom. A pair of binoculars can be useful for scanning roofs and chimney stacks. If things look bad from below, they are probably worse up there, and inside too.

If any major re-roofing or repairs have been carried out, find out what, when, and whether any guarantees were attached. For a flat roof, find out how long ago it was laid (felt roofs last about ten years, asphalt up to 30).

Points to look for or ask about include the following.

Roof

- look for any loose or broken slates or tiles, particularly near chimneys and roof valleys. Walk down the garden or to the other side of the road and have a look at any roof valleys that may be visible (if they are cluttered with slipped slates or tiles, the whole roof may be likely to need rehanging)
- do chimney stacks look in good condition or is the brickwork in need of repointing?

Main walls

- are there any bulges or cracks? (may be caused by settlement of the foundations or by tree roots – own or neighbour's). A way of checking for bulges is to stand very close to a wall and look along it. If any part is out of true, perhaps you should look at another house.
- what is the state of the pointing between the bricks? (it should look smooth and full: gaps or cracks allow damp to penetrate). Are the bricks themselves in good condition?
- is there a damp-proof course (not all old houses have one)? Are there signs of damp at ground level? If a damp course has been injected, ask for the inspection report and guarantees. Confirm that the work has been carried out to specification

- guttering and downpipes: are there signs of rust or leaking, stained or green walls? (damp could penetrate the brickwork, or cause wet rot)
- when were the walls last painted? with what material? will they need doing immediately? and how often thereafter?
- is the paint peeling very badly? (there may be a damp problem)
- are walls covered with a cement rendering? what condition is it in? (it will be an expensive maintenance item).

Doors and windows

- do they fit well? do all the windows open and close easily?
- does the woodwork look in good condition? is there any rust on metal frames?
- what is the condition of the paintwork?
- when were they last painted (or varnished)? (every three years is the recommended interval, more frequently in south-facing walls or if the house is at the seaside).

If you go ahead to the stage of having a professional survey done, tell the surveyor of anything you have noticed that you think may be sinister. If he or she confirms your suspicions, you can ask for an idea of how much it would cost to be put right.

Heavier maintenance and repair costs are likely with an older house, so it is even more important to have an old house surveyed and to get an idea of how well it has been looked after over the years.

Some prefabricated reinforced concrete (PRC) house-types have been designated as defective. Before buying a PRC home, a prospective buyer should check with the local authority whether the dwelling is one of these. If so, find out whether it has been repaired in compliance with the Housing Defects Act 1984 and carries a warranty issued by NHBC. If not, the buyer will have difficulty in obtaining a mortgage and in re-selling, and would probably do better to look for another house.

The garden

How important is a garden to you, as a gardener, for general recreation (sunbathing, barbecues), and for the children?

- is it the right size/too big/not big enough?
- how sheltered is it?

- how much sun does it get?
- is it suitable for a child to play in? are there any hazards? (trees, pond, stream, unsafe access to road)
- is it easily accessible for a pram?
- can you keep an eye on it from the house?
- is it on a steep slope? easy to maintain?
- what state is it in? (if not yet laid out, this could be expensive: purchasing topsoil, laying a lawn)
- is there much grass to cut/hedges to be kept trimmed? (would this present a problem?)
- is there somewhere to store garden tools?
- if outhouses or a greenhouse are included in the sale, what condition are they in?
- is there a standpipe or tap for watering? (may involve additional water charge)
- is it possible to reach the garden at the back of the house without having to go through the house? (also relevant for dustbin emptying).

Trees can be a hazard if they have grown too big or been planted too close to a building or walls (including the neighbour's). Roots spread underground, growing outwards generally in proportion to the canopy of the tree and can affect the foundations of a building and damage drains. Poplars, elms and willows are especially greedy (willows can signify a very damp environment or underground stream).

In some areas, trees in private gardens have tree preservation orders placed on them, prohibiting the owner from lopping or cutting them down without first getting permission from the local authority. Ask the owner if this applies to any tree on the property and get your solicitor to check. All trees in conservation areas are automatically subject to a preservation order.

The boundaries of the property may be marked by walls, fences or hedges, for some of which the owner may be responsible. If the piers of a brick wall or the posts of a fence are on your side, it is more likely than not that the wall will be yours and your responsibility. In any case, it is sensible to inspect the state of any brick walls, wooden fencing or gates. Replacing them can be costly. An unstable brick wall is a danger to life.

Garaging the car

- is there a garage?
- how far is it from the house?
- will your car fit in? (the size of garage is not usually stated in estate agent's particulars; be sure to know the measurements of your own car, including its width with the door open and the height if it is a hatchback)
- are the garage doors easy to open, keep open, shut, lock?
- is there light and a power point inside?
- what is the approach to the garage made of? what sort of upkeep will be necessary?
- what is the access from the driveway/garage to the road like? if the road is narrow, will a car parked on the opposite side stop you getting yours out? Is there clear visibility? (so that you can enter or leave the road safely).

If there is no garage:

- is there a legal access to the property? Planning approval is necessary for a new vehicle access
- is there a car port (a roofed-over area at the side of the house)? can your car be parked in the garden, yard or on the road? (this affects the insurance premium)
- is there plenty of parking and turning space?
- are there parking restrictions outside? or a residents' parking scheme? (involving an annual charge)
- is there space and access to the road for you to put up a garage (needs planning permission)
- where can visitors park?

Chapter 4

Agreeing terms

This section covers both using a solicitor and handling your own purchase.

Before making an offer

If you like what you have seen, check out some practical aspects before you make an offer.

Ascertain approximately when the seller is able and willing to move out. He or she may be waiting to sell before starting to look for a house or may be waiting for a mortgage or be part of a lengthy chain. If timing is important to you, this will affect your decision.

The legal and financial set-up will have to be investigated later when it comes to the conveyancing (the legal side of house-buying). Meanwhile, there is still much to check at this preliminary stage. Some points are so important that they may stop you buying the house.

Freehold or leasehold?

If it is a leasehold property, ask about any annual or other financial commitments such as:

- ground rent payable (how much? fixed or subject to review?). Normally this should be no more than a token few pounds a year
- maintenance charges for repairs or redecoration (is any payment imminent? Has the seller been informed of any future expenditure, and what payments have been made over the past three years or so?)

If it is freehold, there may nevertheless be annual charges for maintenance – for example, roads on a private estate.

Covenants and rights

Are there any restrictions on the use of the house – for example, on hanging out the washing or keeping a pig? Restrictive covenants are obligations imposed by covenant on the owner of a property, forbidding certain activities on the property, such as running a business or putting buildings on parts of it. (You may in any case need planning permission if you want to carry on a professional business from your home address.)

Covenants last indefinitely. It is never safe to ignore them, even if they were imposed many years ago. There is always the risk that someone may try to enforce them. On a housing estate these rules may be part of a 'building scheme' which means that fellow residents can insist that you obey them.

Do other people have rights such as to walk across part of the property? This should come to light when your solicitor receives the draft contract or details of the lease at a later stage. But if there are any indications of this sort of thing, tell your solicitor so that more enquiries can be made.

Consent for building work

Has planning permission for all alterations to the property been applied for? If granted, what work was carried out and by how much did this increase the size of the house? (This could affect your need for planning permission for any future alterations.) If permission was refused, why? Has an enforcement notice been issued?

If you think you would like to make alterations – for example, add a large extension or put in new windows – visit the local planning department to try to discover, before you get too involved, what the local planning authority's attitude is to such alterations.

Also, you can find out by going to the local authority planning department whether there are any plans (or projects) for local buildings, new roads, motorways or industrial development. Every local authority keeps a register of planning applications and the register is open to inspection (as is the register of enforcement proceedings).

Similarly, all building work must comply with the Building Regulations (see page 98). If it does not, your own safety may be affected and the building control department can take enforcement action.

Many of these investigations are covered as a matter of course by solicitors' searches.

Other environmental matters

Environmental policies are gradually moving towards greater protection for members of the public. Since April 2000, local authorities have been obliged to operate a register of contaminated land, so that it is possible to find out whether, for instance, the house has been built on the site of a municipal rubbish tip or the land is otherwise contaminated. Such local enquiries will enable you to find out whether the immediate area has a history of land use which could cause you problems.

You or your solicitor can make numerous other enquiries over matters as varied as flight paths, road improvement proposals, planning zones, commons, oil pipe lines, limestone workings, coal, tin or clay mines, radon (especially in Cornwall), rivers and canals, and Ministry of Defence activities.

Council tax, water and sewerage charges

The council tax band, or perhaps the council tax payable, may have been quoted in particulars you have been provided with by the agent or seller. If not, ask for this information. If only the council tax band has been given, you can find out from the finance department of the local authority what the council tax for that band is likely to be.

Water and sewerage charges are levied separately by the water companies and are either metered or based on the old rateable value. Individual companies set their own tariffs, subject to price caps set by OFWAT, the supervisory body.

Vacant possession and sitting tenants

Normally, a house is sold with vacant possession: when it becomes yours, the seller leaves and it will be empty, ready for you to occupy. But if there are already 'sitting' tenants in the house – that is, the owner has let part of it to other people – you should assume that you cannot get immediate possession of those parts of the property. (Some sitting tenants even have the right to transmit the tenancy to their widow[er] or another generation.) You would also probably have considerable difficulty in raising the sitting tenants' rent above its present level, should you want to. The subject of sitting tenants is complex and you should get legal advice before you take any steps towards acquiring such a house.

What does the house price include?

The estate agent's particulars may mention specific items which the owner would like to sell with the house. When showing the house, the agent may point out in each room any items being included in the sale, or being offered separately. These would be additional to what are usually termed 'fixtures and fittings', which are accepted as being part of the house. Make sure that all extra items are included in your contract.

Fixtures and fittings

To avoid problems later it is vital to establish clearly which items are, and which are not, included in the sale.

The basic concept is that anything that is part of the fabric of the house is included. Over the years, various removable items, known in law as 'chattels' ('moveables' in Scotland), may be fixed to the house and lose their original nature of chattels by becoming part of the structure. One test is the extent to which the items are actually attached and cannot be removed without causing irremediable damage; the other is to consider what might have been the intention of the owner in installing them. But the distinction between a removable and a not-removable item remains difficult to establish.

For example, a case was brought to court over some garden seats and statues which were free-standing on their own weight and not fixed to the ground. These were judged to be essentially part of the architectural design of the garden and so were not removable (i.e. they were fixtures). In another court case, valuable tapestries had been firmly fixed to the walls of a house in such a way that they could not be removed without causing substantial damage. These were, nevertheless, held to be removable because the aim in attaching them was to enjoy them as tapestries and not that they should form part of the house. So it is not easy for the seller or buyer to know exactly what the law would say in a case of dispute.

Many sellers and buyers are ignorant about what they can take or can expect to have bought, so you should be particularly careful on this point. It may not always be practical or desirable to go through all the items on a first viewing, but at a point before you negotiate a price, you should establish exactly what you are buying and be sure that you and the seller are in agreement. Bathroom fittings, light fittings, curtain rails and tracks and TV aerials are commonly disputed items. What has to be done in each case is to clarify what are:

- **items not removable** because they form part of the structure: included in the price
- **uncertain items** which the buyer and seller may regard differently. It should be agreed at the time of making an offer whether they are to be included in the price
- **items removable** since they do not form part of the structure: price to be agreed if sold to the buyer.

Examples of items not removable:

- plumbing and heating installations integrated into the structure
- gas or electric instantaneous water heater
- electric sockets, wall switches and wiring (including lamp socket holders but not light bulbs)
- garden sheds and greenhouses built on foundations
- (usually, unless already moved into containers or specially negotiated) trees and shrubs in the garden.

Examples of items removable by the seller:

- free-standing gas or electric cooker
- fridge, freezer
- dishwasher, washing machine and any similar detachable equipment
- heaters connected to mains supply only by plugs or detachable means of connection
- electrical fittings beyond the point of contact with mains supply
- lamp shades, light bulbs
- carpets, underlay and felt, curtains (though nowadays fitted carpets are normally included and curtains may be)
- free-standing garden furniture and sheds.

Debatable items:

- curtain rails and tracks, including brass/wooden rods and pelmets
- fitted bookshelves and other shelves

- built-in kitchen units/appliances
- built-in cupboards and wardrobes/bedroom furniture (the test being the extent to which they are fixed to the structure)
- electric storage heaters, water softener, wall lights
- decorative door furniture and door chimes
- bathroom fittings, lavatory paper holders
- roof TV aerial/satellite dish (nearly always included in the price)
- free-standing garden ornaments (depends on their purpose).

When you reach the point where you have decided to go ahead with an offer, ask the owner to go through the house with you, agreeing and listing room by room:

- any fixtures and fittings, whether referred to in any particulars or separately agreed between you, which are included in the sale price
- any items the seller is willing to leave but for which you would have to make a separate offer.

You should in due course draw up an itemised list together with the seller, with copies for your solicitors, so that there will be no confusion later. (Check when the time comes that the actual item(s) left for you are not inferior substitutes.)

You should assume that anything not on the list of items the seller is to leave behind will be taken away – indeed, the seller must do this to give you vacant possession.

If the seller's solicitors are using the Law Society's detailed TransAction protocol (see page 247), the seller will be asked to complete a detailed fixtures, fittings and contents form which will make clear what is being left and what is being taken. This forms part of the contract and is legally binding on the seller.

Items bought from the seller

There is no reason why you should not vary any of the 'rules' as to what is or is not removable, provided it is agreed and written into the contract.

Whatever you intend to buy from the seller, inspect it very carefully to make sure that it works or is in good condition (any carpets, for instance, where rugs may have been covering up worn areas, any garden tools or lawn mower which may not have been well maintained) and is not going to cause you additional expense.

List of items included and excluded

Tick either INCLUDED or EXCLUDED where applicable

	INCLUDED	EXCLUDED
Windows		
double glazing	_____	_____
curtains	_____	_____
curtain rails and rings	_____	_____
curtain tracks and fittings	_____	_____
pelmets	_____	_____
blinds	_____	_____
Electrical		
immersion heater	_____	_____
switches, points	_____	_____
wall and ceiling fittings	_____	_____
night storage heaters	_____	_____
fitted electric fire	_____	_____
TV aerial	_____	_____
Bathroom		
bathroom cabinet	_____	_____
bathroom heater	_____	_____
glass shelves	_____	_____
towel rail	_____	_____
toilet-roll holder	_____	_____
heated towel rail	_____	_____
mirror	_____	_____

Kitchen

kitchen cupboards _____ _____

wall utensils _____ _____

Garden

greenhouse _____ _____

garden shed _____ _____

garden trees, shrubs, plants _____ _____

flowers and garden produce _____ _____

garden ornaments _____ _____

garden furniture _____ _____

pots and containers _____ _____

General

fitted carpets _____ _____

fitted mirrors _____ _____

door bell _____ _____

door chimes _____ _____

heating oil _____ _____

solid fuel _____ _____

fitted gas fire _____ _____

fitted shelves _____ _____

Any others (list them below)

. . . . _____ _____

. . . . _____ _____

. . . . _____ _____

. . . . _____ _____

The prices for any separate items have to be agreed on the basis of their original cost, the wear and tear the items have had and their condition now, and what a replacement would cost today. The actual figures are generally wide open to negotiation. But whatever is agreed should be confirmed in writing (tell your solicitor, too).

The owner may try to get you to buy some items which you do not want. If they duplicate what you already have, you are in a better position to refuse them politely. If you do not want them for some other reason – they are not to your taste, perhaps – you will have to judge whether buying them or not would affect your chances of concluding the whole deal.

The seller will probably be pleased if you agree to buy any residual coal, heating oil or liquefied petroleum gas (LPG); the value of these will have to be worked out later, but the principle can be agreed now. However, quite often these are included in the price.

Making an offer

When you decide that you want to buy a house, make an offer for it without delay. If the seller is offering the property through an estate agent, put the offer to the agent (who can then tell other potential buyers that the property is under offer). Do this even before you have had a survey done – the offer does not commit you provided it is made 'subject to contract and to survey'.

A TRUE STORY: James and Jane got on well with the people who were selling a plot of land to them. 'You don't want to see a solicitor,' said the sellers. 'They just charge a lot of money and you have nothing to show for it.'

The sellers' friend prepared the documentation.

James and Jane signed up – then went to a solicitor who found that the plot of land was not the same area as the one on which planning permission had been given.

The sellers bungled the documentation. Fortunately, that let James and Jane off the hook, but they had signed documents without proper investigation. They had many sleepless nights before the problems were resolved.

You must make it clear that your offer is subject to contract – whether it is an oral offer or in writing – so that you are covered if:

- you are unable to raise the necessary mortgage or loan
- a survey decides you against continuing with the purchase
- subsequent enquiries disclose some insuperable drawback: e.g. road-widening or compulsory purchase by the local authority
- you change your mind for some other reason.

If there is any objection to the deal being on a subject-to-contract basis, do not proceed. And do not sign any kind of contract at this stage without taking legal advice.

Agreeing the price

Most sellers fix a price which they believe to be the maximum they dare ask, and most will be prepared to come down unless several would-be buyers are competing.

To decide whether you are willing to pay the asking price or to make an alternative offer, you must take into consideration:

- how much you can afford to pay
- the state of the property market (the more potential buyers there may be after the house, the less scope there will be for bargaining; the fewer potential buyers, the more likely the seller will be to accept a reduced price)
- how the price compares with that of similar properties in the area
- how much you want the house and are prepared to pay over the odds to get it.

Having made your offer, it may be accepted straight away or you may have to sit back and wait: the seller may have other prospective buyers about to make offers, or may still want to show the house to other viewers. You can try to persuade the seller that your offer is so good that it would make sense to accept it, at least provisionally. It all depends on the personalities involved and the state of the market. A seller who has been waiting for six months for a single offer is unlikely to be difficult.

A strong bargaining factor is whether you can act quickly because:

- you have a mortgage certificate guaranteeing the offer of a loan
- a buyer has been found for your own house
- you have ready money.

If the sale of your own house is likely to be delayed, it may be worth getting the promise of a bridging loan from your bank (or other source) to put you in an advantageous negotiating position. However, in a poor market your bank is unlikely to offer an 'open-ended' bridging loan. Except in very unusual circumstances, you would be ill advised to embark on buying a new home without tying up the sale of your present one.

Saving on stamp duty land tax

Whether the buyer has to pay stamp duty land tax on the transfer of a property depends on the price of the house. The duty is 1 per cent on the whole price when this is over £60,000, (e.g. price £70,000, stamp duty £700) with higher rates as the price increases. At or below £60,000 no stamp duty is payable, and stamp duty exemption applies in certain areas for properties worth under £150,000 (see page 23 for more information).

If the price, including fittings such as carpets and curtains, that you are asked to pay is just above £60,000, ask the seller to separate the price of the house and that of the fittings if deducting their value reduces the house price below the stamp duty threshold. However, the value allotted to these fittings must be a realistic one. It could amount to a fraud on the Inland Revenue if you inflate the value of fixtures to avoid stamp duty.

Preliminary deposit

At the point when you make a firm offer, an estate agent will ask you the name and address of your solicitor or conveyancer (if you are using one) and may ask you to pay a small deposit (say, £250) as a token of your intent. This initial deposit has no legal standing and cannot, by itself, bind either party to the transaction. If you decline to pay a preliminary deposit, it is highly unlikely to affect your chances of buying. If you do pay such a deposit, you should get a receipt stating that the deposit was paid subject to contract and to survey. You will not at this stage have had the house surveyed. If a survey reveals any defects requiring attention but not serious enough to deter you or your source of finance, you may want to reduce your offer.

If the sale falls through before contracts are exchanged, a sum paid by way of initial deposit has to be returned in full. Estate agents are required to have a separate 'clients' account' with the bank, into which clients' monies are paid. But be careful. Not all estate agents are members of professional bodies. People have lost deposits when estate agents defaulted.

Valuation for mortgage

A buyer who is applying for a mortgage should notify the building society, or other mortgagee, that he or she has made an offer for a property, and ask that the lender's valuation be carried out as soon as possible. You will have to pay the required fee for the valuation, which is based on the price of the house. (If you lose the house before the valuer has been to it, tell the lender to cancel the visit and to return the fee or keep it ready for your next attempt.)

The valuation is carried out on behalf of the lender to assess whether the condition and value of the house is adequate security for the loan the lender has been asked to make.

The valuer takes into account:

- age, type, accommodation, fixtures and features of the property
- construction and general state of repair
- siting and the amenities of the locality
- tenure, tenancies, if there are any, annual payments or other liabilities.

Planning potential will normally be disregarded.

Valuation for mortgage purposes is the amount at which a qualified valuer believes the property would sell in the open market at the date of the inspection. It is not a structural survey, and in no way guarantees that the house is structurally sound and without defects, nor that it is worth the purchase price being asked. If, in the building society's valuer's opinion, the house is worth less than the purchase price, the proportion that will be lent may be calculated on his or her figure – and the amount of loan offered to you may therefore seem a strange percentage of the purchase price.

Low valuation

The offer of a loan may be withdrawn after the valuation survey. You would then have to start again, with a different property – or a different lender. But most mortgage applications ask if you have already applied for a mortgage on the same property, so it is unlikely that you will get an unconditional mortgage from another source for that house.

The valuer can include a recommendation to the lender not to make a loan unless specified work is carried out, such as putting in a damp-proof course or treating all timbers against rot. He or she may advise the lender to withhold an amount (say, £5,000 retention money or even £10,000) which will be paid out only when the work has been carried out satisfactorily. This can be a problem if you do not have spare cash available – the seller will want all his or her price on the nail. This is where a bridging loan may be needed.

If the lender does lay down such conditions and substantial expenditure is involved, it may be worth getting a second opinion from another surveyor, or there may be an opportunity to re-negotiate the price with the seller. If an agreement cannot be reached, it might be better to pull out of the transaction.

With more minor items of repair, the building society may ask you to give an undertaking to carry these out within, say, six months of completion of the mortgage.

Surveys

One of the most common misconceptions is that mortgage lenders carry out surveys. They do not. They carry out valuation surveys, which are very different. The lenders are solely concerned with whether the house/flat is worth the amount being borrowed, not with its precise condition.

Buyers should want to know the exact condition of the property they are buying. Yet only 15 per cent of buyers commission a proper building survey or structural survey. This is partly because many people think the lender's valuation will protect them and partly because they do not want to spend the money (usually between £300 and £700).

Most building societies allow or even encourage an arrangement whereby the surveyor who does their valuation carries out a survey for the buyer at the same visit. The fee for your survey would be slightly less than it would otherwise be, in view of the fact that the surveyor is already going to visit the property for the building society.

When the 'home information packs' are introduced (see page 144), the documentation provided to a prospective buyer will include a surveyor's 'home condition' report. Buyers will still have to pay for a valuation and might have to commission a more thorough structural survey.

House-buyer's report

There are standard forms for house-buyers' valuation and survey reports used by surveyors who are members of the RICS. If you want to have your own survey done earlier (so as to avoid delay if there are many other potential buyers), and the RICS report is acceptable to the lender, no further valuation report is needed (nor is a further fee payable).

The standard house-buyer's report completed by a building society surveyor when doing the mortgage valuation is not a structural survey. But it provides comments on the condition of parts of the property that are readily accessible or visible and gives an opinion of the market value. These reports contain extensive exclusion clauses: they are not full investigations. They may include recommendations for further tests or investigations that seem to be called for. The fee is about half-way between that for a straight mortgage valuation and that for a full survey.

A house-buyer's report is unsuitable for many older properties and buildings of unusual construction – pre-1900 buildings, buildings over 200 square metres in floor area and buildings over three storeys in height.

Structural survey

A structural survey should be carried out by a qualified person who specialises in this kind of work, such as a building surveyor or architect. A qualified surveyor may be a member of the Royal Institution of Chartered Surveyors (RICS)★ (with the letters FRICS or ARICS after the name) or the Association of Building Engineers (ABE)★. These professional associations are responsible for maintaining standards within the profession. They can be asked for the names of any of their members in a given area who are qualified building surveyors.

Your solicitor may be able to advise on the choice of an appropriate surveyor if you are buying locally, or a friend may recommend one he or she has used. It is preferable to engage a surveyor local to the property being inspected since he or she may know of any relevant conditions in the area which might affect it. The estate agent/surveyor acting for the seller is not allowed to carry out a survey on the house (because of a conflict of interest) but may recommend a surveyor.

Ask the surveyor how soon he or she can do the survey and discuss how comprehensive a survey to carry out. You should obtain written confirmation from the surveyor setting out the extent of the inspection: this may avoid misunderstandings at a later date. The extent of the survey will depend on the age and condition of the property – and on how much you can afford. It is not only for old property that it is desirable to have a survey done: a recently built house can have serious defects too, through bad design, bad workmanship or neglect.

The extent of a full structural survey is described in *Building Surveys of Residential Property*: a *guidance note* available from the RICS (price £30). If you want a full structural survey, refer to this publication.

The cost of a structural survey

Fees are usually by negotiation and relate to the time taken to inspect the property and write up the report. Generally speaking, the larger the property and the worse the condition of the building, the longer the professional survey will take.

The written report accounts for a large part of the cost, so if you are content to have oral comments, or a less detailed survey taking note only of any major structural defects, you would pay less. However, beware of relying on oral comments only. If defects show up later, you may have difficulty in establishing just what the surveyor actually said.

Be prepared to have to pay for a survey more than once during your house-hunting, not only because a survey may show that a property is not worth buying but because a deal may fall through for reasons beyond your control (gazumping, mortgage delay, seller withdrawing).

The survey report

Give the surveyor as much relevant information about the property as you can, particularly details of any doubtful points you noticed when you viewed it (such as damp patches, odd smells, cracks, obviously recent repairs, state of party walls) and on the siting of the house regarding potential flooding or subsidence.

If you plan to make any alterations or improvements, inform the surveyor before the survey in case there are any snags which he or she might spot. If, for example, you plan to demolish an inside wall to enlarge a room, this may turn out to be a load-bearing wall which it would be inadvisable, or very costly, to remove. And if you are planning complete redecoration, or a rewire or replumb, tell the surveyor. You will save his or her time and your money.

What a structural survey includes

You are likely to get a general description of the construction and materials used, and comments on the condition of:

- roof – timberwork, cladding, tiles, slates, chimney stacks, flashing, rainwater gutters, insulation
- walls – plasterwork, brickwork, pointing, insulation, decoration, any cracks, damp, bulges
- foundations – soundness, damp-proof course and external soil level, any subsidence, settlement
- windows – state of frames
- floors and joinery – soundness of timber, ventilation, any evidence of wet rot, dry rot, woodworm
- plumbing – bathroom and WC, fittings, waste pipes, tanks and cylinders
- drains – soil and rainwater
- electrical installation – age of wiring
- chimneys and flues
- garden – state of paths, fences, outbuildings.

The report which the surveyor gives you should summarise the condition of these items in as much detail as you have agreed, together with any faults and their importance.

If the house is furnished at the time, it may not be practicable to make a very detailed inspection, which would involve lifting carpets and floorboards, for example. Much depends on how thorough an inspection the vendor permits.

The survey of the electrical installation may be confined to a 'visual examination'. Much of the wiring is hidden behind skirting boards and under floorboards, and it is possible that the surveyor will draw his or her conclusions only from what can be seen. He or she will say so in the report, but you should be aware of the limitation.

Do not hesitate to discuss the report with the surveyor, who will be able to put the defects into perspective. Ask him or her to explain any technical terms that you do not understand.

Ask the surveyor to tell you the approximate cost of putting right any faults which are found and to give you an estimate of how much you would need to spend to put the house into good structural order. Then try offering the seller a price reduced by that amount. Explain why, and be prepared to negotiate. If the seller will not budge, you have to decide how badly you want the house. Your offer being subject to contract and subject to survey, if you decide that you do not want to buy the house, you are not obliged to go ahead: simply tell the estate agent or the seller direct that you are no longer interested.

Specialist tests

There is a distinction between an 'inspection' and a 'test' of such services as the drains, the heating system, the wiring and timber. In particular, discuss with the surveyor whether the central heating system should be inspected or tested.

Where a house is old or appears to be in poor state of repair, the surveyor may recommend specialist tests. He or she will offer to call in specialists (and you have to pay for them). The fact that a test has been recommended may be sufficient reason for you to incur this extra expense – usually, a potential problem has been diagnosed. If the surveyor has found evidence of serious problems, you will have to accept that you are likely to commit yourself to a lot of expenditure. If that worries you, this could be the point when you start looking around for another property.

Guaranteed treatment

If your surveyor's report shows that specialist treatment is recommended (and you are still likely to buy the house), you can get estimates (usually free) of the cost from specialist firms. For example, a list of their members is available from the British Wood Preserving and Damp-proofing Association (BWPDA)★. It is worth getting more than one such estimate. You may want to offer less for the house to allow for the cost of treatment and other work needed.

Members of the BWPDA can insure their guarantees on their customers' behalf through the Guarantee Protection Insurance Company Ltd (GPI)★. If the contractor goes out of business before the expiry of his 20-year guarantee (figures indicate more than half of contractors do), in the event of any problems the insurer will stand in his place and undertake to have guaranteed remedial work done again by a suitable company. The one-off fee for treatment costing up to £5,000 is about £55 to £60. For treatment costing £5,000 to £10,000 it is about £80.

Treatments which can be guaranteed include wood-boring beetle, wood rot, chemical and electrical damp course treatment, wall ties, lateral restraints, wall stitching and resin repairs to trusses. GPI also have a list of specialist structural waterproofing contractors whose work they will also insure, to cover items such as basements and homes built into hillsides. This type of work carried out under NHBC or Zurich schemes is required to have a GPI-insured guarantee.

Compulsory arbitration for chartered surveyors

Home owners and buyers who are let down by negligent chartered surveyors, be they estate agents, building surveyors or managing agents, no longer have to risk court action to get compensation. A compulsory arbitration scheme for all members of the RICS came into effect on 1 September 1998. Chartered surveyors are also required to have a proper in-house complaints procedure.

Claiming compensation from surveyors is now simple, quick, informal and inexpensive. Each party presents a written statement of its argument in the dispute. A specially trained arbitrator then looks at all the evidence and, if necessary, personally inspects the property. The arbitrator's decision will be binding on both sides.

NHBC Buildmark Scheme

If the house is less than ten years old, check whether it is covered by the NHBC★ Buildmark Scheme. (This in itself is no reason for not having a survey.) Find out how many years there are left on the NHBC scheme. The balance is transferred to a new owner, but only for defects which appear after the house is sold. Defects which are (or could have been) apparent before the purchase will not be remedied by NHBC unless the previous owner has already claimed. If your surveyor notices anything that may come under the NHBC scheme, it is the seller who must make the claim. Besides, you should be very cautious about buying a house with known defects.

Zurich Insurance scheme

This is similar to the NHBC scheme outlined above (see page 32).

Existing guarantees

The previous owner may have employed specialist firms to carry out remedial work for which a guarantee has been given – for instance, treatment for woodworm, for dry or wet rot or rising damp, or the use of special protective coatings for roofs or external walls. Such a guarantee can normally be transferred from one owner to the next, although you may have to notify the company concerned and pay a registration fee. Sometimes a formal assignment of the guarantee is necessary. You should get the original document eventually, usually through your own solicitor, but ask whether the surveyor can see it before inspecting. Make sure you ask your solicitor to obtain not only the guarantee but also the original report and estimate on which the guarantee is based. This will detail what work was (or should have been) done and any qualifications to the guarantee.

Guarantees for damp treatment are often conditional on other works being carried out (such as replastering in a special way or lowering the ground levels outside). These tasks are not usually carried out by the treatment company. If any problem arises, it is often easy for the treatment company to put the blame on someone else.

Some guarantees are for long periods (20 years or more). However, the company which carried out the work might not last as long as the guarantees it gave. If it goes out of business the guarantees will become worthless, unless backed by insurance, such as that afforded by the Guarantee Protection Insurance Company Ltd★. The Guarantee Protection Insurance Company Ltd policy lies with the property and does not need reassigning when the house is sold.

The steps on making an offer

Step 1: see the house you like, go home and think/talk it over.

Step 2: go to view it again (preferably at a different time of day and day of the week). Find out as much as you can about the neighbourhood, development plans and all environmental matters.

Step 3: in a buyer's market, put your own house up for sale.

If everything is still all right (and it looks as though you will get a buyer for your own house):

Step 4: make an offer at a price you can afford (or a little less) via the estate agent or direct to the seller. Decide who is to do the conveyancing: ask what your solicitor's or conveyancer's fees will be; tell your chosen solicitor/conveyancer of your offer and give him or her the seller's name and address and that of the solicitor. When the 'home information packs' are introduced (see page 144), the relevant documentation will be obtained at this stage.

If your offer is accepted:

Step 5: put your own house on the market if applicable (and if not already done). Contact the building society (or other lender), complete the application for a mortgage; ask when the valuation can be done (and the name of the surveyor if you want him or her to do a report for you at the same time).

Step 6: confirm your offer in writing 'subject to contract and to survey' to the seller direct or to the estate agent; copy to your own solicitor or conveyancer.

Step 7: return the mortgage application with the valuation fee.

Step 8: let your solicitor or conveyancer have relevant details of any potential problems; find out when the seller can move out; warn your bank manager (if a bridging loan is likely to be needed).

Step 9: if your own survey is required, contact the surveyor, discuss the extent of the survey, draw attention to any aspects of the building you are uneasy about and/or want checked out in particular; decide how detailed a report you require (written/oral; specialist tests); confirm your instructions in writing; ask what his or her fee/expenses will be.

Step 10: await the outcome.

After making an offer

What happens at this point of the transaction depends on the house, the buyer and seller concerned, and the state of the market. The best would be that your offer gets accepted straight away. The house is then 'under offer' and the seller should be asked to agree not to entertain any other buyers. Ask the owner (or the agent you are dealing with, if he or she knows) whether the house is on the books of another estate agent as well as the one who has told you about it. If so, you may be pipped at the post from another quarter without you or your agent being aware of the likelihood.

Newspaper advertisements cannot be cancelled immediately; also, people who have viewed before you may make an offer subsequent to yours. So, expect some bargaining to go on after your first offer.

If you are told, or you sense, that your figure is being matched or surpassed by another, decide fairly swiftly whether to withdraw or to increase your offer, and by how much.

During the period between making an offer and exchanging contracts, neither the buyer nor seller has entered into a legally binding contract. As long as the buyer's offer is still subject to contract, the estate agent handling the sale is under a duty to pass on to his or her client, the seller, all other offers made – right up to the day when contracts are exchanged. So, it is possible for a new buyer, or a previously unsuccessful underbidder, to enter the field offering an acceptable price which the agent has to notify to the seller.

Contract races

If two or more people want to buy the same property, the seller will sometimes tell his or her solicitor or conveyancer to send out a second (or even a third and fourth) set of contracts to the would-be buyers' solicitors. The buyers then have to race each other, and the first to send a deposit and signed contract gets the house. Solicitors/conveyancers are required to tell the legal representatives of all the known would-be buyers when there is a contract race.

Should you run in a contract race?

Contract races are usually only prevalent at times of shortage of houses or rising prices (or both). However, it is not uncommon for banks or building societies, when selling houses they have repossessed, to use contract races to get the best price from a buyer who can exchange contracts quickly. This informal 'auction' can cause great distress because many may take part (and incur large expenses) but only one can win.

Contract races are undesirable contests for buyers. The seller is not even legally obliged to sell to the winner. You could incur survey fees, search costs and legal bills yet have nothing to show for it. The advice is: take part only if you feel you have a really good chance of buying the property.

Gazumping

In the unattractive practice of 'gazumping' a seller, tempted by a higher offer, goes back on the agreement with the potential buyer and accepts a later, higher bid. This tends to occur during a rising market with more buyers about than houses. As the law and practice of house purchase now stand, a buyer is not protected against gazumping until he or she has entered into a binding contract. You have to weigh up whether the consequences of binding yourself to a contract prematurely before you have made all the proper enquiries will be more serious than the chances of being gazumped.

A decision by the Court of Appeal in 1993 may give some protection against gazumping in a situation where the seller has agreed not to sell to anyone else provided contracts are exchanged within a specified period. This is known as a 'lockout agreement'.

There is a legal requirement on mortgage lenders to obtain the highest price when selling property. This means that gazumping is an even bigger risk than usual. The best advice is to try to speed up the exchange of contracts as soon as your offer has been accepted.

Gazundering

The equally unsavoury practice of 'gazundering' may occur in a falling market. This happens where a buyer, just before exchange of contracts, offers a lower price, in the hope that the seller will accept it, rather than lose the sale of the house.

Pre-contract deposit agreement

The Conveyancing Standing Committee set up by the Law Commission* has recommended a pre-contract deposit agreement which is designed to help deal with the problem of gazumping. The principle is that each side pays a preliminary deposit of 1½ per cent of the purchase price to a stakeholder and signs an agreement that there will be a final exchange of contracts within four weeks. If one side withdraws without good enough reason (the form of agreement specifies the precise grounds), both deposits are released to the other. So a gazumped buyer will at least have some compensation for the expense incurred. The government has, however, shown no enthusiasm for this suggestion.

The Conveyancing Standing Committee's recommended form of pre-contract deposit agreement, with an explanatory leaflet and guidance notes which should be read before signing, is available free from the Law Commission.

The shortcoming of the scheme is that if the seller receives a substantially increased offer, it will still be worthwhile to lose the deposit. Nevertheless, the agreement may be some inducement to both the seller and buyer to keep their word.

Another way to beat gazumpers

A workable way of avoiding gazumping has been put into practice by some solicitors: the seller gives the buyer the exclusive right to buy the house in return for a fee and on condition that contracts are exchanged within a specified time.

The boxed example opposite shows how it works.

The problem with this is that the vendor may decide to sell elsewhere, in which case the buyer has to be content with compensation.

Limiting the scope for gazumping
The following steps will reduce the likelihood of gazumping occurring:

- reducing the length of time between any tentative agreement and the final contract. This can be done by pre-qualifying for a mortgage and appointing a conveyancer before an offer is accepted
- enquiring of the estate agent whether it has a policy on gazumping.

Mary wants to buy Rose Cottage from Peter. Peter is ready to sell, but Mary cannot exchange contracts yet as she is waiting for her mortgage offer and she has not exchanged contracts on her own sale. She is certain that all these things will be dealt with in the next few weeks. How does she make sure that Peter sells to her and no one else, and that he does not put the price up in the meantime?

The solution is for Peter to agree with Mary that she can buy Rose Cottage at the agreed price as long as she exchanges contracts within X weeks. Peter must be compensated for freezing the price and taking the chance that Mary will at the last minute not go ahead with the deal. He will therefore charge quite a large sum for committing himself to the sale before Mary does – say, £1,000. Mary will lose that money if she does not exchange contracts but not if she goes ahead. Peter should agree to reduce the purchase price by the amount of the option price (the £1,000).

Note: such an agreement should not be attempted without a solicitor (the buyer has to be protected by the agreement being registered in the Land Registry or Land Charges Department).

Some agents ask their clients to sign an agreement stating that they will not gazump

- keeping the estate agent informed about progress in obtaining mortgage finance and getting a survey
- use of the proposed home information pack, due to become mandatory in all residential sales in 2007 (see page 144).

Buying on a second attempt

After a series of negotiations, perhaps, which can be nerve-racking for a would-be buyer, who at this stage wants very much to succeed with a purchase, you may be disappointed and have to start all over again elsewhere. But after a seller has accepted a bid and the losers have been informed, it is not uncommon that some weeks later the prospective buyer has to withdraw from the transaction for one reason or another. At this point, a disappointed under-bidder may find himself or herself being contacted by the seller or his or her agent to ask if he or she is still interested and willing to re-start negotiations.

If you are bitterly disappointed at being outbid for a particular house (you had already mentally moved in), it is worth telling the owner or the agent so that if anything goes wrong with the first transaction he or she will remember how keen you were. And do not just leave it to the agent – if the board stays up a while without 'Sold' being stuck over it, a reminder might be to, literally, ring the bell at the right moment. Both agent and seller will now want to settle the matter without further delay and you could be in a good position to succeed at a second attempt.

Chapter 5

Carrying out work on your new house

It is clearly much easier and quicker to renovate or even decorate a house if it is empty. If financial and other circumstances permit, it may be worthwhile delaying your move for a few weeks to enable work to be carried out. Consider whether you can manage to have completion for purchase (of your new home) earlier than completion for sale (of your old home), even at the cost of a bridging loan. This would allow a period for work to be done while your new house is empty.

If the house is empty (because the owners have already moved, or it is derelict), it might be possible to obtain permission to start work as soon as contracts are exchanged. Whether this will be possible will depend on the goodwill of the sellers.

Even if you 'move in with the builders' you will still need to know before exchange of contracts what will be involved and how much it will cost.

There is often a considerable delay in setting up building works. Planning permissions and building regulation consents take time to apply for and to approve. Sometimes, builders are not available to start straight away. If you are buying a house that needs repairs, it is best to get started as soon as terms are agreed (but remember that if the purchase falls through you may have incurred expense to no avail). In any event, you will need to know, before you commit yourself, how much you are likely to have to spend. For detailed advice, see *Getting the Best from your Builder*, from Which? Books★.

Applying for planning permission

For some structural alterations or improvements, you have to obtain planning permission. Apply in good time: it can take some weeks or even months to come through. You can apply even if you do not own the house, but, of course, if you do not buy the house you will lose the money you have spent on applying.

Forms are available from the local planning department. You will also have to submit several copies of site and location plans, along with detailed drawings showing the work you intend to carry out.

Planning permission is usually necessary only for significant changes in external appearance but you should ask at the local planning department whether what you propose needs planning permission.

The Office of the Deputy Prime Minister (ODPM)★ publishes a free booklet, *Planning: a Guide for Householders*, available from its Publications Centre★, at council offices, Citizens Advice Bureaux and housing advice centres. Booklets called *Making Your Planning Appeal* and *A Guide to Taking Part in Planning Appeals*, also available from the Publications Centre, describe the procedure you can follow after a refusal.

Advice on how to deal with difficulties, refusals or objections can be obtained from chartered town planners, architects and surveyors. Members of the Royal Town Planning Institute (RTPI)★ include not only local authority planning officers but also consultants. The RTPI will be able to suggest where to get specialist advice.

If you want to use part of your house for a business or build on part of the plot, you will need to find out about the planning history of the house and the local authority's policies. The RTPI's regional leaflets, *Where to Find Planning Advice*, can help you select a suitable consultant.

Do not let any work start until you have the necessary planning permission, listed building consent and building regulations approval, where these are needed.

Building regulations

The Building Regulations, which have the force of law, operate throughout England and Wales.

The various building regulations are concerned mainly with material work, health and safety, services and fire precautions. They apply to new buildings and extensions, structural alterations to existing buildings and installation of controlled services or fittings.

A copy of the Building Regulations can be consulted in local authority offices or in most public reference libraries. Although the regulations are shorter and simpler than they used to be, and more flexible and easier to use, a layman would almost certainly need guidance to interpret them. Free and priced booklets and publications on different aspects of the regulations – loading, preparation of site, ventilation, insulation and so on – are available from the Office of the Deputy Prime Minister (ODPM)★ and also from the Stationery Office publications centre★.

For some kinds of building work, you do not need to apply for Building Regulations approval or to give notice. For instance, you do not need to if you are merely repairing a building or replacing drains, sanitary fittings or solid fuel or oil heating appliances, where no structural work is involved. Also, the regulations exempt certain small detached buildings and extensions. Contact the building control officer of your local authority to find out whether the work you are proposing to have done requires approval or a building notice. If so, the officer can let you have the necessary notification form and tell you what details and drawings are required.

You have to pay prescribed fees to the local authority, in two parts if you deposit plans for approval (on application and an inspection), or once on inspection if you give a building notice. There are flat-rate fees for small extensions (up to 40 square metres) and for loft conversions; fees for other work are based on estimated cost.

Scotland has its own Building Standards (Scotland) Regulations. You apply for a building warrant – for which you have to pay a lodging fee – and the work is inspected before a certificate of completion is issued.

Timber-frame houses

If the house is of timber-frame construction, it is advisable to check what can and cannot be done when carrying out any type of d-i-y or extension. For more information, the *10 Tips for Self Builders* leaflet is available free of charge from the UK Timber Frame Association (UKTFA)★, which also provides information and advice about issues such as surveys, planning and design.

Restrictions on alterations and demolition

If the house is a listed building or is in a conservation area, demolition or structural alteration of any kind would need consent from the local planning office. It is a criminal offence to demolish a listed building without consent. This covers not only the house but also outbuildings and boundary walls.

Some properties are restricted as far as the development or use is concerned by covenants in the title deeds, mostly laid down when the house was first built. A covenant may, for instance, stipulate that certain alterations or additions shall not be made or can be made only with the consent of the person who sold the land on which the property was built. (Some covenants cannot be enforced but, if in doubt, consult your solicitor.) Also, mortgage deeds have a clause stipulating that the building society's (or other lender's) approval must be obtained for any proposed alterations to the house. If a property is leasehold, the landlord's consent will probably be required.

Professional advice on structural work

For older property, particularly for property constructed before 1850, the Society for the Protection of Ancient Buildings (SPAB)★ can be asked for general advice. SPAB publishes technical pamphlets and information leaflets on treatment and installation in old buildings, and maintains a card index of architects, surveyors, engineers etc. (usually members of the Society) who have experience with work on historic buildings.

It could be useful to have a word with someone at the local authority planning department or engineers' or technical department, or the building control office, who may be able to let you see plans for recent work carried out at the property – layout of drainage, for instance – or of previous structural work or adaptations.

If you want a considerable amount of repairs done, or perhaps some alterations or modifications, it is worth getting preliminary advice from a professional – an architect, building surveyor or similar consultant. For new work – such as extensions, creating new rooms, kitchen layouts – use an architect who has special skill in economic layout and design. If the work is largely remedial and repair, a building surveyor may be a suitable consultant.

Architects and building surveyors offer a range of services – preliminary discussions, preparation of designs, provision of documents or drawings, applications for approval from various authorities. They will obtain quotations and arrange the details of contracts with builders, inspect the work periodically and authorise payments. You can make use of all these services, or seek professional advice at selected stages only. The contracts are signed by the employer (that is you, the person for whom the work is being carried out) and the builder; the architect may however be able to give you a rough idea of the costs, including his or her own fees.

The fees charged by an architect or surveyor are determined by the extent of the services provided. Where the work is extensive, fees are a percentage of the total cost (which cannot be known until the work is completed). Some services may be charged on an hourly basis at an agreed hourly rate or, if the client prefers it, all fees may be charged on an hourly basis. Before an architect or surveyor starts working for you, you should, in order to avoid misunderstanding, agree the basics of the charge with him or her in writing.

Architects

An architect has to be registered with the Architects Registration Council of the UK, must have specific academic qualifications and has to adhere to a code of professional conduct.

Most architects are members of the Royal Institute of British Architects (RIBA)★. Other professional bodies of architects to which an architect may belong are: the Architectural Association★; the Royal Incorporation of Architects in Scotland★; the Royal Society of Ulster Architects★; and the Royal Society of Architects in Wales★.

No architect has to belong to a professional body and some do not belong to any. Architects who do not belong to a professional body, but who are qualified, are known as 'unattached architects'. The fact that an architect elects to belong to a professional body is a matter for him or her and does not confer any additional qualification or status. The registration qualification is exactly the same for all architects, whether they belong to a professional body or not.

Registered architects in private practice can be found in the *Yellow Pages*, and some local planning authorities keep a list of local architects. RIBA has regional offices with lists of local members, and its office in London has a free clients' advisory service. Advice for clients considering using an architect is included in the RIBA publication *Guide to the RIBA Forms of Appointment* (price £15).

All the professional bodies of architects also provide an advisory service to help people find the right architect for their project, and provide booklets relating to terms of appointment and scale of fees.

These various booklets are advisory only, in that they are the basis for negotiation, and no professional body of architects compels its members to work to a fixed scale of fees.

Most (but not all) architects carry professional indemnity insurance. They are not legally required to do so. If you are employing an architect, check first that he or she has adequate insurance with a reputable insurance company. If not, it would be better simply to employ another architect who does. If things go wrong, it might be difficult or impossible to bring a successful claim against someone who is uninsured.

Building surveyors

If you had a structural survey done of the house, the surveyor who did that should also be qualified to advise on building work. If not, you can contact the Royal Institution of Chartered Surveyors★; the Royal Institution of Chartered Surveyors in Scotland★; or the Association of Building Engineers. These bodies provide an advisory service to help people find the right building surveyor for the job; and all suggest a voluntary scale of fees.

Building or design consultants

Firms and individuals who call themselves consultants of various types – architectural, building, design, architectural surveying – are not formally qualified and not registered as architects, but carry out work similar to that of registered architects. They are not bound to adhere to any professional code and may not be insured for negligence. You should ask the consultant during an initial discussion what his or her charges are likely to be based on. Check that the person you want to use has adequate professional indemnity insurance cover.

Builders

Generally, the best way to get a good builder is through recommendation. If you have just moved into a new area, ask neighbours and local estate agents. If you are consulting an architect or building surveyor, he or she should be able to advise you on a suitable builder, as part of the service. Some builders advertise, or put their names on boards outside houses where they are working.

The Federation of Master Builders (FMB)★ can supply the names of members. Those on the National Register of Warranted Builders (NRWB, contactable at the FMB) are bound by a code of practice and offer a warranty that provides Work in Progress cover, and, at the end of the contract, protection for two years against defective workmanship or materials as well as protection for a further eight years against major structural defects. Under the warranty, such defects will be put right by that builder or another registered builder. The warranty also provides payment (maximum £10,000) towards any reasonable additional costs if the builder ceases trading while your work is in progress. The cost of the warranty is 1.5 per cent of the contract price – payable either by you, as the person commissioning the work, or by the builder. Cover is provided by Allianz Cornhill plc.

The National Federation of Builders (NFB)★ has seven regional offices throughout England and Wales which can provide a list of reputable builders in each area. Member companies of the NFB have satisfied stringent entrance criteria to join the organisation, which includes providing seven references from customers, suppliers and financial institutions. An optional extra is the 'Benchmark Plan' – a members-only insurance scheme which pays out the cost of correcting any building work defects for periods up to 20 years. The NFB also operates a Code of Conduct to safeguard customers. The Scottish Building Employers Federation (SBEF)★ covers all areas north of the border. It can supply the names of suitable member firms or send a full list from which you can make your own choice.

If possible, estimates should be obtained from two or three builders, particularly if extensive work is involved. Write out a list of the work you wish to be done, so that each one can estimate for exactly the same job. If you want the new work to match in with the existing building, you must make this clear.

According to the Office of Fair Trading, more official complaints are made every year about rogue builders than about used car salesmen. The most publicised cases involve dishonesty, often coupled with intimidation and preying on the old and vulnerable. Builders have extorted huge amounts of money from people by claiming that they need work done on non-existent problems, then failing to correct the 'defect'. The sums involved run into billions of pounds.

As the law stands, local Trading Standards departments cannot even warn consumers against firms and individuals about whom they have had scores of complaints – legal action is hampered by rogue traders winding up companies and starting up again almost immediately, having evaded their previous creditors and liabilities.

The government is considering various proposals to improve standards.

Organising the repairs and alterations

It helps to keep a special notebook (small enough to fit into your pocket or handbag) for recording names and addresses of suppliers, brands and prices of articles, and other relevant information. Discipline yourself to use only this notebook and not have recourse to backs of envelopes and other scraps of paper.

It is important to plan the correct sequence in which to do the various jobs, or arrange for them to be done. List all the jobs, then draft a programme, day by day and week by week over the period before you move in, in the sequence in which everything would probably be best carried out. Keep the programme/timetable by the telephone, so that appointments with service men, workmen, delivery men or officials can be put down at the time they are arranged. Note the name of the person you have spoken to when booking appointments by telephone, also the date of the call (written confirmation of instructions is an added safeguard).

Some items have a long delivery time and you may need to place your order as soon as contracts are exchanged – for example, for replacement windows, central heating, fitted carpets, kitchen units – and make the delivery date a part of the sale agreement: get a commitment from the suppliers in writing.

While the house is empty, you will have to make arrangements about getting keys to the workmen and making sure that someone is there when the delivery men are due to come.

Do not make your timetable too utopian: allow for non-delivery, late delivery, workmen's errors, your errors, unexpected snags, sickness, strikes and other malignant acts of man or fate.

The work – and the mess

Knocking down walls, dismantling wooden fitments, getting at pipes or wiring and so on are all jobs which create an amazing amount of dust, dirt and débris. Any floor coverings should be protected or removed, and any fittings in the house or flat covered or moved away, ideally before any workmen start.

If fitted carpets have to be lifted, see that these are rolled, not folded, so that they do not become badly creased. Watch out that builder's rubble is not 'tidied' under floorboards, in the roof space or even on to a neighbour's flat roof.

Any work that involves making holes in the wall, putting things into or behind walls or ceilings (particularly plumbing or electrical work) is likely to necessitate replastering afterwards and probably repainting. Such work should, therefore, be done before redecorating and final cleaning.

Where a large amount of rubbish and builder's rubble results from demolition work, make it the builder's responsibility to remove it.

Heating and insulation

You may be able to get a grant towards the cost of installing central heating if it is part of a comprehensive improvement plan for your house – but not if you are installing central heating only, or central heating combined with inessential other work. Apply to the local authority for this grant.

Installation may necessitate:

- estimates and preliminary discussion
- up to two weeks' work, depending on the type and size
- having the water supply temporarily turned off
- using a plumber/electrician/plasterer.

The Association of Plumbing and Heating Contractors★ and the Heating and Ventilating Contractors Association★ can be approached for the names of members in any area.

Grants are available to private householders from local authorities in some circumstances to pay a percentage of the cost of insulating an inadequately insulated loft and for lagging pipes and water tanks. A Department for Transport, Local Government and the Regions leaflet about the homes insulation scheme is available free from the local authority and Citizens Advice Bureaux.

Damp, rot and woodworm

A builder may be able to find and deal with minor localised problems caused by a defective damp-proof course; putting in a new or replacement damp-proof course is a specialist job. An improvement grant from the local authority may be obtainable to help pay for this, but remember that it takes time to get such a grant and you must not start work before it is approved. *The Which? Book of Do-It-Yourself* (published by Which? Books★) advises on treating damp (including the installation of a new damp-proof course) and rot.

If you are getting a mortgage, the building society or other lenders may require that damp, rot or woodworm problems be dealt with immediately, as a condition of the loan. They may want a guarantee for the work, in which case it will have to be done by a specialist firm (preferably backed up by the Guarantee Protection Insurance Company Ltd★ in case the firm goes out of business for any reason).

Names of specialist firms who are members of their relevant trade association can be obtained from the British Wood Preserving and Damp-proofing Association★.

Roof repairs

It is worth checking the roof again at this stage for any signs of loose tiles or gutters blocked by leaves and dirt. Overflowing gutters are often the cause of damp soaking through walls or under eaves. Fitting mesh guards will prevent leaves from being washed into the tops of downpipes.

Chimneys may need to be repointed, or the flashing replaced. Check that any television aerial is securely attached, but is not damaging the chimney itself. If any chimney is used to flue-in a gas appliance, it is worth having a 'cage' put over the chimney pot, to save having to call in the RSPCA or fire brigade to release a trapped bird.

Electricity

Plan what lighting you would like in the new home at an early stage, in case any new wiring – for spotlights or wall lights, for instance – will be necessary.

Depending on the age of your new home, it may be a precondition for obtaining a mortgage that its electrical installation is examined in detail to confirm its safety (previous owners may have altered it incorrectly).

In any case, if the house is more than 30 years old, the wiring will almost certainly need replacing if this has never been done. Switches, socket outlets and pendant light cords that are more than about 15 years old are also likely to need replacing.

The electricity company or a private electrical contractor will survey the wiring and provide a report or an inspection certificate. You can get the names of approved electrical contractors from the National Inspection Council for Electrical Installation Contracting (NICEIC)★ or from your public library or electricity company shop. The list also indicates those which are members of the Electrical Contractors' Association (ECA)★. SELECT★ will supply a list of its members in Scotland and has free leaflets offering advice to householders.

The survey will also tell you how the electrical installation is arranged and enable you to plan what lighting, additional socket outlets (for portable appliances) and fused connection units (for stationary appliances) you would like, in case any additional wiring is necessary. Sockets to provide power for electrical power tools or portable devices, such as lawn mowers, must be fitted with a special safety device.

Consider the electricity consumption of lights which stay on for a long time, to illuminate a dark corridor or staircase, for example. Fluorescent lamps use considerably less electricity than tungsten bulbs of similar light output, and have a longer life and in some situations recoup the initial higher cost quickly. Low–energy halogen bulbs are also widely available. They fit into normal sockets.

An advantage of rewiring completely, whether this is absolutely necessary or not, is that it gives you the chance to increase the number of socket outlets or to re-position existing ones, according to how you want to use them and where you plan to put your furniture.

The Electrical Installation Industry Liaison Committee has recommended the following minimum number of socket outlets to be provided in homes:

kitchen 4	single bedroom/teenager's room 3
living-room 6	landing/stairs 1
dining-room 3	hall 1
double bedroom 4	store/workroom 2
single bed-sitting room 4	central heating boiler room 1

Rewiring or extending electrical circuits, putting in or moving a socket may mean temporary disconnection of the electrical supply and replastering after running cables under the plaster or through ceilings.

When completed, a new installation (a new circuit for a first-time electric cooker, for instance) or a major alteration should be tested by a qualified electrical engineer (a member of the NICEIC) and a formal test certificate issued. You should notify the electricity company, which may inspect before connecting or re-connecting the supply.

Plumbing

The existing plumbing may need to be modified to install a new sink or basin, an extra WC or shower or to plumb in an automatic washing machine or dishwasher, for example.

A new installation or renewal of plumbing may mean replastering and having the water supply temporarily turned off.

Sanitary plumbing and drainage has to comply with the Water and Building Regulations; if you are in any doubt, consult your water company or local authority's building control department.

Any water fitting to be installed (a shower, for instance) has to comply with the Water Regulations, to prevent waste, misuse, undue consumption and contamination of water. The installation of fittings is subject to the approval (and possible inspection) of the local water company, which interprets and enforces its own bylaws, and which should be notified at least seven days before work starts on the installation. (*The Which? Guide to Plumbing and Central Heating*, published by Which? Books,* covers both basic and more complicated jobs.)

The Institute of Plumbing* maintains a register of plumbers and can supply a list of registered plumbers in business in a particular area (send an s.a.e.). The register is continually monitored by the British Standards Institution under the PRIMA (Public Register Inspection Maintenance Assessment) scheme. The Institute also publishes an annual business directory of registered plumbers (available in public libraries).

Floors

Wooden floors should be checked for loose joists or supports, loose boards or nails, projecting knots and warping, and big holes or cracks which would have to be filled in.

Flooring has to be laid after any piping for central heating or any rewiring has been completed. Ensure that nails are not driven into pipes or wires running underneath. It is a good idea to mark the floorboards with the position of cables and pipes beneath; this will make them easier to find if anything goes wrong later.

Kitchen flooring – other than carpets or carpet tiles – should be laid before floor-standing kitchen units are fitted and before a dishwasher or washing machine gets plumbed in.

Carpets and underlay should not be laid until floors have been finally cleaned and allowed to dry thoroughly. It is easier to lay new carpets before moving in, but make sure that they will be protected during the move.

Telephones

In most older houses, wiring for the telephone is on the surface along skirting boards or picture rails. The telephone wiring can be concealed in conduits or channels built in while a house is being structurally modified. If the house has an old-style telephone, new plug-in connections can now be installed or extra sockets added to an existing line.

Once you have one plug-in socket and line installed by BT, you can yourself add other sockets if you wish by buying a d-i-y kit from BT or from a telephone shop. Or you can get an electrician to do the connection for you.

A wide range of telephones is now available to use in a plug-in socket; these phones, for sale through BT, shops and other outlets, vary in shape, colour, sophistication and price.

Any telephone or socket kit you buy should be one approved by the British Approvals Board of Telecommunications as suitable for use with BT lines, and which therefore carries the BABT approval label with green circle.

The Telecommunications Industry Association* can provide information about specific items of equipment and the names of independent contractors.

Burglar alarm

It would be sensible to review the security of your new home as soon as possible.

Each house presents different problems. You can ask at the local police station for a crime prevention officer (CPO) to come and give you free advice on the security measures that would be appropriate to your home. Burglar alarms, usually installed by specialist firms, can be fitted to doors and windows, and so can special locks. Some burglar alarms are triggered by pressure mats under carpets or flooring and should be placed in position before carpeting is laid and in places where they will not be set off by any pieces of furniture when these are later put in their permanent places.

The National Security Inspectorate maintains a register of companies that it has approved as alarm system installers.

Inadvertent damage may be done to an existing burglar alarm system during building work, so check it carefully when all the work is finished.

House-cleaning and decorating

Redecoration of any room is considerably easier, quicker and less messy if the room is empty of furniture, carpets and curtains; a professional decorator should therefore charge somewhat less.

Thorough cleaning of the house includes washing paintwork, walls and insides of cupboards, scrubbing floors and cleaning windows. (For more information see *Which? Way to Clean it* from *Which? Books**.) Firms specialising in general cleaning work will supply people to do the cleaning with the appropriate equipment. Ask for estimates first.

Carpet–cleaning firms will clean fitted carpets *in situ*. Have this done after all other work is finished but allow a few days for them to dry before furniture is moved in. Loose carpets and rugs can be taken away for cleaning on the firm's premises, to be returned before moving–in day. Various types of carpet shampooers can be hired. Some removal firms undertake carpet–cleaning.

Doing your own repairs, alterations and decoration

If you are a d-i-y enthusiast, you may look forward to doing a lot of the necessary work in the home. There are some factors you should take into account when deciding whether or not to do any of these jobs yourself.

How difficult is the job?

This may depend on your age, fitness and temperament, as well as your previous d-i-y experience, and what tools and equipment you have.

If it is something you have not done before, you will need to spend some time learning about the job – how systems work, how to design your own, what equipment to use, how to go about it, and so on. The bigger the job, the more diverse the range of small tasks it is likely to involve. *The Which? Book of Do-It-Yourself* is a complete illustrated guide to the full range of d-i-y tasks. *Which? Way to Fix It* covers household and appliance repairs. (Both titles are published by Which? Books★.)

Plastering and advanced carpentry are two jobs which require skill and practice.

Would d-i-y save you money?

Doing it yourself saves money mainly because you do not have to pay for someone else's time, overheads and profit on materials. The most profitable jobs to do for yourself are those for which the professional rates are high.

D-i-y risks

You could, of course, hurt yourself while doing the job. The results of some d-i-y jobs could be dangerous, particularly electrical work. *The Which? Book of Wiring and Lighting* explains how to do your own electrical work safely and to professional standards.

Only qualified gas fitters are allowed to connect a gas supply to an appliance: for example, a member of the Council for Registered Gas Installers (CORGI)★.

Hiring equipment

You may need equipment for repairs or decorations which you would not normally use and so would not want to have to buy and store. There are d-i-y hire shops in most large towns. If you do not know of one, look in the local paper or under 'Hire contractors' in the *Yellow Pages*.

Empty or uninhabitable houses

It is worth notifying your local authority if a property is to be vacant for any length of time because a council tax refund may be payable. If you are carrying out building work which makes the property uninhabitable for a considerable time, you should check with your local authority as no council tax may be payable.

You should inform the building's insurer: cover for some risks, such as vandalism or theft, is restricted when a property is unoccupied. Also, arrange for contents insurance for any items (carpets, curtains, kitchen equipment, furniture) that you bought from the previous owner and which are in the empty house. Contents insurance may exclude theft cover if premises are left unoccupied for an extended period.

Curtains give a house a lived-in look and may be a form of safeguard against intruders. Leave some curtains up at your old home if it has not yet been sold, and put some up at your new one as soon as possible.

To prevent anyone who is working in the house from running up telephone bills, you can ask your telephone company to bar outgoing calls – until you inform them that you want to revert to normal calling out.

Chapter 6

The mortgage

Very few people can afford to buy their first home without having to borrow at least part of the cost. Loans to home-buyers are usually in the form of a long-term mortgage.

A mortgage is a loan secured on a property. You cannot sell mortgaged property without repaying the loan – and if you do not keep up your payments, the lender ('mortgagee') has the right to go to court for a possession order against you, the borrower (or 'mortgagor').

You pay interest at the lender's standard variable rate or at a fixed, capped, discounted or base rate tracker rate, depending on the type of mortgage.

Before lending any money, the lender will want to make sure that you, the borrower, can keep up repayments and that the house you want to buy is worth enough to cover the loan if you default on your repayments.

How much you will be able to borrow will depend on:

- your disposable income – and therefore how much you can afford in mortgage repayments
- the value and type of home you want to buy.

How much can you borrow?

Most lenders work out the maximum they are prepared to lend by using a multiple of your annual income before tax. For instance, a single person might be allowed to borrow between 3 and 3.5 times his or her annual income. So, if you earn £25,000 a year, you would be allowed to borrow up to £75,000 or £87,500 depending on the multiple used. A few lenders will allow you to borrow up to 4 or 5 times your income, in limited circumstances.

A couple who are both earning would usually be able to borrow up to 3 or 3.5 times the higher income plus 1 times the lower income. (Lenders are not allowed to discriminate against women by applying the larger multiple to a male partner's income when it is not the higher of the two.) Sometimes a different formula, adding the two incomes together and multiplying by 2.5 or 3, is used. Couples and single people alike could also find variations in the amounts on offer from different lenders.

Unmarried couples are in most cases treated in exactly the same way as a married couple. Other couples or groups of friends can apply for joint mortgages too. But you may need to shop around because lenders are likely to be rather more cautious and the maximum loan could be smaller than the total of your incomes might suggest. If you are thinking of applying for a joint mortgage with friends, remember that each of you is responsible for paying the whole mortgage. If one of you cannot afford to keep up payments or moves out, the other (or others) will have to take over the payments. Sometimes a lender might be reluctant or even refuse to release a borrower from a loan obligation.

What counts as income?

Broadly, 'income' is your basic salary before tax or other deductions. Some lenders will include overtime payments, commission or bonuses but only if they are guaranteed: the lender will probably want confirmation from your employer that these payments are likely to continue. In exceptional circumstances, some lenders may take into account future increases in salary or promotion prospects.

Income from investments is not usually counted and neither (normally) is income from social security or other benefits.

Account may be taken of such ongoing financial commitments as hire purchase debts or payments under a court order.

If you work on short-term contracts, your lender will usually want to get some indication that the contract will be renewed by your current employer or that you will easily find other contract work.

Self-employed borrowers

If you are self-employed, the amount you can borrow will usually be based on the average of your earnings over the previous three years or so. Some lenders may base it on your last year's profits but will look at previous years to make sure it was not an exceptionally good year. The lender will not simply take your word as to what your annual income is but will want to see your annual accounts and/or your tax assessments, and may call for information from your accountant.

If you are newly self-employed or have been in business for a relatively short time, you may well find it difficult to get a mortgage. And even if a lender is prepared to grant a mortgage, it may be for a relatively small amount. Your chances are much better if you can contribute a significant chunk of the purchase price – more than, say, 25 per cent. Some lenders specialise in lending to self-employed people and are thus more flexible in their attitudes than traditional lenders. For example, if you put down a large deposit (between 10 and 25 per cent, depending on the lender), you may be able to get a 'self-certification' mortgage without the usual need to verify the amount you earn. Don't lie about your income, however, as this would constitute fraud.

But how much can you afford?

Just because a lender is prepared to give you a mortgage of a certain size, do not be led into thinking that you can afford it. Lenders' formulae are based on averages, and your situation could be far from average: for example, if you have exceptionally high travelling costs to go to work, you will have far less income available than someone who lives only one mile from the office.

Also consider whether your income is likely to drop soon – for example, because you plan to give up work to care for children. Think carefully too about what else you want to spend your income on – you may enjoy taking frequent holidays or long-haul travelling or have an expensive hobby and decide that a big mortgage is not for you.

If you already have heavy financial commitments (such as a car loan), it could mean that you do not really have enough spare income each month to cope with the maximum loan a lender will make. Also, bear in mind the costs of equipping and running a home (particularly if you are a first-time buyer): there are council tax and water charges to pay, repairs and maintenance, and unexpected expenses – things you need for the house, from doormats to a dining-room table – to allow for.

What is the value of the home you want to buy?

Buyers are not usually able to borrow the whole of the purchase price (or the amount the property is eventually valued at). Lenders have to make sure that they would get their money back if the buyer does not keep up the mortgage payments and they have to get a court order to repossess and sell the property.

This means that the lender is unlikely to lend you the full price even if this is within the amount you can afford to repay. Instead, you will be allowed to borrow a percentage, known as the loan to value (LTV). Lenders have a normal maximum percentage that they will offer without qualification. This maximum varies periodically according to market conditions.

Most major high-street lenders will lend up to 95 per cent, although a few will consider 100 per cent loans. The maximum percentage may vary with the mortgage deal. With many lenders you get a cheaper deal if you borrow, say, 75 per cent than if you borrow, say, 95 per cent.

The percentage you can borrow is not a percentage of the purchase price but of what the lender's valuer reckons that the property is worth. If the valuer reckons the house is worth less than the asking price, even a mortgage of 100 per cent might not be enough to enable you to buy

Responsible lending

From October 2004, most mortgages will be governed by the Financial Services and Markets Act 2002. This will require most lenders to comply with compulsory new rules and guidance issued by the Financial Services Authority (FSA)*. A principle of 'responsible lending' will be imposed on mortgagees which will require lenders to have regard to the interests of their customers and to treat them fairly. The idea is, according to the FSA, 'that customers should not be exploited by lending in circumstances where they are self-evidently unable to repay through income and yet have no alternative repayment plans.' Although the rules are still being worked out, they are likely to include:

- a requirement that the lender show that account was taken of the borrower's ability to pay
- a restriction on the level of charges that the lender can lawfully impose. As regards early redemption, the lender will be able to charge only a reasonable pre-estimate of the costs incurred; the same applies to charges on arrears. With reference to extortionate credit charges, the current Consumer Credit Act regulation will be replaced by a general obligation not to charge excessive sums which

are contrary to the interests of the borrower. The lender will have to pay attention to the amount of charges made by other institutions

- forthcoming new measures which are intended to reduce the occurrence of arrears and repossessions. Clearer and more detailed information will be given to intended borrowers to allow them to consider whether they can afford the repayments, explain the risks if the repayments are not made, and direct them to sources of advice if things go wrong. Lenders will also have to publish their own policy and procedures for dealing fairly with a borrower in arrears.

Policy and procedures

The draft lender's policy and procedures prescribed by the FSA are more defined and extensive than the current Council of Mortgage Lenders guidance and are likely to include:

- providing to the borrower, within five working days of the arrears becoming known, details of: the missing payments; the arrears charges likely to be incurred; actions that the lender can take, and how willing it is to discuss any proposals put forward by the borrower; and organisations that provide free advice to those in arrears
- using reasonable efforts to negotiate with the borrower a new structure of repayment as an alternative to taking possession of the property
- taking possession of the property only when all other reasonable attempts to recover payment have been taken
- consulting with the borrower's adviser (e.g. Citizens' Advice Bureau or other debt counselling agency) regarding the arrears
- supplying to the borrower in arrears a monthly statement of payments due, arrears amassed and charges incurred
- taking a reasonable approach to the time within which the arrears are to be repaid and devising a plan which is tailored to the borrower's financial circumstances
- allowing the customer to change the repayment date of the mortgage instalments and the method by which payment is made
- before going to court for a possession order, providing the borrower with an update of the information already provided and some guidance about obtaining local authority housing.

Mortgage indemnity guarantees

If you borrow a high percentage of the property value, the lender will want to protect itself against the increased risk. A lender may be prepared to accept anything as extra security which could be turned into enough cash if needed, such as a charge on a second property or share certificates, but the usual way is to charge a 'high lending' fee. The lender can use this to pay for an insurance policy, called a mortgage indemnity guarantee, which guarantees to pay the lender the outstanding balance of the loan if the home has to be repossessed and sold for less than the amount of the mortgage. This charge used to be applied to loans exceeding 75 per cent LTV, but most major lenders no longer charge unless you borrow over 90 per cent LTV, and some lenders no longer charge a mortgage indemnity guarantee at all.

Note that even though you pay the premium, not only do you receive no cover from the policy but the insurance company can pursue you personally for reimbursement if it has to pay up under the policy. The cost of the premium varies – depending on the lender, the size of your mortgage and the size of your deposit – but can add up to hundreds or several thousand pounds.

What sort of home is it?

The amount you can borrow will also be affected by the sort of home you are buying. If the house is unconventional or unusual in its construction and therefore likely to be difficult to sell, the loan could be based on a lower than usual percentage of the valuation, or the term allowed to repay the mortgage could be shorter than usual.

In England and Wales a lot of property (mostly flats and maisonettes) is leasehold: you are buying the right to live in the property for a certain number of years, after which it reverts to the landlord. You should find no difficulty getting a mortgage on a leasehold property, although the lender will need to check the lease and be satisfied about two things in particular. First, there needs to be a clear and legally binding agreement about who pays for the repair and maintenance of the building. Secondly, most lenders will lend only if there is a reasonable amount of the lease left after the end of the mortgage term. Many lenders want at least 20 years left at the end of the mortgage term; with others, it could be as much as 40 or 50 years. The result of this is that it could be difficult to get a mortgage on a leasehold property with less than 50 or 60 years, or even longer, to run on the lease.

You could also experience difficulty in arranging a loan if the property is used partly for business and partly for living – for example, if it is a case of living over the shop.

How many years to repay?

In theory, a mortgage term (by the end of which the loan has to be repaid) can be as little as five years. But the usual term is 20 or 25 years; longer-term loans – 35 years or more – are available from some lenders. It is good practice for lenders to check that a mortgage finishes before you reach retirement age, and some of them may insist on it.

If you are buying a leasehold property, the length of the lease may affect the length of the term. For example, if the building society requires 40 years of the lease to be left at the end of the mortgage and the lease has 60 years to run, then the maximum length of loan will be 20 years.

Interest rates

Most lenders have a 'standard' variable interest rate, which usually increases or decreases roughly in line with base rate changes, although not all changes in base rates will be passed on to borrowers. It is worth shopping around as there is now a lot of competition between banks and building societies. (See later in this chapter for more about the type of interest-rate deals lenders may offer.)

All lenders issue brochures or mortgage packs. It is not easy to compare like with like, but they all have to show the APR (annual percentage rate) in their printed information.

The APR, introduced by the Consumer Credit Act in 1974, was supposed to help consumers compare the different deals available – simply, the higher the APR, the more expensive the deal. But what started out to be a straightforward calculation became less reliable as a tool as financial products became more diverse and complicated. The APR is generally higher than the quoted rate of interest: it includes one-off charges such as arrangement and valuation fees, and takes into account the way interest is calculated on a repayment mortgage. Some mortgage lenders tempt new borrowers by offering a low interest rate or fixed rate for an initial period of, say, two or three years. Under regulations that came into force in 2000, lenders have to use a calculation that uses the initial low or fixed rate and then assumes the current standard variable mortgage rate for the remainder of the term. For example, if a lender offers a mortgage with a fixed rate of 5 per cent for two years and the lender's standard variable rate at the time of the agreement is 7 per cent, the APR must be calculated assuming that the rate of interest is 5 per cent for two years and 7 per cent for the remainder of the term (even though in reality the standard variable rate will vary over time). If you want a quote for a mortgage with a fixed or initial discounted rate, get quotes for both this rate and the standard variable mortgage rate – this will at least give you an indication of what you might pay after the initial period.

If you want to compare current interest rates and conditions for mortgages from various sources, try looking at what is available on the Internet (see page 134).

Types of mortgage

There are two major decisions to be made when choosing a mortgage: the type of repayment method and whether to choose a special interest rate deal (see page 124).

When repaying a mortgage, you have to pay back the money you have borrowed (the capital) and pay the cost of borrowing the money (the interest). The two main ways of doing this are by a **repayment** mortgage or an **interest-only** mortgage. With a repayment mortgage you repay the capital in instalments, along with the interest, so that at the end of the term of the loan you have paid off the capital. With an interest-only mortgage, you pay interest on the whole amount of the loan for the full term and usually make additional payments into some sort of savings scheme to pay off the capital at the end of the term. Endowment policies were frequently used in the past. Now an alternative option is to link an interest-only loan to an individual savings account (ISA) or possibly to a stakeholder pension.

Repayment mortgages

With this type of mortgage, how much you pay each month depends on how much you have borrowed, the interest rate charged and the length of the loan. The longer the period of the loan, the longer there is to pay off the capital, so the smaller the monthly repayments. But over the course of the whole loan, your total payment will be much higher because you are paying interest for longer.

In the early years of a repayment mortgage, much of each payment you make goes to pay the interest on the money you have borrowed and a smaller part goes towards paying off the capital. But, as the years go by, the capital you owe reduces and so the proportion of interest in each payment goes down and the proportion that is paying off the capital goes up – until in the last few years only a very small part of each payment is interest.

Mortgage protection insurance

If anyone is financially dependent on you, or if you are buying a house as a couple, you will need insurance which will pay off the loan if you (or your partner if you have a joint mortgage) were to die. In fact, some lenders insist on this. A mortgage protection policy is a relatively cheap form of life insurance because the amount the policy would have to pay out goes down as you pay off your mortgage. If you have a joint mortgage, it may be better to take out a joint life policy which pays out once – on the first death. Or, you could consider taking out two separate policies – one for each borrower.

What happens if you move?

With a repayment mortgage, you pay off the loan when you sell your house with the money you get from selling it. If you are buying a new home, you then get a new mortgage for that.

Interest-only mortgages

With an interest-only mortgage, you do not pay back any of the capital until the end of the term. You pay interest on the whole amount of the loan throughout the term and you usually also have to pay separate premiums on an investment or savings plan. At the end of the term the loan is repaid from the proceeds of the investment. Some lenders may allow you to take out an interest-only mortgage without putting a savings plan in place. However, you would have to be sure that you could pay the capital back by other means.

As the amount you owe does not change, you will be paying interest on the whole loan for the entire term.

The mortgage is usually linked to a savings policy for which you have to pay regular (usually monthly) premiums to the provider for the whole term of the loan. The policy is taken out for a period to coincide with the term of the mortgage so that, at the end of the loan term, the policy 'matures' and the proceeds are used to pay off the capital. However, there is no guarantee that your investment will achieve this.

If you have dependants you will have to arrange life cover, but with an interest-only mortgage the amount you have borrowed remains the same throughout the term, so a policy where the life cover decreases over the term will not be sufficient. Instead you will need to arrange a term assurance policy where the level of cover remains the same until the end of the term. This does not apply if you are using an endowment policy as the savings vehicle to repay your mortgage because endowment policies automatically include life cover.

Endowment policies

Low-cost endowments were, until recently, the most common policy used as the means of repaying an interest-only mortgage. The policy contained both life cover and savings and was supposed to grow enough during the term to build up sufficient capital to pay off the mortgage. Often these policies were sold on the basis that there would even be extra capital available after the mortgage was paid off as a 'nest egg'. While people who took out endowments in the 1970s saw their policies mature with more than enough money to pay off their policies, endowments are now struggling. Today many thousands of these policies are falling behind and will not produce enough to pay off the capital owed. A large number of people with endowment mortgages have had to make decisions about whether to increase their premiums, or put in place alternative arrangements to cover the shortfalls.

The problem with endowment policies sold in the past was that they had very high charges, which often meant that little or no investment would take place in the early years of the policy. This made them very poor value if you were forced to stop paying or cash in during the early years. They were also very inflexible. You could not decrease the premiums or extend the term, and if you increased the premium you incurred yet more charges. This meant that often, if you increased or extended your mortgage, you would have to take out yet another endowment to cover the new mortgage, rather than being able simply to restructure your original plan. Despite this, endowments were sold as the 'flexible' option, with many advisers criticising repayment mortgages for their rigidity.

Today it is rare to find any provider or adviser recommending an endowment policy. *Which?* magazine suggests that most people should avoid them because they are risky, expensive and inflexible.

If you think you may have been mis-sold your endowment policy, *Which?* has a free website, *www.endowmentaction.co.uk*, that will give you all the information you need in order to decide whether you should make a complaint. The Financial Services Authority (FSA)★ also has several factsheets concerning endowments.

Pension mortgages

You can use a personal or stakeholder pension as the policy to repay your mortgage, but it is an expensive route to choose. Personal or stakeholder pensions allow you to take up to 25 per cent of the pension fund you build up as a tax-free cash sum when you reach your retirement age. The idea is to structure your policy so that the tax-free cash sum you build up is enough to pay off your mortgage at your retirement date.

The advantage of using a pension plan to pay off your mortgage is that you get tax relief (at your highest rate of tax) on the contributions you make to the pension. You can also include life cover on your plan and receive tax relief on the amount you are paying for life cover. But there are disadvantages. The most important one is that you are using part of your pension fund to repay your mortgage loan, so a smaller sum will be available to provide you with an income when you retire. And you may be tying yourself to taking your pension at a fixed date in the future, even though this may not be convenient. Also, it will be much more expensive than if you were funding a savings policy purely to pay off your mortgage, as you can take only a quarter of the fund you build up as the tax-free cash sum. So if you had a mortgage of, say, £50,000, you would have to build up a pension fund of at least £200,000 to achieve this figure.

If you do decide to go for a pension-linked mortgage it is essential to check what growth rate the provider has used to set the premium. Some providers use high rates to keep the premiums low and more competitive, but they may not be able to sustain this level of growth over a long period of time. This was a common problem with endowment policies too, and is one of the reasons why so many policies are falling short of their target amount.

Pension-linked mortgages are quite specialist, so always take advice from an independent financial adviser who has pension knowledge (not just mortgage knowledge) before proceeding.

ISA mortgages

Here again you pay interest only on the loan. In addition, you pay contributions to a stocks and shares ISA (Individual Savings Account). An ISA is a tax-free 'wrapper' within which you can invest in shares, collective investment schemes (such as unit trusts), corporate bonds, insurance funds and cash. The proceeds are then used to pay off the mortgage, but there is no guarantee that your ISA will be worth enough to repay it all.

The main advantage of an ISA mortgage is that, as the proceeds from an ISA are tax-free, it is a tax-efficient way of building up a fund to pay off the mortgage. ISAs are much more flexible than endowment policies because you can increase and reduce your contributions and withdraw part of the funds without cashing in the whole plan. In addition, the set-up and management charges are lower. At the time of writing the maximum contribution per person to an equity ISA is £7,000 a year, although this limit is set to reduce to £5,000 in April 2006. However, ISAs, just like any investments linked to shares, carry a risk that there will not be enough funds to pay off the mortgage. A separate life cover policy may also have to be set up if the lender insists.

Interest-only versus repayment

The problem with using any type of pension or savings plan that is linked to share-based investment is the risk that the plan may not build up enough cash to pay off the mortgage. Share-based investments can go up or down, and the more risk you take the higher the potential gains but the bigger the potential losses. If you want an absolute guarantee that your mortgage will be paid off by the end of the term you should choose a repayment mortgage.

Interest-rate deals

A mortgage at the standard variable rate (see page 119) is the basic mortgage product – many lenders also offer a range of special deals with different, and attractive, interest rates, for which you may have to pay an arrangement fee. These may have strings attached such as compulsory insurance through that lender or hefty penalties for those who want to switch to another lender or deal within a set period. These are known as redemption penalties or early repayment charges, and fall into two types – those that apply only for the length of the special deal (for example, two years during the fixed, capped or discounted rate) and extended redemption penalties. Extended redemption penalties apply beyond the special deal and tie you in to the lender's standard variable rate for a number of years after the special deal has expired. Avoid deals with these types of extended redemption penalties if you can. They may seem attractive as the interest rate is often lower than on other deals, but remember you'll be tied in to the lender's standard variable rate which the lender can alter at any time it likes.

Fixed-rate mortgages

Fixed-rate mortgages guarantee that the interest rate will not change for a stated period. Most loans of this kind have fixed interest for between two and five years but can go up to ten or longer. When the fixed rate expires, the interest rate reverts to the lender's standard variable rate.

Fixed rates are ideal if you want the security of stable repayments for the first few years, especially if you would find it hard to cope with rising interest rates. Your decision as to whether to fix, and for how long, will be influenced by your view on the outlook for interest rates. If variable mortgage rates turn out to be below your fixed rate you will lose out. Of course, you will benefit if interest rates rise steeply.

Discounted-rate mortgages

Discounted-rate loans apply a set discount to the standard rate for a stated period (usually one to five years), so the rate you pay will move in line with the standard rate but will always be the set amount below it. Some deals offer stepped discounts: for example, 3.5 per cent discount for six months then 0.5 per cent discount for two and a half years. After the discount period ends, you revert to the lender's standard rate. Some one- or two-year discounts tie you to the standard rate for several years afterwards.

So, discounts do not protect you from rate rises, but you benefit from any falls. The shorter the period, the bigger the discount. A large discount during the first year will help at a time when money may be tight. On the other hand, you can avoid the 'payment shock' of suddenly facing much higher payments after one year by opting for a more modest discount over, say, three years. Consider a discount if you are not bothered about stable payments, and if you think that your discounted rate will average out at below the available fixed- and capped-rate deals.

Capped-rate deals

Capped rates are a variation on the fixed-rate theme: the interest rate is guaranteed not to rise above a certain level during the capped period, often between three and five years. In addition to the advantages of fixed rates, your repayments will go down if your lender's standard rate becomes lower than the capped rate. However, if standard rates do not fall below the capped rate, you often pay more than for an equivalent-length fixed rate.

Base rate tracker deals

Base rate trackers, as the name implies, 'track' the bank base rate (the interest rate set by the Bank of England each month) at either a set percentage above or below. So, for example, if the bank base rate is 3.75 per cent, a mortgage that is 0.5 per cent above base rate for two years will start off at 4.25 per cent. Base rate trackers are available for anything from a few months to the term of the mortgage. Their main advantage is that there is less discretion on the part of the lender than with standard variable rate mortgages – with base rate trackers your rate must move in line with the bank base rate.

Cashbacks

Many lenders offer large 'cashbacks' shortly after you start paying your mortgage, in the form of a cheque which you are free to spend on whatever you choose. Usually, you will be charged the standard variable rate and receive a percentage of the loan, usually between 2 and 8 per cent, as a cashback.

Cashbacks can be useful if you are short of funds to finance your move, perhaps because of lack of savings or negative equity in your current property. However, you should avoid cashbacks if you do not really need the money. They tie you in to the lender's standard rate for a long time and can be expensive in the long run.

More modest cashbacks, say £400, are often offered as part of fixed-rate or discounted-rate deals. This can be useful if, say, you want to switch lender but are put off by the valuation and legal costs involved.

Mix-and-match deals

Some lenders allow you to combine different interest-rate options. For example, you could borrow part of your mortgage at a variable rate and part at a fixed rate. Compared with taking out the whole mortgage on a fixed-interest basis, you would gain some benefit if interest rates fell, though, conversely, you would suffer some increase if interest rates rose. Compared with taking out the entire mortgage at a variable rate, you would face a smaller increase in payments if interest rates rose but also a smaller decrease if interest rates fell. Mix-and-matching is therefore a way of hedging your bets.

Penalty-free deals

Most fixed, capped, discounted and cashback deals come with hefty penalties if you repay your loan early or switch to a better deal. When selecting a deal, check how long you must stick with the same lender to avoid penalties (often between two and five years).

Penalties can mean repaying all the benefits received from a special deal (such as free legal fees) and/or paying either up to six months' interest or a set percentage (up to 5 per cent) of the amount you owe or the total amount originally borrowed. Either way, the charge can be prohibitive. For example, on an £80,000 loan, six months' interest charged at 5 per cent comes to £2,000.

If you do not want to be tied to one lender for years, or if you intend to repay your loan quickly by paying off lump sums, it may be best to avoid all these deals and pay a slightly higher interest rate to get a deal with no penalties. Some lenders now offer competitive deals with no penalties for repaying part or all of your loan. You could also consider a 'flexible' mortgage that allows increases or decreases in your monthly payments.

Flexible mortgages

Traditionally, most lenders adjusted the balance on which you paid interest annually, usually at the end of each calendar year. If you have a repayment loan, your debt falls each month as you make your payments. However, under this annual interest system you do not get any credit for reducing the debt, in terms of the interest charged, until the start of the following year.

More and more lenders now calculate the balance on which you pay interest more frequently – usually daily, but it can be fortnightly or monthly. This is better than the old annual system in terms of cost and flexibility, allowing you to pay off your mortgage more quickly and save interest.

The daily interest system has also allowed the development of flexible mortgages that let you repay your loan more quickly through modest increases in monthly payments, rather than having to save up lump sums.

As well as offering the facility to increase monthly payments, flexible mortgages can have a number of different features, such as:

- a flexible payment schedule allowing you to pay fortnightly or in 10 monthly payments per year rather than 12
- the ability to make withdrawals on previous over-payments, or even take 'payment holidays' (where you pay nothing for a few months)
- the ability to make reduced monthly payments
- no redemption penalties if you pay off your mortgage
- a loan 'draw-down' facility that allows easy access to extra secured loans, without your having to go through the formal further advance application process.

However, many flexible mortgages offer only some of these features and you may find that some have restrictions attached. For example, you may have to make overpayments before you can take a payment holiday. There are also fewer special deals to choose from than with a standard mortgage – although you can get discounted, variable and fixed-rate flexible mortgages – and you tend to pay more for the flexible features.

Where to get a mortgage

The first rule is to shop around: there are over 150 UK mortgage lenders.

Make sure you know what sort of loan you are being offered; check what costs are involved; find out whether life insurance is included or not or is compulsory; check the redemption penalty. Are you tied to the standard variable rate for several years after your special deal runs out? Do you have to buy the lender's building and contents insurance or payment protection cover? Do not take on too big a loan just because the lender offers you that much. You may decide you do not want to give up a large percentage of your income on paying your mortgage.

Study the literature of potential lenders: different building societies, banks, insurers and other financial institutions.

Lenders

Mortgage lenders such as banks and building societies sell mortgages direct to borrowers as well as through intermediaries. If you go to them for advice they can recommend and sell a mortgage from their own range only. This limits your choice.

Building societies

At one time, almost all mortgages for home-buyers came from building societies, which funded the loans from people's savings with them.

Each society has its own guidelines regarding whom it is prepared to lend to, how much to lend and on what type of home. Branch managers may have some discretion to vary the conditions and it is worth discussing your particular case with the manager even if it looks as though the guidelines seem to rule out a loan to you.

Banks

Banks have now become prominent in the mortgage market, particularly for large loans. All the high-street banks offer mortgages, including the 'mortgage banks' that used to be building societies; less well-known foreign banks are also in the market.

Other lenders

Insurance companies that offer life insurance may also be in the mortgage market.

Direct lenders – some banks and building societies have set up branchless, direct arms that operate via the telephone or Internet.

Local authorities have to give mortgages to council tenants who want to exercise their 'right to buy' option. A few authorities may offer mortgages to people prepared to buy and renovate derelict houses.

Employers, particularly banks and other financial institutions, often offer mortgages to their staff, usually at low interest rates, as a fringe benefit. But before you take one, check what would happen if you were to leave and change jobs: would you be allowed to keep on the loan and, if so, at what interest rate would you have you repay it?

Finance houses and credit companies may be prepared to lend you more than other lenders, but at a higher interest rate. They are unlikely to offer repayment mortgages. There may be a high redemption charge if you want to pay off the mortgage in the first few years (in order to move to a cheaper lender, perhaps). They also seem to be faster off the mark than building societies in starting repossession proceedings if you are in arrears.

Centralised lenders specialise in mortgages for quite specific markets (e.g. self-employed, self-certification, etc.), usually through intermediaries. They often offer very competitive deals, but check the size and duration of redemption penalties and how the standard rate compares to other lenders.

Builders or the developer of a new site may offer to arrange mortgages for prospective buyers, perhaps offering to get 100 per cent mortgages or lower-than-normal interest rates for the first year as part of a package to induce you to buy. Some schemes depend on the solvency of the builder and should be treated with caution.

Private mortgages are no longer common, but are a possibility. If a relative or friend offers to lend you money to help you buy a home, at a low interest rate, or none, it would be a cheap source of finance. But make sure a proper business-like arrangement is made between you, with a mortgage deed.

You should be careful if the person from whom you are buying a house offers you a loan. It may be just because the seller is desperate for a quick sale but it could be because he or she knows that getting a mortgage will be difficult due to structural or other problems. Get your solicitor to check the terms carefully before agreeing, and make sure the house is properly surveyed.

Mortgage intermediaries

Mortgage intermediaries (or brokers) do not themselves lend money but make arrangements for you to borrow from someone else. As the range of mortgage deals is now so vast a good intermediary can help you find the best one to suit your circumstances.

Intermediaries vary from those who are tied to one financial company and can sell only that company's regulated products (such as endowments or life insurance) at one end of the scale to independent advisers at the other. If you pay the intermediary a fee you are more likely (but not guaranteed) to get some impartial advice. Mortgage intermediaries can usually arrange loans from any lender, although they may have a panel of, say, six with which they place most of their business.

Under the mortgage code, advisers must tell you whether they usually arrange mortgages from a selection of preferred lenders or from the market as a whole. They must also tell you whether they'll be paid a fee by the lender for arranging the mortgage and, if it is more than £250, how much the fee is. If you don't take up the recommended mortgage within six months, the maximum fee you can be charged is £5. This right is given to you by the Consumer Credit Act 1974.

A good intermediary should give you a choice of mortgages to suit your circumstances. Get written quotations setting out all the payments involved (including any arrangement fee) and study the figures carefully. If there are quotes on special interest deals, find out what your payments would be at the current standard variable rate to get an idea of how they might change at the end of the deal. If you are in any doubt about anything, ask for an explanation and get your solicitor to look over any document you have to sign. And there is nothing to stop you going to a second intermediary to see what that one has to offer you.

Most mortgage intermediaries have signed up to the Mortgage Code and are registered with the Mortgage Code Compliance Board★, which maintains a register of intermediaries. A condition of the Code is that they must also be members of an arbitration scheme to help provide redress for customers in dispute with intermediaries.

Estate agents

The selling agents may also act as mortgage intermediaries. Many estate agents are owned by or tied to particular insurers, banks or building societies, which means that they can offer you endowments, pensions or life insurance only from that particular company, although they may be able to offer you loans from any lender.

Getting information on mortgages

As soon as you start looking for a house to buy, it is worth going to visit several potential lenders or intermediaries to discuss a loan. The

Mortgage Code of Practice lays down the information that lenders and intermediaries must give to customers. When getting advice on a loan, ask whether the lender complies with the Code and ask for a copy. Most lenders and intermediaries have signed up to the code.

Information you should find out from booklets or a personal visit includes:

- the standard interest rate and what special deals are available – and whether there will be an arrangement fee
- what payment you have to make per £1,000 borrowed
- when and how payments have to be made:
  - in the first month?
  - in the rest of the financial year?
  - thereafter?
- what will happen when the interest rate changes
- what percentage of valuation the normal maximum loan is
- what insurance must be bought as a condition of the loan (contents, buildings, mortgage protection, etc.)
- whether there will be a redemption charge if you pay off the mortgage within so many (how many?) years

---

Beware of poor mortgage advice

Many people turn to an adviser for guidance on which type of mortgage is best for them. However, obtaining good advice can be hit and miss. A *Which?* report in May 2001 found that much depends on the individual adviser rather than who he or she works for. Researchers for the magazine discovered that some advisers did not fully take clients' needs into account or find out their attitude to financial risk-taking, while others failed to explain the range of deals available – behaviour which contravenes the Mortgage Code. Other problems included misleading claims about the pros and cons of repayment *vs.* interest-only mortgages and a lack of information about redemption penalties. If you are considering using an adviser it is important to do your homework carefully. Read up about the deals on offer, consider whether you are comfortable with risk, and think carefully about your long-term needs – for example, whether you are likely to want to move to a bigger property.

- whether the firm offers 'information only' or an advice and recommendation service on the best mortgage for your individual needs. This should be disclosed under the Mortgage Code. You have more comeback if you go for the advice service – and you are not obliged to accept the advice if you do not like it.

Under the Financial Services Act, firms that sell endowment, ISA or pension mortgages have to be authorised to carry out their business and have to abide by a set of detailed rules. One important feature of these rules is that firms have to make it clear whether they are giving completely independent advice to their customers on what their best choice is, or are tied to selling one company's products.

Regulation of mortgage advice

Since 1997 the mortgage industry has been self-regulated through the Mortgage Code of Practice. Most lenders and intermediaries have signed up to the code. However, from 31 October 2004 the Financial Services Authority (FSA) will take over the regulation of mortgage advice and information. The voluntary Mortgage Code of Practice will cease to exist from this date.

The new regulations are being introduced to try to improve the quality of advice and information, and will cover most mortgages entered into after the end of October 2004. The regulations won't, however, cover buy-to-let mortgages or second charges.

What protection you can expect from the regulations
- Before lending to you, a lender must check your ability to repay the mortgage.
- Your mortgage adviser will provide you at the outset with an initial disclosure document, explaining whether he or she is giving you advice or information only and providing information on how you'll be charged.
- You will be provided with a Key Facts Illustration (KFI) for each mortgage you're interested in. This will give the costs and terms and conditions of the mortgage in a standardised format and is designed to help you compare mortgages from different providers. You'll be provided with an updated KFI at offer stage.

- Where you have asked for advice, your adviser must ensure the mortgage he or she recommends is suitable for you and, of the ones available from the firm, best meets your needs and circumstances.
- Advertising and marketing materials will have to be clear, fair and not misleading. Cold calling will be banned in many circumstances.
- Only advisers who search the whole mortgage market and who offer you the choice to pay a fee for their advice will be able to call themselves independent.
- Advisers who are paid on commission must disclose this to you.
- You will be able to make any complaint about mortgages to the Financial Ombudsman Service.
- You will also have access to the Financial Services Compensation Scheme in particular circumstances.
- Protection will be given from unfair and excessive charging practices.

Finding a mortgage online

A vast array of information about mortgages is available on the Internet. Most lenders have their own websites giving information about their products and deals. And there's a host of websites that help you compare mortgages and let you search for products that have the features you are interested in. These vary in terms of how much of the market they cover. Some let you go on to apply for a mortgage online, although most consumers prefer to take out a loan the traditional way. Which? has its own interactive mortgage search – available free to anyone – at *www.switchwithwhich.co.uk*. It provides access to a database of over 8,000 mortgage products to help you find a good deal.

There is also plenty of independent information about mortgages and what to look out for when you're choosing one. For background information, the FSA site (*www.fsa.gov.uk*) is a good source of impartial guidance, while the Council of Mortgage Lenders (*www.cml.org.uk*) provides detailed advice on home buying and the products available. To look up standards of good practice for lenders, check out the Mortgage Code online at the site of the Mortgage Code Compliance Board: *www.mortgagecode.co.uk*. The Code will remain in force until 31 October 2004, after which it is being replaced by statutory regulation through the FSA (see page 133).

Product comparison sites

CharcolOnline *www.charcolonline.co.uk*
MoneyXtra *www.moneyextra.com*
Moneyfacts *www.moneyfacts.co.uk*
Moneynet *www.moneynet.co.uk*
Moneysupermarket *www.moneysupermarket.com*
UK Mortgages Online *www.ukmortgagesonline.co.uk*
Which? *www.switchwithwhich.co.uk*

Websites are correct at the time of going to press, but note that details may change. See also the property websites on page 312.

Applying for a mortgage

You may be asked at an early stage to fill in a form giving some details of your income and commitments. Many lenders offer a **mortgage certificate** to potential borrowers. This states how much they would be prepared to lend you (subject to the value of the property you will want to buy) and could be useful if you need to persuade a seller that you are a serious buyer who will have the finance to proceed. It is worth noting that a mortgage certificate is not a guarantee that the lender will give you the money for the property you want to buy. Whether it agrees firmly to lend you the money will depend on the exact details of the property, the accuracy of the information you've supplied, and the outcome of credit checks.

To apply for a mortgage certificate, you'll need to complete a form and may need to give details of your employment, income and financial commitments. The lender may contact your bank or employer to check that you are a credit-worthy and reliable person.

A self-employed person may have to submit audited accounts. If you are freelance or working on an irregular basis, you may find it difficult to get a loan unless you can produce a large part of the purchase price yourself. With what is known as a 'non-status' mortgage, the amount borrowed is not related to earnings, but some evidence of financial stability will be required, such as an accountant's or bank's reference, and the interest rate may be higher. Mortgage certificates are usually valid for only a limited period of time, typically three weeks.

When you have found the house you want

Once you have made an offer for a house, you will have to apply formally for the loan.

You have to give details of the house you want to buy, including the price. You also have to say how much you want to borrow and may be asked where the rest of the purchase price is coming from. As well as completing the form you will need to supply a variety of documentation to back it up. Exactly what documentation will depend on the lender involved and your circumstances, but might typically include payslips, bank details, and proof of identity and address.

Once you have filled in the application form, you will have to pay for the lender to value the property. This is a valuation only, not a full structural survey, although most banks and building societies offer you the opportunity of arranging through them a house-buyer's report or a full structural survey. The fee is based on the purchase price (or the valuation, if that is higher). If the lender decides not to give you a loan as a result of the valuation, you will not get the fee back. Neither can it be refunded if you decide not to go ahead with the purchase, whatever the reason. However, nowadays many mortgage deals include a free valuation, or a refund of the valuation fee after the mortgage is finalised.

When the valuation has been done, and the status enquiries are complete, the lenders will let you know whether they are prepared to lend, how much and on what terms.

Mortgage conditions

Conditions will be laid down by the lender which the borrower has to undertake to observe. These will in most cases include:

- keeping the home in good repair
- not letting all or part of the home without the lender's permission (this means you would need to ask before you have tenants in the basement, for example, or take in lodgers or paying guests)
- not altering the property without the lender's permission
- informing the lender of any local authority proposals which would affect the property
- keeping the property insured
- not applying for an improvement grant without proper permission.

They may also include:

- undertaking to carry out certain repairs or improvements within a specified period
- not taking out any further mortgage without permission.

Insurance

Insurance for fire and other risks to the building is always a condition of granting a mortgage. Some building societies and banks arrange the insurance with a selected insurer, or the borrower is entitled to choose from a number of insurers named by the lender. With others you can use an insurer of your choice, although you may have to get the lender's approval (and may be charged for this, typically £25). Some insurers will pay this fee for you.

The loan

If the amount you are offered is enough to allow you to go ahead, you should have no problems. But you could be turned down or not be allowed a large enough loan to enable you to complete the purchase.

Turned down for a loan?

If your application is rejected, you should ask the reason. It could be:

- because of your circumstances (your income, credit record, age or occupation)
- because of problems with the property such as its condition or type.

If the problem is you or the house, a different lender may well use different lending criteria – though you may be asked to disclose whether a previous application has been turned down.

If the problem is a bad report on you from a credit reference agency, you should ask the lender for details of the agency concerned. You are entitled, on payment of £2 to the agency, to a copy of your record. If it is incorrect, you can ask for it to be put right.

For older properties, particularly those in need of repair, the loan may be a lower percentage of the price than normal. Most lenders stipulate that the loan is conditional on repairs being carried out within a specified period, and may hold back some of the loan until these are completed and the lender's inspector has approved the work.

Need a larger loan?

If the reason for the offer being low is your income, do think carefully whether you really can commit yourself to the loan you were requesting. Perhaps if you looked at a cheaper home, you would have no problems in getting the (smaller) loan you would need.

Cost of obtaining a mortgage

The costs which have to be paid by you, the borrower, are:

- the lender's valuation fee
- the lender's solicitor's fee for handling the mortgage application
- your own solicitor's fee for handling the mortgage.

The lender's solicitor's job is to check the legal ownership of the property, carry out necessary searches and enquiries and to draw up the mortgage deed laying down the conditions of the loan.

Your own solicitor may also charge you a fee for providing the lender with the documents about the ownership, and for checking the mortgage deed.

If you are getting a building society or bank mortgage, your solicitor will usually act for both you and the building society. Most solicitors include the necessary mortgage work within their charge for the purchase rather than charging separately for it.

Possible additional costs

If you have:

- a special deal mortgage (particularly fixed and capped rate) from a bank or building society, you may have to pay an 'arrangement fee' when you take it out
- a second mortgage or top-up loan, there may be a charge for obtaining this and the bank or insurance company solicitor's fee for handling it; your own solicitor may also make an extra charge, especially if he or she is not acting for the second lender
- a mortgage indemnity guarantee or high-lending fee (required if your loan is for more than a certain percentage of the value of the

property), this would entail a single premium, payable as a lump sum or added to the mortgage loan

- a stipulation by a lender for repairs (for example, eradication of damp or woodworm), and, if the lender retains a sum out of the mortgage loan until the work has been done to its satisfaction, there may be a fee for inspection
- a bridging loan from the bank to make up the purchase price if you buy before selling, or have to wait until repairs are carried out before taking up your loan, the bank makes a charge for arranging such a loan
- a mortgage other than an endowment, premiums for a mortgage protection policy to provide cover for the sum being borrowed may have to be paid throughout the period
- a newly built house which is still being constructed, and the lender is releasing the mortgage loan in stages, you have to pay a fee for the lender's surveyor's inspection and certificate at the various stages, and will have to pay the interest on the earlier parts of the loan from the time you first receive any money
- other surveys/inspections required by the lender's valuer (tree reports, structural engineers' reports, and so on), these will require further outlay.

Insuring in case of hard times

Many lenders offer insurance policies which pay your mortgage payments if you are unable to earn because of illness or unemployment (mortgage payment protection insurance – MPPI). These are often available only to their own borrowers but there are a few policies from lenders or through mortgage intermediaries which are available to anyone. These policies are not cheap. Read the small print carefully before signing up to one of these.

The wider the circumstances in which you can claim, the better. Some policies pay out only if you are unable to work because you are ill or have had an accident. Others include redundancy – though not usually if you volunteer for redundancy. A few policies cover a wider definition of unemployment – for example, if you are sacked or lose your job but are unable to claim redundancy, perhaps because you have not worked for the firm for long enough.

Make sure that your work is covered by the policy. Some do not pay out if you normally work part-time, even if you earn good money in that time and have been doing so for several years. Most policies cover self-employed people for unemployment only if they involuntarily cease trading and tell the Inland Revenue.

Some policies do not pay out on redundancy or unemployment if you have been with your employer for less than a certain time or if you are on a fixed-term contract. Most policies will cover mortgage payments only for one year, some for two years; you are unlikely to find policies paying out for longer than this.

The Association of British Insurers (ABI)* has drawn up a code of practice requiring its members to make sure that customers understand what they are buying and that policies recommended to them are suitable. However, if a policy is sold through a lender or mortgage intermediary who has little knowledge of the details of the policy, you should normally be given a written summary of the cover. It is very important that you read it and check that the policy is suitable for you.

Pitfalls of mortgage payment protection insurance

Although taking out this form of insurance is advisable, it is no guarantee of financial security. Research carried out for the Office of the Deputy Prime Minister which was published in 2003 showed that:

- some 12 per cent of borrowers experience difficulty with mortgage repayments, but only 1 per cent make an MPPI claim
- 30 per cent of claims are rejected (for example, because of a pre-existing medical condition) and appeals are rarely successful
- 20 per cent of successful claimants still fall into mortgage arrears due to the time lapse between the claim and the eventual payout under the policy
- the rise in house prices means that premiums have become prohibitively expensive
- the claim process can be delayed if former employers are slow to provide details, and the insurance company's administration is inefficient.

Benefits and mortgage payments

Income Support and Jobseeker's Allowance are Social Security benefits to help people on low incomes. If you qualify for either benefit, you may get limited help to meet your mortgage payments, service charges and ground rent. The government will pay only the interest, not the capital, repayments. Moreover, there is an upper limit of £100,000 on the size of the mortgage which is eligible. If the mortgage is larger than this, assistance may be given only on the first £100,000. Restrictions may be imposed if your housing costs are considered to be excessive. The payments are made directly to your lender. One restriction, for example, is that the payment is limited to the average national interest rate. If you pay more than that, then the excess will not be covered by the state. Hence, you will face a growing mortgage debt. If you experience this shortfall, contact your mortgage lender immediately.

Rules that came into force in 1995 stipulate that if your mortgage was taken out before 2 October 1995, generally no help will be given with housing costs for the first eight weeks, 50 per cent of eligible interest will be paid for the next 18 weeks and 100 per cent thereafter. This does not apply to pensioners. If the mortgage was taken out after this date, no help will be given for the first 39 weeks of a claim. After that time, the full amount of eligible interest (subject to the £100,000 ceiling) will be paid. The 39-week rule does not apply to pensioners. Other categories of claimants may receive special treatment. For further information contact your local Benefits Agency, housing centre or Citizens Advice Bureau.

In addition, a new mortgage-interest 'run on' benefit has been introduced, the imaginatively named 'extended mortgage interest income support run on'. This operates when you or your partner have been claiming Income Support, Incapacity Benefit or Jobseeker's Allowance for 26 weeks, have been receiving help with mortgage payments and have started full-time work that is expected to last for five weeks or more. It continues the previous mortgage interest payments for a further four weeks. The idea is to overcome barriers to taking up work caused by the gap between pay day and repayment day.

You cannot claim for:

- premiums on mortgage payment protection insurance policies
- payments towards buildings insurance
- interest exceeding the national average rate
- interest payable during ineligibility periods (eight weeks or 39 weeks as appropriate)
- any amount relating to capital repayments (e.g. premiums of an endowment policy)
- interest relating to borrowings in excess of £100,000.

Problems with mortgage payments

The early years of the 1990s saw an unprecedented number of homes being repossessed by building societies and other lenders. If you find that you cannot keep up your mortgage payments, do not assume that you will automatically lose the house. There is much that can be done to help the situation. You should tell your lender as soon as possible and try to work out a way through your problems together. The Mortgage Code commits lenders to treating cases of hardship sympathetically and positively; and the new FSA regulations will also require the fair treatment of borrowers who are in arrears and facing repossession. As part of this, lenders will be required to provide an FSA information sheet to borrowers when they first go into arrears. The

---

Hints on how to avoid losing your home

- If you are unemployed and/or are claiming Income Support, ask for assistance from your local Job Centre or Social Security office to help with interest payments (not capital repayments).
- If you fall behind with your payments, contact your lender at once (before he or she contacts you) and explain the position. Some lenders now have helplines. Ask for advice on what can be done. Mortgage lenders normally prefer to come to an arrangement with the borrower than take possession proceedings.
- Alternatively, try the National Debtline*.
- *Do not* ignore letters from the lender. Respond promptly.
- Consider going to a debt counsellor. Many Citizens Advice Bureaux offer this service free of charge.
- Be very wary about borrowing more to pay off the arrears, particularly if you are being offered a loan by a finance company. Interest rates on such loans are often much higher, and you could find that you simply get deeper into debt.
- If court proceedings are issued, comply with the time limits and go to all court hearings. Writing a letter to the court explaining your circumstances is never sufficient. Courts do have wide powers to suspend possession orders if there is a realistic prospect of the arrears being cleared within a reasonable time. This generosity does not exist when there is negative equity.

---

way forward will to some extent depend on the type of your mortgage. Contact your local Citizens Advice Bureau or look in the *Yellow Pages* for support and information if you are having difficulty with payments.

The negative equity trap

Owing to the fall in property values in the early 1990s, many people found themselves owning houses of a lower value than the amount outstanding on the mortgage. Because, traditionally, lenders have insisted on loans being repaid as a condition of agreeing to a sale of a house, this prevented many people in that situation from moving house – even those who had maintained all their monthly payments and were not in financial difficulties. This phenomenon could arise again with the advent of another recession.

Many lenders have introduced schemes to help those with negative equity. If you have to move – for example, because of your job – you may transfer the negative equity from your present to your new home (but you would not be allowed to increase your loan).

There are no easy answers, but if you find yourself in that situation, it probably does no harm to point out to the lender that it shares some responsibility for the situation (by virtue of lending too much) and invite a shared approach to resolving it.

Chapter 7

Finding a buyer for your house

Having taken the decision to sell, you can either handle the sale yourself or commission one or more estate agents to find you a buyer.

An agent will do some of the work for you but you must be prepared for this to cost considerably more than if you do it all yourself. Without an agent, you will be spending time rather than money – at a time when you are probably occupied with buying as well as selling a house. It may not take longer to find a buyer privately than if you engage an estate agent, but it could do.

If a new industrial or office development is imminent and a firm is likely to be importing new staff, it will probably do its house-searching through an agent. Local people, on the other hand, have more opportunity for studying local newspapers and 'For Sale' boards.

If you advertise your house extensively and do not manage to sell it, you may have difficulty persuading an agent to take over from you. This is not a matter of the agent being nose-out-of-joint but of practical experience: a house known to have been on the market for a long time is likely to be much more difficult to sell, and it may be suspected that there is something wrong with it – even if this is not the case.

From 2007 sellers will have to compile information about their house for prospective buyers – the home information pack.

Home information packs

Home information packs (HIPs) are also called 'sellers' packs', and will be introduced in 2007. The intention is that they will increase openness and transparency, shortening the period between offer and contract (from an average of three months to just over three weeks, it is hoped) and reducing the number of factors that can cause a transaction to collapse after the initial agreement of terms, including gazumping. The packs will help sellers calculate a realistic selling price and demonstrate their seriousness to buyers as well as helping buyers commit to a purchase.

It is expected that the cost to the seller of putting the pack together will be around £600. Although precise details are not yet finalised, the pack is likely to include:

- copies of title documents
- replies to standard enquiries made by the buyer
- replies to searches made of a local authority
- copies of any planning, listed building or Building Regulations consents and approvals
- copies of any warranties and guarantees
- a surveyor's home condition report
- a draft contract.

Preparing the house for sale

Your house is your home – somewhere that, presumably, has reflected your way of life and your taste while you have lived there. When it comes to selling, you need to put yourself in the position of the people viewing and pick out all the faults that *you* can live with but which could lose you your sale.

This can be an uncomfortable experience, but making an effort and maybe spending a little money now, before you start showing the property, will pay off in terms of both the speed at which offers come in and the price ultimately achieved. Consider allowing two or three weeks to bring your property up to presentation standard.

If you find it difficult to see your home with the eyes of a stranger, look at other houses (whether or not they are for sale) and consider what would appeal to you or put you off. What you are aiming for is a tidy front (and back) garden and fresh exterior paintwork, plus an attractive entrance and a well-decorated, clean, uncluttered interior. Although it is not necessary for your potential buyers to fall in love with all your decorative schemes, they will be more likely to make an offer if they feel they could move in straight away without having to endure months of disruption while the place is being brought up to standard.

Garden

Here, the priorities should be to blitz the weeds, mow the lawn and trim the edges, clip the hedges, and get rid of any rubbish – you might need a skip, or a few trips to the dump, if this includes builders' rubble, relics from long-forgotten forays into do-it-yourself, parts of cars, defunct bicycles or household appliances, or accumulated garden refuse that has been piling up over the years.

If the family pet has made a mess of your lawn, consider patching – or even, if it is not a large area, laying new turf: a lush, well-manicured expanse of green is always a pleasing sight. Remove other signs of pets – bones, rubber rings and so on – and stow away the children's toys and the clothes-line when viewing is imminent.

If none of the plants is in flower, or you have bare patches of earth, a few pounds spent on bulbs or bedding plants could greatly improve your front garden.

Front entrance

If your front entrance is dominated by a dustbin, the family's outdoor footwear and the dog's water bowl, replace them with some colourful house plants or, outside, planted-up containers. If you do not have any suitable tubs or other planters, buy cheap flower-pots or improvise with a discarded wheelbarrow, coal scuttle, stone sink or wicker basket. If the paint on the front door is dull and scratched, repaint it – first impressions matter a great deal.

If you are expecting people at dusk or later, switch the external light on and have some lights on in the house: it will look much more welcoming.

Inside the house

Clear as much away as you can: viewers will be trying to imagine their own belongings in these surroundings, but if every shelf and surface is currently overflowing they will find this difficult. 'Edit' your displays of ornaments and books, pack away almost all the bottles and jars in your bathroom and clear the kitchen worktops, perhaps leaving out just a few token items that are attractive in their own right.

Move furniture back against the wall. In short, try to create an impression of space, everywhere. If storage is a problem (you might of course be moving out because you want more space and storage yourself) ask a neighbour, friend or relative to take a few items short-term – and make sure it is only short-term. Or fill your car with stuff you want to get out of the way. Remember, one person's treasures are another person's clutter.

Don't forget that you will probably have to open the doors of some of your built-in cupboards, so be sure you can do this without releasing an avalanche of the contents.

Consider adding a wall mirror or two to increase the illusion of space or reflect light back into a room that doesn't get too much of it.

Carry out essential repairs and do some redecoration if necessary – avoiding controversial colour schemes and picking pale, neutral shades (cream and white are always safe) to enhance the feeling of spaciousness. If the hall and stair carpet is looking particularly worn or shabby, it could be worth recarpeting, to make the initial impact on viewers one of newness; or, if you have decent floorboards, go for polished boards, which are very much in vogue and will be preferable to clapped-out carpet.

Replace dead or missing light bulbs and fix any broken fittings. Dripping taps also call attention to themselves, so try to sort these out too before any potential purchaser comes through the door.

Certainly you should scrub the place like it has never been scrubbed before – woodwork, toilet bowls, washbasins, kitchen surfaces, windows – and make sure the house smells clean. If you think there may be lingering food smells, use furniture polish, bake some bread (one food smell that everyone likes), use a room spray, burn a scented candle or roast some coffee beans to overcome unwanted odours. This will create the impression that boiled cabbage and fry-ups have never once been on your household menu.

If the grouting between your kitchen or bathroom tiles is dirty-looking or flaking away, re-grout: this is quick and simple job and will freshen up the appearance of any tiled area.

Draw attention to features of the rooms that you want the people viewing to notice by having background light switched on in advance. If you have an open fire and the weather is cold, get the fire going – nothing is as welcoming. And bring in some fresh flowers (these are never 'clutter'). All in all, you need to imagine that you are styling your house for a magazine photo-shoot. The result may not look like everyday life as you and your family know it, but it should achieve the objective.

Focusing attention on what matters most

Keep pets and children under control. If Bonzo bounds across the garden to welcome your viewers with a playful lunge, they may simply decide to pass on your property. Ideally, try to arrange that your children are neither eating nor in the throes of a messy or noisy activity while the viewers are in the house. Some people love animals and children, but even so, this is not the time to distract them from appreciating what your house has to offer them.

Selling without an agent

If you want to sell your house privately, these are the steps you will have to take:

- prepare your house for sale
- decide on an asking price
- decide which items are to be included in the sale, and prices for them
- draw up the particulars to give to potential buyers
- spread the word
- answer all enquiries
- arrange the appointments to view the house
- show round all viewers
- evaluate the merits of rival bids
- negotiate a final price with the buyer you choose.

Fixing a price

A do-it-yourself seller may not be as knowledgeable as a local estate agent on what would be the right price to ask. An agent's expertise lies in knowing current market trends, what similar local property is selling for, and in judging what would be an attractive but appropriate price for a particular house and any of its contents.

If your house is one of several similar ones – in a post-war estate, for example – it is easier to judge a price than if it is an older one which may be in a better or worse state of repair and redecoration than neighbouring ones, or a house for which there is no comparable one in the immediate area.

To find out current asking prices in the neighbourhood, study the windows of local estate agents, and advertisements in local papers for similar houses. Remember that the price asked is not necessarily the figure at which the property gets sold.

What neighbours or friends report as the sale prices of neighbouring properties may not be reliable.

The condition of the house itself ought to be considered before a price is settled. If you have decided not to repair or decorate, and your house needs attention, you should expect a lower price than for an identical house in good order.

Valuation

You can ask a local estate agent to give you a valuation for your house. If you are not selling through the agent, there may be a charge: ask first what this charge would be. If you do decide to have a valuation, make it clear that you are asking for a valuation – not giving an instruction to sell. It is advisable to get the arrangement and fee confirmed in writing.

If you are uncertain about the saleability of your house – for example, where there are structural problems that could deflate the price or make it difficult to sell – ask a surveyor to look over the house. The survey may reveal one or more faults which would justify a buyer in asking for some reduction on account of them. If so, build into your asking price some allowance for this and keep in mind what figure would finally be acceptable. If, however, you make clear to potential buyers any defects you are aware of, you should not have to reduce the price because of them later – though the price is always a matter for negotiation, and you cannot force a buyer to accept a particular price.

Bargaining

Make the asking price as attractive a figure as possible: £94,500 or even £94,450 is better than £95,000. It is sensible to set the asking price higher than the one you expect to settle for, so that there is some room for manoeuvre. If you want a quick sale and think a little bargaining will attract a buyer, you can quote a figure and add 'o.n.o.' (or near offer) – and wait for one. Any buyer hopes to start negotiating at a somewhat lower figure than he or she is prepared to settle for and the parties may finally decide to compromise.

The buyer may ask for a reduction because you are not having to pay an agent's commission on the sale, or may try to get as many extras as possible included in the price.

What to include in the price

You may have included in the asking price items in the house which you wish to sell with it. Alternatively, a separate price can be asked and negotiated for these. In either case, as the seller, you should be quite clear about what will be regarded as fixtures and what you are entitled to take away with you.

You should also consider which items belong to you rather than the house, but which it would be more sensible or convenient to sell with it, such as a washing machine or dishwasher already plumbed in, the fridge or cooker.

If the kitchen contains units constructed to house a particular size or brand of equipment, it may be more sensible to leave these where they are. As a selling point, a well-fitted kitchen comes high on most people's list and to remove specially designed equipment could be short-sighted. A decision on this may also depend on whether you know yet what you need in your new kitchen.

Made-to-measure curtains, perhaps with matching pelmets, are often best sold with a house since they are unlikely to fit satisfactorily into a different one, and adapting them may be uneconomic. Similarly, all fitted carpets are better left in position for the next owner. Curtains and carpets are usually included in the sale price. If you do want a separate price paid for them, the condition they are in should be taken into account when fixing a second-hand price for them. Bear in mind also what the buyer is saving by not having to buy new carpets.

Fixtures

By law, you must sell as part of the house anything that is a fixture, (unless it is specifically agreed between the buyer and seller that particular fixtures are excluded). For full details of the legal position regarding fixtures and fittings see Chapter 4.

List of items for sale

When you have reviewed the house and garden, and decided what to sell, make a list, pricing items according to their quality, original cost, age and current condition. When you show the house, point out these items specifically.

To avoid misunderstandings or subsequent queries, it may be worth your while to duplicate a list of any items which you are selling separately, together with other information about the house, along the lines of the 'particulars' which estate agents draw up.

When it comes to final negotiations, you may find that the buyer does not want some of the items you want to sell. He or she is quite entitled to reject these but, if you want to stand firm, you are in a stronger position – it depends on how badly the buyer wants the house: he or she may feel obliged to buy the contents you offer.

How to prepare sale particulars

All estate agents prepare sale particulars describing, usually in glowing terms, the properties they are selling. Although it is by no means essential to have sale particulars when selling privately, they could well help to sell the house, especially if you are advertising out of the locality.

There is no set format to preparing sale particulars, but it is usually best to start with a general summary giving the address, type of house (bungalow, semi-detached, chalet etc.), number of bedrooms, locality and price. Add a sentence or two on situation ('set back from road', 'quiet cul-de-sac'). Do not be tempted to give the kind of misinformation which some agents go in for (for instances of this see page 46). It is safer and better to describe the house as it is. Exaggerated claims will lead to disappointment. Nevertheless, do mention all the selling points: for example, if the house has recently been renovated or has central heating, say so.

Next, include a description of every room in the house. Plan this so that when you later come to show people round, they can follow the order set out in your sale particulars.

Give measurements (which must be accurate) for main rooms (no need to give the size of the cupboard under the stairs unless it is very spacious). As you go through each room, highlight any special features, as well as facilities such as the number of radiators, electrical sockets and telephone points. Do not include in your sale particulars any item which is not included in the price.

Remember to describe the whole house. Cupboards, attics, cellars should all get a mention, along with plus points (double glazing, burglar alarm, cavity insulation, roof insulation and so on).

Having dealt with the inside, move on to a description of the garden, garage, fuel store and outbuildings. Again, do not include items which you plan to remove.

Similarly, if you intend to take fixtures which would normally be included in the price, say so in the particulars. If you leave it till later, you could cause annoyance and this might upset the progress of the sale.

Next, deal with things which are not included in the sale, but which you are prepared to sell: for example, 'the carpets may be purchased for the price of £1,000 (or to be negotiated)'.

You can either fix the price or invite offers 'in the region of' or 'not less than' £000. If the market is uncertain, you can leave the figures blank in your master copy, and add them later. That will save you having to advertise too loudly that you have made some price reductions.

Make sure you include directions for finding the house (including the nearest public transport).

Finally, it is helpful to give additional information, including the mains services which are connected (and those which are available but are not connected), the type of heating and the actual amount of council tax and water rates payable. The name and address of the local authority is also useful. If planning permission has been granted for an improvement – a conversion or extension, perhaps, or a garage – which has not yet been carried out, do not forget to mention this.

End with your own name and telephone number, and an indication of the arrangements you offer for viewing.

Producing the sale particulars

Plan the layout, allowing for one or more photographs to emphasise the main features.

The particulars should be typed out or wordprocessed neatly. This will be your master copy, which should then be photocopied. Do not expect hundreds of enquiries, but have maybe two dozen sets prepared for your first edition. You can always have more copies made later. A buyer who is really keen might need several sets of the particulars to show to his or her solicitor, mortgage broker, surveyor etc.

Photographs

If you have a camera, there is no reason why you should not produce your own photographs – in colour. A few simple rules will enhance

> **WARNING: misrepresentation**
>
> You must make very sure that your sale particulars are accurate. If you make incorrect statements, even innocently, you could lay yourself open to being sued for damages for misrepresentation, or cancellation of the contract (or both). This applies equally to any information given orally to a proposed buyer.
>
> By all means put in a disclaimer like this: These particulars are believed to be accurate, but they are intended as a guide only and do not form part of a contract. (But it will not necessarily get you off the hook if the particulars are misleading.)

the effect of your photograph. Avoid elementary errors, such as incorrect focusing and wrong exposure.

Frame your picture so that it shows the best features of the house. A close-up of the dustbins and septic tank may have practical significance, but will not bring the punters rushing to buy. Cut out unnecessary intrusions: parked cars in the foreground or the gas works in the distance are bound to be off-putting. On the other hand, if you can successfully frame the photograph with elegant foliage, then do so. Do not confine yourself to outside views. If there is a feature which would photograph well (like a well-equipped kitchen or attractive living-room), a photograph of this should also be included.

It is best to experiment. Run off a whole film, then look critically at the results. With luck you will have some good pictures from which to choose two or three for your sale particulars. Get your local film shop to run off the necessary numbers of prints of these and stick them to your particulars – photocopies never really come out well. With a digital camera, images can be put on a website and sent in emails.

Advertising

Before you can have any hope of selling your house, you must tell the world it is on the market. Do it in a way which makes people interested enough to come and take a look.

Among the many different ways of letting it be known that you have a house for sale, some are cheap, others expensive. You need to plan a campaign. Here are the choices.

'For Sale' sign outside the house

Some people are reluctant to take this step. They feel it might encourage burglars or nosey neighbours. The decision must be a personal one, but there are many advantages. Many house-hunters tour the neighbourhood and a 'For Sale' sign might be the first indication they see that your house is, indeed, for sale. The sign will also help people who have already contacted you to find the house. There could well be people in the locality looking for a house, either for themselves or relatives.

If you are concerned about being pestered by people who do not have an appointment (or burglars), you can always put on your sign: 'For Sale – please telephone for appointment on xxx xxxx.' You can easily make your own sign or, if you want a more professional appearance, some stationers' shops stock signs, or you can have them made up specially.

Cards in local shops

Many newsagents' shops and sub-post offices (and even supermarkets) have a window or wall set aside for advertisement cards. This is a very cheap way of advertising. If you want it to be eye-catching, take the same care with your card as with your sale particulars. Use fluorescent card, and add a colour photograph.

To reach as many people as possible, place cards with a number of shops. Inevitably, this is a limited way of advertising – but you could be lucky.

Property shops

You may be able to use a 'property shop' in your area. You have to fill in a fairly detailed form giving information about the property and allow it to be photographed. You pay a fee for the details and photograph of your house to be displayed in the 'shop'; some shops charge per week for displaying property. Most include indefinite

---

WARNING: size and number of signs
Prosecutions have been successfully brought where 'For Sale' signs do not comply with the law. You are permitted to have either one board up to 0.5 square metres in area, or 2 boards 'conjoined', together not exceeding 0.6 metres.

---

display in their initial charge. Some property shops computer-match available properties with prospective buyers. The seller and any interested purchasers get in touch with each other direct and negotiate individually. There is no commission to pay on a sale, but the fee you pay is not refunded even if you fail to sell.

In a few places, property centres have been set up by local solicitors. At such a centre, details of properties are shown and one of the centre's solicitors undertakes the selling transaction for you. The fee you are charged is based on the selling price of your house and includes display of the property and the conveyancing. The Solicitors Property Group★ can tell you where to find such centres.

Your notice board/email at work

If your employer has a notice-board for use by employees, consider putting up one of your cards there too. Email 'ads' are another possibility, if permitted.

Newspaper advertisements

Newspaper advertising can take many forms. At its lowest level, you can simply place a classified advertisement in your local paper. The next step up would be an advertisement in the regional paper for your area.

If you want to reach a wider public, you can advertise in one of the specialist magazines, such as *Exchange & Mart*, *Dalton's Weekly*, or *Loot*. Many national daily and Sunday newspapers have property sections. Top-of-the-scale advertisements go into the glossy magazines such as *Country Life* or *The Field*.

The medium you choose depends to some extent on the prevailing conditions and the kind of house you are selling. In boom times, you have only to whisper that your house is on the market before you have dozens of prospective buyers arriving at the door. Most of the time the property market is quieter, which requires active marketing. You should budget to spend quite a large sum of money on advertising. How much depends on the type you will use. Consider the alternatives.

Local paper

People who intend to move into an area frequently buy the local paper to find out what is available. You are therefore likely to reach not just the locals. Because this is the cheapest option, it gives you most scope. You need not confine yourself to three abbreviated lines. You could well include a photograph and an eye-catching description. Look at other private advertisements and improve on them. Try to arrange it so that your advertisement appears on the same page as estate agents' advertisements – perhaps with a bigger photograph than the agents use to advertise their houses. Most local papers will arrange the typesetting for you and can give advice on the wording. It is best to plan to advertise for several weeks, rather than exhaust your budget on one big advertisement.

Regional paper
The regional paper will cover one or more counties. Because of its wider readership, its rates will inevitably be higher than the local paper – so you are unlikely to be able to create the same 'splash' with your advertisement. It is still worth considering as it is cheaper than national advertising.

National advertising
Consider this if you have a house which has something unusual; perhaps you own two acres and offer an opportunity to join the 'Good Life', or you are in an area where prices are still low and you are trying to encourage people to move or retire to your house.

Drafting an advertisement

An advertisement should include the following basic information:

- type of house (e.g. detached, semi, terraced, bungalow)
- location
- number of bedrooms
- number of living-rooms
- number of bathrooms/separate WCs
- heating system
- garage
- garden
- freehold or leasehold
- price
- telephone number for appointments to view
- possibly also the number of floors, council tax band and any desirable amenities, such as proximity to station, schools or if it is in

a conservation area, etc. If some features are out of the ordinary or would make good selling points, include these.

The length of your advertisement will be dictated by price. You can probably afford to be quite expansive in a local paper, but may have to cut your wording to the bone if you advertise nationally. Find out the cost before you start preparing the advertisements.

Using too many of the abbreviations listed below will condense the entry to such a degree that it becomes virtually unreadable, and certainly not eye-catching. Compare the two advertisements (both for the same house) which follow:

> Arch. des. det. hse. 1975. 4 lge bdrms, 2 bath, 2 WC, 30 ft sit rm, sep d/rm, study, mod. kit/brkrm. gas CH. Dble gge. patio. ¼-acre walled gdn. £00,000 FH. Tel. . .

> Architect-designed house, detached. Built 1975 in wooded area 10 mins from town centre, standing in ¼ acre of own ground. 4 large bedrooms, one with bathroom ensuite; 1 other bathroom, 2 WCs, sitting-room 30' x 14' with picture window on to patio, separate dining-room, study; kitchen recently modernised, pine wall units and breakfast area. Gas CH. Double glazing throughout. Double garage. Well-stocked walled garden. Freehold £00,000. Tel. . .

Making a video or using a digital camcorder

More and more people own video cameras or digital camcorders. If you are one of them and are trying to attract interest from outside the

---

Some common space-saving abbreviations used in property advertisements

CH = central heating	clk = cloakroom
p.b. = purpose built	gge = garage
CHW = constant hot water	exe. con. = excellent condition
conv = converted	rm = room
FH = freehold	c & c = carpets and curtains
rec = reception	lge = large
GR = ground rent	f & f = fixtures and fittings
kit/brkrm = kitchen/breakfast room	det = detached
WC = loo	o.n.o. = or near offer

area, consider making a short film of your home, using the following guidelines.

Do not spend too much time on the technicalities. All you need to do is give a general impression – both inside and out, though if you are aiming to send the pictures to people not familiar with the area, you might include a few opening shots of your town/village or neighbourhood.

Take views of the outside of the house from different angles, including the road. Home in on the features. Hold your shot for long enough, but not for too long. You do not want your buyers to fall asleep while watching.

Use it to complement your sale particulars inside the house. Show the special characteristics, but do not zoom in on every socket and radiator. If you do a commentary, be sparing unless you are sure you are good at it. It is probably best simply to say where and what you are filming, rather than attempt a travelogue voice-over.

Digital recordings can be played back on television, and both digital and analogue recordings can be edited using a computer. Video clips can be put on to a website.

Other means of selling

There is no limit to the ways in which you can advertise your house – from a large advertisement painted on the side of your car, to handing out leaflets in a shopping centre (but watch out for breaches of the law or bylaws), local radio or teletext or even creating your own home page on the World Wide Web. You can try anything if you have the imagination and resources.

Answering enquiries

All being well, your advertisements and publicity will start to produce results – in the shape of enquiries and telephone calls. Arrange for someone to be on hand to answer any enquiries. (If you are available only during evenings and weekends, say so in the advertisement.) Keep a pad by the telephone to record names and times of appointments – you will probably find it easier to deal with one viewer at a time (although having two viewers looking round at the same time creates a competitive environment and could improve your chances).

Do not try to judge your enquirers by the sound of their voices. The surly voice at the end of the line may turn into the most enthusiastic would-be buyer. The objective is to get him or her to come to see the house. Sound helpful, but not too enthusiastic (even if it is the first caller for a month). Viewing should, ideally, always take place in daylight.

It goes without saying that you should be ready for the appointment. The house should be in tip-top condition – and you should be there! Nobody will buy your house if they travel 50 miles to find it locked up.

Preparing an information kit

Have to hand essential information about the running of the house, such as heating and electricity costs. Your bills for the last two or three years are a good indicator. If you are not on mains drainage, your buyers will need to know how often the septic tank has to be emptied and how much it costs to do so. Add to your pack documentation about guarantees, servicing of central heating, and instructions for any equipment which will be included in the sale (central heating, water softener, waste disposal unit etc.).

It is helpful to give local information, such as details about schools, shops, churches, local recreation facilities etc. Your tourist information centre or local authority may be able to let you have local guides and maps at little or no cost. Prospective buyers, especially those from outside the area, will find these useful.

The viewing

You will probably find that your first few attempts are a little difficult. It is hard to remember to point out important features in a place which you may have come to take for granted. Don't worry about this. If you sound hesitant or nervous that could well create a good impression. Most people do not take kindly to 'hard sell'. On the other hand, don't let your nerves keep you talking non-stop. Follow the general guidelines below.

Invite the visitors into your living-room or lounge. Start your grand tour with the inside, beginning with the downstairs and moving upstairs (if applicable). Generally, try to follow the order of rooms in your sale particulars. It is a good idea to say that you are doing this. If they do not have a copy, offer them one, and a pen to make notes. Show the main rooms (living, dining, kitchen) first and the bedrooms

---

WARNING: security

A few unscrupulous people use the invitations in house-sale advertisements to plan burglaries, or to steal whilst posing as prospective buyers. Be vigilant. One elementary precaution you can take is to show the house by appointment only. Ring back everyone who contacts you – even casual callers. You can use the pretext, when asking for the number, of needing to check with your wife/husband for convenient times to view. In that way you will at least have the name and telephone number of anyone who arranges a visit.

Do not leave valuables or jewellery in easy reach when showing people around.

---

and bathroom next. After they have seen the inside, take them outside (have an umbrella ready in case it pours with rain) and show them the garden and any outbuildings.

Point out the features, but do not over-sell. The fireplace you like so much may be the one thing they will want to remove! Indicate what is and what is not included in the price. If there are items you want to sell as extras, tell the viewers about these too.

Once you have shown them round, offer them a coffee and ask them if there is any information they need. Here your information pack will be useful. You should be able to have at your fingertips answers to most questions which are raised. Remember to offer a local guidebook or leaflet if it is available, especially if the viewers do not live locally.

Should you let them look round by themselves? Many people would welcome the opportunity to view a house on their own. They can then feel free to look more closely at the house, and discuss it privately together. You will have to make your own assessment as to whether it is safe to allow them to go round the house unaccompanied. On the whole, it is a good selling ploy to allow this. You will, of course, still be in the house, and should be able to see if their coats are bulging with hidden loot when they leave!

At the end of the viewing

Do not press your visitors for a decision. If they are wavering, you could easily push them the wrong way. Simply ask them if they have any more questions. It is the house, after all, which will sell itself if they like it.

Make it clear that they are welcome to come back to have another look (some prospective buyers inspect a house many times) and offer to supply them with any further information they might need now or later.

Before they go, make sure:

- that they have your sale particulars (more than one copy if they want them)
- that they have your telephone number, and know how to contact you at all times (at work, for instance)
- that you have their name, address and telephone number.

Don't build up your hopes

Appearances are deceptive. Enthusiastic enquirers often disappear without another word. Others, who appear to show no interest at all, could buy the house without even bargaining over the price. The chances are that your first visitors will not buy, and you may have a long wait before you even receive an offer. Take advantage of the opportunity to practise your guided tours and your sales pitch.

Selling through an estate agent

The advantages of using estate agents to sell your home are:

- they take some of the work and worry off the shoulders of the seller
- they have more experience in judging the market value of a house and how best it should be sold (and whether by private treaty or auction)
- they have better facilities for publicising the sale, and ready access to more would-be buyers
- they offer better security – for example, an elderly person or someone living alone can ask for the agent's representative to accompany all viewers
- they can ask if an interested buyer has adequate means or mortgage facilities already arranged and will, if required, negotiate a mortgage on behalf of a buyer.

The agent's prime concern is to achieve a speedy and, as far as possible, a trouble-free sale, for all parties concerned. If an applicant's 'buying power' is established at the outset, it is to the benefit of all concerned. Agents have access to mortgage funds from a variety of sources.

The use of computers by groups of estate agents is increasing. Details of your property are fed into the multi-list computer system and are then available to all agents participating in the scheme, who can offer the property immediately to prospective buyers over a wide area.

Finding an estate agent

If you have already found a house to buy through an agent, do you then go on to ask the same agent to sell yours? There is something to be said for doing this: the agent will have more to lose if he or she cannot sell your house. But be careful that the agent does not down-value your house in order to achieve (effectively) two quick sales.

To compare local estate agents, find out:

- what type of property they sell
- whether they belong to one of the professional associations (see below)
- the extent of the services offered
- on what basis they charge and what is included.

Studying shop windows, newspaper advertising and the display boards of different estate agents will give an idea of what business they handle, how extensive it is, and whether it covers a special market or deals with all types of housing. The style and flavour of the text may reflect the style of the firm.

The number of 'For Sale' boards in the area reflects agents' activities and the number of 'Sold' stickers their effectiveness. But some local associations of estate agents agree that none of their members will erect 'For Sale' boards, and the local authority may impose restrictions.

Most estate agents belong to one or other of the professional associations: the Royal Institution of Chartered Surveyors (RICS)★, the National Association of Estate Agents (NAEA)★ or the Association of Building Engineers (ABE)★. They have codes of conduct for their members, who have to participate in indemnity schemes protecting the public from fraud.

Be wary of unqualified estate agents, some of whom are unscrupulous. Estate agents do not have to be registered to carry on business, but if convicted or found in breach of certain obligations under the Estate Agents Act 1979, they can, in the last resort, be prohibited from doing estate agency work by order of the Director General of Fair Trading. Any complaints should initially be made to the local authority trading standards department.

The Ombudsman scheme for estate agents was set up in 1992 by the large chains of corporate agents. In January 1998 it was expanded and made available to smaller, independent agents who are members of the RICS or NAEA, both of which have agreed a Code of Conduct for their members. The Ombudsman has the power to award up to £25,000, although most awards are under £500. The Ombudsman will act only after customers have tried and failed to obtain redress from their estate agent. The most common grievance concerns the refusal of the agent to pass on the buyer's offer unless the buyer agrees to obtain financial services from the agent.

Estate Agents' Code of Practice

The Ombudsman for Estate Agents (OEA)★ has issued a new Code of Practice for estate agents, which came into operation in 2003. The key features of this Code are:

- agents must not deliberately misrepresent the price of a property or recklessly make misleading statements
- at the outset, agents must give clients a written copy of their customer contract as well as details of fees, expenses and business terms. Information about how the agreement can be cancelled must also be given
- as appropriate, agents must explain the phrases 'sole selling rights', 'sole agency' or 'ready, willing and able purchaser'
- clients must be informed of the Ombudsman for Estate Agents scheme, and given access to the Code of Practice free of charge
- agents must not harass or cause offence in order to gain instructions
- agents must not erect a 'for sale' sign, allow unsupervised viewing or give out keys without the client's permission
- all offers made should be recorded and passed on to clients as soon as is reasonably practicable
- prospective purchasers must not be discriminated against on the grounds that they will not take financial services offered by the estate agent

- agents must tell the seller if the purchaser does take advantage of their services, and thereby disclose any potential conflict of interest.

The estate agent's inspection

Ask someone from the estate agents to call to look at the house. It is a good thing to ask specifically who will be dealing with your house and to meet him or her personally at the outset. (It may well not be the senior partner with whom you deal.) The agent should make a thorough inspection in order to be able to assess the value of the house, taking into account its position and condition. You can then discuss, and get advice on, what would be a suitable and attractive asking price – not necessarily the same figure as the valuation. (If you seek advice from more than one agent, do not automatically give instructions to the one who suggests the highest asking price. It could just be a not-very-ethical ploy to get your instructions.)

The agent should take measurements of rooms, and note other details, such as heating, special features and so on, for the description to be circulated. You should have ready details of council tax and water rates, any ground rent payable and any service or maintenance charges.

If you want, the agent will offer advice on which items to leave in the house, what price to ask for them, and whether to carry out renovations. (See pages 145-8 for tips on how to present a house for sale.)

Get the agent to tell you what arrangements will be made for advertising the property. These could be:

- insertion in the agent's list of houses for sale, fed into a computer, mailed to buyers on the register or handed out at the office
- a special circular dealing only with your property
- an advertisement in a local, regional or national paper or magazine.

The agent may arrange for photographs to be taken for publicity purposes. The cost of a specially printed brochure, with photographs, may not be included in the fee, and you should check what this cost will be.

If there are special circumstances (for example, you are selling because of financial problems or a marriage breakdown), tell the agent; point out that there could be circumstances where, through no fault of your own, you may have to abandon the sale.

An energetic agent will return to the office, draft the particulars, print them out and mail them – often on the same day – and perhaps also telephone any buyer who might be interested, and who might visit even before seeing the particulars.

Agents do not necessarily confirm with the seller (or even show him or her) the house description or an advertisement. You should say if you want to vet the text before it is printed or duplicated. It is worth doing so, even if it causes a day's delay, to make sure that the particulars are accurate.

The estate agent's fee

Under the Estate Agents Act 1979, you must be told in advance in what circumstances an estate agent will charge you and what the fee will be (or at least how it will be worked out) and you must be told if the estate agent or any of his or her associates has a personal interest in the transaction.

Estate agents generally base their fees on the selling price of the house and according to the type of agency contract you have with them. For sole agency, you might pay 1.5 or 2 per cent of the final selling price; for multiple or joint-sole agency fees are negotiable between 2 and 3.5 per cent. Charges can vary markedly according to area. An agent may more rarely operate a sliding scale, charging, say, 2.5 per cent on the first £20,000 of the selling price, 1.5 per cent on the rest. An agent sometimes charges a flat fee, irrespective of the selling price. It is worth shopping around; it is possible to negotiate a fee.

In some parts of the country, fees are all-inclusive. Elsewhere, you may find that commissions are lower but that you have to pay certain expenses up-front. These may include advertising, printed particulars and occasionally even the cost of a sale board. You must be given an itemised bill for these extras.

Even where an estate agent has approached you direct asking if you are willing to sell because he or she has a client anxious to buy your house, you will be charged commission if you do so.

Sole agency

You may instruct more than one agent to sell your house, but an agent may reduce the fee if you grant sole agency – this means that you put your property exclusively into that agent's hands. It is quite common to give one agent a sole agency for a limited period of, say, six weeks. If, after the agreed time, no buyer has been found, you can appoint another agent instead of or in addition to the first. It is important to ensure that any sole agency period is quite short. Otherwise, the agent may neglect your sale in favour of properties where there is multiple agency, when he or she is competing against other agents for a higher fee. Start with, say, four weeks with an option to renew. In any period of sole agency, it is important not to instruct another agent, otherwise you may find yourself having to pay commission to both.

There should be clear agreement about the basis on which the agent will receive commission: namely, that the agent must have introduced the buyer who actually completes the purchase. Do not undertake to pay commission to an agent for introducing a buyer 'ready, able and willing to buy': this would mean that if anything went wrong and the sale did not go through, you might still have to pay the agent's fee. Nor should you agree to any agent having 'sole selling rights' – this would entitle him or her to a commission, even if the eventual buyer was not introduced by him or her. The Ombudsman for Estate Agents scheme requires the agent to explain these arrangements in clear language.

Unpleasant court cases have resulted where two agents have claimed commission for the same sale, or where an agent has tried to claim commission where no sale has happened. The wording of the agent's letter confirming instructions is very important. If you disagree with what is said, get the matter cleared up then. Do not simply hope for the best. In some circumstances, it may be sensible to ask your solicitor to advise you on the wording of the agent's terms.

Extras

VAT is payable on agents' fees and on any advertising costs. Ask the agent which services are included and what will be extra. If advertising costs are not included, do you have to pay all, or only those above a certain figure? Ask the agent whether advertising is in local or national papers or magazines – costs differ a lot.

If details of the advertising costs which will be incurred, either broken down to the column centimetre rate or per advertisement, are given to you at the outset, you can be aware of the precise charges for which you will be liable. You can set your maximum for extra publicity costs and instruct the agent accordingly.

Some estate agents make a charge for the 'For Sale' board. Do not automatically accept this, and certainly do not agree to pay for a 'Sold' sign. (Some agents will even pay the householder for the right to erect a 'Sold' board.) Whatever agreement you make with the agent, get it confirmed in writing. The agent may well ask you to confirm acceptance of the charges, in writing.

Showing the house

Estate agents usually leave the job of showing viewers round a house to the owner, saying that he or she is best fitted to do it. So, even when selling through an agent, you have to be prepared to give up time for this. You may be able to make appointments ahead, or you may find the agent sending round viewers from the office who want to be shown round immediately. If you are out at work all day, appointments will have to be made for evenings or weekends.

If you can never be at home at the time potential buyers might want to view, you may consider leaving a spare key with the estate agent. Always check on their key policy however (see below).

Keys for viewings

When trying to sell a house, many people opt to give their estate agent a set of keys. Working people who are out all day may find this unavoidable as the agent can best show potential buyers around during the day. However, too many agents are not sufficiently careful with their clients' keys, and instances of maladministration are regularly reported to the Ombudsman for Estate Agents. In the worst cases people have found items missing from their home after it was shown to buyers. In one extreme case a garage remote control was taken from a flat to which the agent had the keys and a valuable car was stolen – all without any signs of a break-in. Unfortunately, it is virtually impossible to prove burglary of this sort, so prevention is the only cure.

Maintain strict control of the house keys, ideally by *not* giving the agent a set at all. You are within your rights to insist on being in the home when people are being shown around, and if the agent will not accommodate your timetable find another one who will – or sell privately. If you must hand keys to an agent, ask for a written statement on the company's key-handling policy. If it does not have one, consider using another agent.

When the buyer's surveyor comes

Expect to have to put yourself to some trouble when the time comes for the valuer or surveyor to inspect. He or she is unlikely to come on a Saturday or Sunday, and will not come in the evening, because the inspection needs to take place in good daylight. A valuation for a lending institution may take only 15 minutes or so, but a full structural survey on a big house will take some hours. When the appointment is made, enquire how long the surveyor is likely to take, so that you can organise your day accordingly.

It will do no harm to prepare for the surveyor. Have steps or a ladder available if possible; make sure all doors and windows are unlocked, including the garage; check that the roof hatch can be moved; check that inspection covers can be opened; have the hot-water system running, and the central heating too, in the winter. Finally, get someone to take the dog for a walk and keep the children occupied, or *vice versa*.

Selling an empty house

A house which is furnished and, better still, occupied, is a more attractive proposition to viewers than an empty one. Even if the furniture and decorations are not to others' tastes, the house itself will make a better impression. But the situation can arise when you have to move, taking your furniture with you, before finding a buyer. All that will remain in the house you are selling will be the fixtures and fittings and any items which you are hoping to include in the sale.

When the house is empty, it would be advisable to appoint an estate agent to help with the sale. You should agree with the agent in writing:

- that all viewers be accompanied by the agent or a member of staff
- arrangements for the custody of the keys (squatters in the guise of potential purchasers have been known to have keys copied)
- a list of the items to be included in the sale, and the price of any others which are being offered separately.

Preparing an empty house

If a house is left vacant during the colder months of the year, consider leaving on some kind of heating to prevent the place getting too damp or pipes bursting (not to mention a cold reception for any viewers). A house which has been left empty and shut for any length of time tends to smell either fusty or damp, particularly at a time of year when it would normally be heated.

If a little ventilation can be arranged without making it easy for trespassers to enter, this is helpful. In winter, if heating is not possible, the water system must be drained. Remove the telephone or safeguard it against unauthorised use, so that you will not get a bill for calls made to Australia by some unidentified person. See that someone visits regularly to clear the stuff that comes through the letter box – having to push the door open against a mountain of circulars creates a bad impression.

Negotiating a house sale
Through an estate agent

There is no need to enter into negotiations about price with a buyer if you have appointed an estate agent – this is what you pay the agent for, to act as pig-in-the-middle, passing offer to seller and reconsidered price to buyer. If there are several interested buyers, the agent will try to encourage offers and counter-offers between them. It is in the agent's interest to get as high a price as possible because the commission is based on the selling price. But the agent may prefer to go for a quick sale at the expense of an extra £100 or so of commission.

Your estate agent may suggest that, as a token of intent, the buyer whose offer you have accepted should put down an initial deposit of perhaps £250. This is of no advantage to you (or your buyer), and it is not as common as it used to be. You (or the estate agent) must get the buyer's full name and address, and that of his or her solicitor/conveyancer, and give him or her yours.

Without an estate agent

If you are not selling through an estate agent, you yourself must act as negotiator. The chances are that the first offer will be less than your asking price. If it is so much less that you could not accept it under any circumstances, you will have no difficulty in rejecting it. Before you do, take stock. Is there a reasonable prospect that you will receive a better offer from this buyer or another? Are you sure you have not pitched your price too high? Could you proceed at that price if you had to (bearing in mind your other commitments and the price of any new property)?

It is sensible to consider all offers calmly. Do not rush to accept or reject any offer.

With or without an estate agent

The following are factors to consider.

Your mortgage and financial requirements

How much is owing on your present mortgage? How much can you afford to borrow on your next property? You should obtain a redemption figure on your existing mortgage and see your lender to obtain an indication of what will be available to you, having regard not only to your means but also the house you want to buy.

The house you want to buy

Have you found a house? If so, have you agreed terms to buy it and are you under pressure to proceed? If you have already agreed to buy another house, there could be more justification in accepting a lower offer for your own house.

What is the market doing?

If prices are rising, you are much more likely to achieve your asking price than if the market is static or falling. If house sales are sluggish, you could be waiting a long time for another offer.

Checking out your buyer

If you are using an agent, that will be part of his or her job, but you are still involved in the decision-making: it is your decision which buyer to go for.

Some buyers are a much better prospect than others. There are even people who obtain a sort of perverse pleasure in making offers for houses which they have no intention of buying. Others are so desperate that they will invent anything to secure the house. You have to assess whether your buyer will really buy your house, at the price agreed and within the timescale you have contemplated. You may not have a choice, in which case you have to do your best with any buyer who makes an offer for your house, but if there is more than one, you might rate them in order of preference as follows.

1 **The buyer who has actually sold his or her house, moved out and been paid for it.** Such people are quite rare, but would be top of the list for reliability, provided, of course, that he or she does not have difficulties with a mortgage. However, such buyers also know they are in a strong position, and can use it to drive a hard bargain.

2 **The first-time buyer.** First-time buyers are potentially reliable as they do not have the problem of selling their own property. But – a big 'but' – many houses are beyond the means of first-time buyers. You will need to know that these buyers really do have the wherewithal to go ahead. Ask for some assurance that they can borrow the necessary money – and can pay the balance that they do not borrow. Make sure that they can proceed without delay.

3 **The buyer who has sold his or her house 'subject to contract'**, i.e. has found a buyer, but nobody has yet committed themselves legally. Many will say at this point that they have actually sold their house. That is not correct, and you should discount such claims. Here you need to know, again, how he or she is going to finance the deal. Can he or she borrow the extra money to make up the price? You should also try to find out whether this buyer is selling to a first-time buyer, or to someone who also has a house to sell. In such circumstances, there is likely to be a chain and therefore problems.

4 **The buyer who has not sold his or her house.** By all means talk to people in that situation. After all, until you find a buyer, it is the same situation as your own. Nevertheless, you would be unwise to negotiate very seriously with someone in that position. It could be months before this individual can proceed. Do not take the house off the market until the situation becomes clearer.

Hard bargaining

Any act of bargaining requires similar skills, whether you are trying to conduct the next wage round with the management or asking the greengrocer to knock six pence off tomatoes. Bluff and counter-bluff often play a part. Both sides make strenuous efforts to show that they are only marginally interested in the transaction proceeding and that there are plenty more houses/buyers available.

The ability to bargain effectively is often the quality which makes the difference between a good and a mediocre estate agent. The chances are that the more you do it, the better you may become. If the buyer is genuinely keen and the price is within range of your expectations, most people can reach a compromise. If you do come to an agreement, be sure to cover the relevant points: the price, and what exactly it includes; extras, such as what they are and how much you will sell them for; and the expected completion date.

Agreeing terms

Try not to be drawn into some unsatisfactory formula, such as agreeing a right of first refusal to a buyer. That ties your hand without giving you any assurance that you will sell the house.

Until you have agreed terms, it is best to consider that the house remains firmly on the market.

When you do reach agreement on all the essential details you will need to move on to the legal procedures. You and your buyer might like to draw up a note of what you have agreed (see example, below).

It is best not to sign this memorandum, in case you exchange contracts by mistake! However, it records your intentions and you and the buyer should each keep a copy. If you are using an estate agent, he or she will produce a similar memorandum and send it out to all concerned. Remember that the transaction is still not legally binding.

Synchronising the transactions

If you yourself are in the process of buying a house, you will almost certainly wish to exchange contracts on your sale and purchase

---

It is agreed **subject to contract** as follows:

Property: Bide a Wee, The Street, Large Snoring, Norfolk (described in the attached sale particulars)

Price: £180,000 plus £1,000 for the carpets as fitted

Sellers: Albert Raven Sleepy and Denise Dozy Sleepy

Buyers: Larry Edward Snodgrass and Melanie Florence Snodgrass

Completion: Aim for 1 July

Buyer's mortgage: £100,000 to be applied for from the Large Snoring Providential Building Society

Buyer's solicitors: Messrs Snoozing, Dreaming and Nightcap, Bank Chambers, Large Snoring (for the attention of Miss Nightcap)

Seller's solicitors: Messrs Fleecem, Screwem and Cheatem.

---

simultaneously. It would, therefore, be unwise to wait until you are ready to exchange contracts on your purchase before accepting a 'subject to contract' offer on your sale: it will take your buyer several weeks to get to a situation where he or she can also exchange contracts.

To speed things up, you can ask your solicitor to send off the necessary forms to initiate the local authority search. When the replies come, they can be sent directly to the buyer's solicitor. Some local authorities take a long time to deal with these enquiries, so this procedure can save time.

Under the TransAction Protocol (see page 247), your solicitor will send off the search anyway.

Steps prior to exchange of contracts

If you are using a solicitor/conveyancer, your next step is to inform him or her that you have a buyer and to hand over the relevant details – the buyer's name and address, his or her solicitor's/conveyancer's name and the address of the firm, the conditions and price you have agreed, particularly the details of any items included in the sale or being sold additionally, so that these can be incorporated in the contract. The completion date will not be agreed until exchange of contracts but, if you have discussed possible dates with your buyer or if you or he (or she) has special requirements, it is always a good idea to let your solicitor know.

The estate agent does not withdraw the house from the market until contracts have been exchanged unless you, the seller, request this. It is your decision whether the property should be left on the market until contracts are exchanged. The estate agent will be in a position to advise you whether or not to leave it on the market in case the initial interested purchaser should drop out for any reason. If any further offer is received, that person must be advised that there is already an offer on the property, and the initial interested purchaser must be informed of a subsequent offer received.

Many sellers are concerned about choosing who will succeed them in the house, and, having found a buyer they like the look of, they do not want to be bothered with any other offers. The agent may not want to disturb your peace of mind, but he or she does have a clear duty to report all offers to a seller, whether or not the property has already been provisionally sold.

If you tell the agent to withdraw the house, he or she will announce that the property is 'under offer' – often adding this notice to the advertising board outside the house and the shop window if the house is displayed there. If you left keys with the estate agent, do not forget to get them back. If your house was on the books of more than one agent, inform them all when you no longer need them.

You can stipulate that the exchange of contracts be within a specified period – for example, one month from the date the draft contract is issued to the buyer is a reasonable time for a registered property. This may be worth doing when the market is good and there are several potential buyers around, but not in a poor market where buyers are few and far between.

Your solicitor/conveyancer prepares the contract in draft form to send to the one on the other side.

Contract races

Where several equally acceptable offers have been made, it is possible for a seller's solicitor to send out contracts to the solicitors of each of these potential buyers, with a note advising them that the first received back, signed, will get the house. This can be efficacious, but contract races can rebound on the seller: once the buyers know that they risk losing the property, they sometimes all pull out.

Breaking the chain

If you are selling through an agent who participates in a chain-linking scheme and there is a threatened break in a chain of buyer/seller/buyer because your potential buyer has dropped out, ask your agent whether the property is suitable for the chain plan. This means that the agent will arrange to buy your house at a discounted price based on a valuation arranged by the agent, so that the rest of the chain can continue. The house is later sold by the agent, who recoups his or her expenses from the proceeds of that sale. (With the *Chainmaker* service, if the house is eventually sold for more than the agreed valuation, the difference usually goes to the original seller.)

Paying off your mortgage

Your existing mortgage must be repaid when you sell your house. Usually your solicitor will deal with the work involved in redeeming (i.e. paying off) the existing mortgage on the house you are selling, and the fee for this work will generally be included in the fee for the sale. A few building societies or mortgage companies employ their own solicitors to deal with the redemption and you will have to pay the charge made by their solicitors. Some lenders charge a mortgage redemption fee (this may be as much as three months' interest) if the mortgage is paid off within the first years. Most lenders will waive this charge if a new mortgage is being taken out on the next property with them.

The mortgage deed stipulates the length of notice you need to give (or what interest you will have to pay in lieu of notice) when you want to pay off what you still owe. If your completion date is sooner, you may have to pay the stipulated interest but lenders do not always enforce this.

Insurance

You must continue with the insurance of the house until exchange of contracts, when the responsibility passes to the buyer, but it would be wise to keep your own buildings insurance policy going until completion day. If the place burns down between exchange of contracts and completion, and the buyer has not insured, a lot of litigation might be needed to get your money.

Under the terms of the TransAction Protocol (see page 247) it remains your responsibility until completion. Keep the contents insurance policy going up to completion day. If you are not going to continue with the same contents policy in your new house, do not cancel it until after the move.

Letting the buyer into the house

After contracts have been exchanged, the buyer may want to borrow the keys to get into the house (for measuring up, for instance). If you are still living in the property, you can arrange for the buyer to visit while you are at home. If the house is empty and the estate agent contacts you about this, tell him or her to ask the buyer to sign that the keys are issued 'for viewing purposes only: I/we will not take possession'. This is some safeguard against the possibility of an unscrupulous buyer moving in and then causing trouble over completing his or her payment, possibly even claiming protection as a tenant. As a general rule, however, it is unwise for keys to be released to a purchaser after exchange of contracts without a written undertaking prepared by the seller's solicitors and signed by the prospective purchaser. A better alternative may be to ask the estate agent or a member of staff to accompany the buyer.

Chapter 8

Countdown to the move

Once you have agreed to buy a new house and to sell your own (if applicable) the procedures for moving house get under way.

Before exchange of contracts

Chapter 7 gives a detailed description of the run-up to exchange of contracts.

In practice, as exchange of contracts approaches, you should:

- be in contact with your solicitor to go through the paperwork and sign the contract
- check that your finances are in order – everything budgeted for and your loan offer received
- make sure that your solicitor knows of everything you want included in the contract. If, as part of the deal, the seller has agreed to carry out work or include extra items in the sale do not rely on a gentleman's agreement. Get it written into the contract before exchange
- pay the deposit to your solicitor (if you are a first-time buyer or the deposit on your sale cannot be used or you are topping it up)
- discuss with your seller and buyer possible completion dates
- if you have not already done so, check possible completion dates and make provisional arrangements with a removal firm, but do not confirm these until contracts have actually been exchanged.

The date for completion must be agreed at the time contracts are exchanged and is specified in the contract. You may well be involved in two completions – one when your new house becomes yours and, if you are selling as well, when your old one ceases to belong to you.

Before fixing the date for completion, both buyer and seller should be certain that they have somewhere to move to on the day.

Ideally, everyone would have two or three days to move from one home to another, but the complex financial arrangements involved in house transfer do not permit this. Unless you are prepared to go to the expense of a bridging loan, you will be stuck with everything happening on the same day. Do not agree to a completion date unless you are sure you can meet it.

If anything should go wrong for the seller's move into his or her new home, he or she cannot expect to remain in the old one: on the date of completion, the seller has to give you vacant possession, and to move out on or before that day with all furniture and belongings (except any that are being sold with the house).

Before completion

The period between exchange of contracts and completion gives you an opportunity to make all your preparations for the move. The moving date is fixed (except, possibly, when you are buying a new home and the contract might specify that the builder will give notification of when the house is ready to move in) and you can confirm the tentative arrangements which you may have made since you first agreed terms for the house.

The legal side of things will be taken care of by your solicitor, but make sure that you stay in contact. There will be plenty of activity on that front.

Practical matters before completion

While the legal matters are being taken care of between exchange of contracts and completion day, there are practical things you can get on with and administrative matters you must not overlook.

Bridging loan

In the rare case where you have to complete your purchase before your sale, your bank or mortgage lender might let you have a bridging loan, provided you have exchanged contracts on the sale of your own property and have a firm offer of a mortgage in respect of the purchase.

But beware of bridging finance – unless you are not having to bear the cost (for instance, because your employer is footing the bill). It is expensive. Most banks charge a setting-up fee of 1 per cent (or a flat fee of £100+) of the loan just for agreeing to lend you the money. On top of that, you will be paying a higher rate of interest.

If you have exchanged contracts on your sale, you will at least know that the end is in sight and you can calculate accordingly. But if contracts have not been exchanged, you will need an 'open' bridging loan, because you have no guarantee that the house will sell quickly (some houses take many months to sell). People who take on open-ended bridging loans can pay out hundreds, even thousands, of pounds in interest. When the market is poor, many banks refuse to give open bridging loans except in very exceptional circumstances. In any event, it is almost never sensible to take on an open-ended bridging loan.

Insurance on the house

With leasehold properties, the landlord sometimes carries the insurance. Make sure that there is no doubling-up of your insurance arrangements.

As soon as contracts are exchanged, ask your solicitor to ensure that insurance cover is in force. However, if the TransAction Protocol (see page 247) is being used, the property may remain at the seller's risk for insurance purposes. This is also usual where you are buying a new house from a developer. There is no point in having two insurance policies on the same property – and it can sometimes lead to difficulty in making a claim.

You have to tell your insurers if you are not moving into the new home straight away. The cover on a home which is not lived in is generally less extensive.

If you are selling your house, you should keep the insurance cover in force until completion has actually taken place. After that, remember to cancel it, and claim a refund of the unused premium.

Check whether the **sum insured** is adequate. The sum for which you insure should not be the market value (the amount you are about to pay for the house or its council tax valuation) but the cost of rebuilding it if it should be destroyed, including the cost of clearing away débris and rubble, the architect's and surveyor's fees. This is what is meant by the **reinstatement cost**. Also, there should be an allowance for permanent fittings such as central heating and double glazing. Your mortgage valuation should say how much the property should be insured for.

The Association of British Insurers (ABI)★ issues a free leaflet, *Buildings Insurance for Home Owners*, available from the ABI and at some building societies, insurers and Citizens Advice Bureaux. This explains how to calculate the amount to insure for on specific sizes and types of houses in various regions of the country, based on rebuilding costs. The figures given in the leaflet are, of necessity, averages. Your house may be more, or less, expensive, than the examples shown. If in doubt, ask a surveyor for an 'estimate of the reinstatement costs': the charge should be reasonable if you request it when arranging the survey.

Bear in mind that in the case of an older house in a terrace, or in a street of houses of similar types, if yours is destroyed by fire, the planning authority will almost certainly insist that the replacement, or

---

Buildings insurance when you move

It becomes your responsibility to insure your new house or flat the day that you exchange contracts to buy the property. However, you should keep your buildings insurance cover on your existing home until completion, in case the buyer defaults. Let your insurer know in writing, beforehand, that you want an overlap. The cost of insurance varies depending on where you live so you may be charged a higher or lower premium. Unusual and listed buildings are more expensive to insure. The move might provide a good opportunity to change insurer, in which case you should cancel your old policy if you pay monthly or, if you paid a year's worth of premiums, you should ask for a refund for the unexpired portion of your existing policy.

Mortgage lender's chosen insurance policy

If you are getting a mortgage, your lender will make it a condition that the property is insured and will probably be keen to arrange cover: lenders get commission for doing so. But you *do not have to stick with the mortgage lender's chosen insurance policy*. Most lenders will allow you to arrange your own insurance, although they will want proof that the policy provides adequate cover for their security, and may charge a fee for checking this. If you have a special mortgage deal which commits you to buying your lender's insurance, you have no choice in the matter, although you may be free to switch insurers after a few years.

---

at least its façade, should be as much like the original as possible. Hence, even a small Victorian terrace house, with a stone bow window, could be very expensive to replace.

Nowadays, nearly all insurers issue index-linked policies, with the sum insured linked to the house-rebuilding costs index and changing automatically as the average cost of rebuilding changes, although the premium you pay does not change until renewal.

You should hold on to the buildings policy for the house you are leaving because you remain liable under the Defective Premises Act: most policies will cover this liability for seven years after the sale.

The cost of convenience
If you are given the option of paying for your buildings insurance by adding the premium to the amount you owe on your mortgage, do not take it. It may sound convenient but not only will you pay interest on the insurance premium, possibly for the full life of the mortgage (usually 25 years), you will also have an extra loan (made up of the insurance premiums) to repay when you pay off the mortgage.

Contents insurance

Notify the insurers of your present home that the cover for 'contents' should be transferred to the new address from the day you move in. If you are moving in over several days, get the insurers to hold the contents covered for both addresses.

If your home is broken into and your television is stolen, you claim on your buildings insurance for the damage to your house but on your contents insurance for the theft of your television. Some insurers will offer you a discount if you take out both buildings and contents insurance with them. This may simplify things when you come to claim, but you will not necessarily be getting the best deal either financially or in terms of getting the cover you require. To find out whether any combined policy deal is worthwhile, you need to get quotes and details of cover for separate policies.

The sum for which you insure the contents may have to be adjusted if you are buying a lot of new things for the new house or are selling a lot on moving out of the old one. The premium you have to pay may also be different because of the different area and type of house to which you are moving.

Motor insurance

Your motor insurers will have to be informed of the new address and whether or not the car will be garaged, which may affect the premium.

Council tax

Council tax on a property in England or Wales depends on the tax band in which the house has been put and the tax charged per band. Information is available from the local authority for the area where the house is situated.

Water

Water charges are levied by the relevant water authority, not by the local authority in England and Wales (in Scotland, water rates are paid along with ordinary rates). For domestic consumers, the charges are generally based, at present, on a percentage of the property's rateable value; if metered, they are based on exact consumption plus a standing charge.

A move to a new house may be the moment to change to metered water consumption if you think this could save you money. The water company for your new area will be able to give you information about its charges.

Even if your water consumption is metered, you have to pay a charge for sewerage and environmental services, at present based on the rateable value of the property. A sewerage charge is not payable if there is no connection to the public sewer.

Apportionment

The seller is responsible for council tax and water charges for the part of the rating year before the completion date, and the buyer for the part after the completion date. For example, if completion takes place on 1 July, the seller must bear the liability for the 92 days which make up the months of April, May and June, while the buyer must accept liability for the remaining 273 days of the rating year.

It used to be a convention for rates and water charges to be apportioned on a day-to-day basis, not weekly or monthly. Nowadays, the local authority or water company prefers to make the necessary adjustments, as this helps it to keep its records up to date.

Accounts

Your bank account or accounts may need to be transferred to a branch in your new area. If you have not already noted the address of the one nearest to your new home, your present branch will be able to find out for you. Your bank manager may require a formal letter asking for the transfer to be made on a certain date. You can arrange this by visiting the branch you wish your account to be transferred to. You will be given a standard 'transfer' letter to sign. Ask for the new branch's bank-code number and your new account number(s) so that you can notify anybody who pays directly into your account or debits it directly. You can go on using your existing cheque book and card until you get the new ones.

With a bank deposit account, it is important to maintain continuity so that no interest is lost. Check in due course that the closing date at your old branch and the opening date at the new one are the same.

Even if you do not need to move your account, you will have to notify the bank of your new address. This applies generally to all savings accounts – such as building society or National Savings.

Charge accounts

If you have accounts which are paid weekly or monthly by post or personally with retailers in the area, write or telephone a request for these to be closed and any outstanding accounts to be sent to you, at either your old or your new address.

If you intend to continue to use a monthly or budget account at a large retail store, you will have to notify it of your new address, so that the accounts will be sent to you at that address. An inadvertent lapse on paying an outstanding bill (sent to the wrong address) may get you on to a computer record as a bad risk without your realising that this has happened. You should also notify any credit card company of your change of address.

Hire of TV

If you hire your television set and/or video recorder, check with the rental firm whether you can take it with you to your new home: if necessary, have your account transferred to another branch. This would be worth doing if you have been paying a reduced rent for an older set. Otherwise, turn in the set and take out a new contract locally for another one.

It is more usual to include a roof TV aerial in the sale of a house – also more sensible. But if you have decided to take it with you, you will have to arrange to have the aerial taken down off the roof (the removal men will not do this) and then to have it put up on your new roof – and will have to pay someone to do this.

Forwarding mail

Redirection forms are available from your local post office. You need to send or take a completed form with the appropriate fee to your local sorting office. You can also do this via the website *www.royalmail.com*.

- letters – for an initial charge (£6.45) for a period of up to one month; for further details see page 25
- parcels – a charge equal to the original postage is generally payable on each parcel on delivery to the new address (only inland parcels will be redirected).

Allow some time before the date you want the redirection to start. The request form must be signed by all those in the household who want their mail redirected, and a separate fee is payable per surname if there is more than one. (As an added precaution, make sure that the new owners know your new address, and ask them to redirect any mail that comes for you.)

The same form contains a section for you to complete for notifying TV Licensing, Bristol BS98 1TL of your change of address.

Change-of-address notification

It is advisable to include both your new and old addresses in messages because if you are notifying organisations which keep geographical lists they will need to trace you by your old address.

To help you estimate how many change-of-address cards you will need, make a check list of organisations you may need to advise. Tick off each one as you send the notification. After your move, you can then check against your list any incoming mail which has had to be redirected by the post office and, if necessary, notify any sender you may have forgotten or ask others to update their records.

You may want to wait to send out messages until you have your new telephone number. Do not tell people your new address until contracts have been exchanged.

The following is a basic checklist for change-of-address notification.

Finance

- bank: if moving to another area, authorise the transfer of accounts to a new branch, cancel any standing orders no longer needed
- current accounts, credit cards, loans, investments, savings: update addresses by phone, post or online
- pension/benefit book: notify your local social security office; nominate a new post office or give the new number of an account for paying in; if your pension is sent quarterly, tell The Pension Service★
- National Insurance: notify your social security office or the Department for Work and Pensions (DWP)★ of the old and new address, giving your National Insurance number (as on your pay slip). If employed, your employer will do this for you
- Inland Revenue: tell your inspector of taxes
- Premium Bonds: complete the notification card attached to your holder's card and send to National Savings and Investments Premium Bonds, Blackpool FY3 9YP
- National Savings Certificates and Save-As-You-Earn: send old and new addresses and holder's number to Savings Certificate and SAYE Office, Durham DH99 1NS
- stocks and shares: write to the registrar (details on share certificate and dividend vouchers); give new bank details if dividend paid directly. Also, inform your stockbroker
- credit card companies, hire purchase company, local authority (council tax), water company.

Insurance

- broker/agent
- life insurance company
- house insurance – contents and buildings
- any other insurers.

Car

- vehicle registration: complete the section on your vehicle registration document and send it to the address on the document
- driving licence: if you have a paper licence, complete form D1 (from most post offices and the DVLA) and send it with identity documents and a passport-sized photograph to DVLA, Swansea SA99 1BY. To apply for a photocard licence; if you have a photocard

licence, complete the section on the paper counterpart and send with your photocard to DVLA, Swansea SA99 1BY.
- car insurer (premium may change)
- AA, RAC or other motoring organisation.

Health
- NHS or private doctor/dentist, private health insurers
- National Blood Transfusion Service: if you are not moving out of the area, notify your present centre
- optician
- hospital, clinic or day centre.

Work and leisure
- current employer
- firm's (and previous firms') pension provider
- trade union, professional association
- TV Licensing: telephone (0870) 241 6468 or visit your post office
- VAT office (if you pay VAT).

Others
- children's school(s)
- clubs, societies or any organisation you belong to, magazine or book club, football-pools company
- charities to which you regularly donate money
- public library (and return all borrowed books)
- mail order firm(s)
- theatre, concert or other mailing lists
- *Which?* (PO Box 44, Hertford X, SG14 1SH) and other subscription publications.

Don't forget to let friends and relatives know your new address, along with any other companies you normally deal with, as well as institutions that may need to know the details.

You could also leave your new address for the incoming occupant with a request to forward mail and redirect telephone calls.

Arrangements for new schools
If you are moving into a new area and want to find a new school for your child, send the details to the local education authority of the area

you are moving to and ask for help in finding a place. The authority should send a list of all available schools in the area, and may send prospectuses of individual schools. You can write direct to the schools for information and to arrange a visit; do not commit your children to a school until you have visited it.

The *Education Authorities Directory* published by the School Government Publishing Company★, gives information about post-primary state schools. The Advisory Centre for Education (ACE Ltd)★ also produces useful publications.

If you want information about private schools, contact the Independent Schools Council Information Service (ISCis)★ or the Scottish Council of Independent Schools (SCIS)★. ISCis has published *the ISC Guide to Accredited Independent Schools 2004* and also offers a magazine and fact pack.

A number of education yearbooks and guides give information about independent schools (for example, *The Independent Schools Yearbook* published by A & C Black; *Which School?* published by John Catt Educational); both should be available in public reference libraries.

Information about approved pre-school playgroups and private nursery schools is obtainable from the local authority's social services department, and information about maintained nursery schools and nursery classes at primary schools from the local education authority. Information about nursery, primary and secondary schools in Scotland is available from education departments at regional council offices.

The Pre-school Learning Alliance (PLA)★ represents and supports 16,000 community pre-schools in England and can tell you about local playgroups.

Telephone

It is worth liaising with your seller (and a kindness to do so with your buyer) to save unnecessary disconnection and reconnection charges or having to be without a telephone for any length of time.

Giving up your existing telephone

Notify your telephone company at least seven working days in advance that you will be moving out. Give the date when you want to stop your telephone service and give the address to which you are moving. At the same time, say whether the buyer of your present house or flat wishes to take over the telephone line from you. He or she will have to apply to take it over. The rental charge will be apportioned between you on your next telephone accounts.

Getting a telephone at your new address

Contact the telephone company as soon as possible, by telephone. Explain what you want: either to have a line installed at the new address or to take over the existing line there.

If your new home does not have the modern plug-in sockets, they will have to be installed. Both British Telecom (BT)★ and the cable companies can install these sockets, so it is worth shopping around for the best deal.

When you are taking over an existing line and it remains unbroken, there is no takeover charge, but if the line is unconnected, even for just a day, there will be a charge.

If you are moving within the same telephone exchange area to a new address, it is usually possible to take your existing number with you if you want to, but you will be charged for doing so. BT also offers a messaging service that informs callers to your old number of your new number.

If you are to have a new telephone line, shop around for the best deal from BT and the cable company operating in your area. A cable company may be much cheaper than BT for a brand-new connection.

Gas and electricity

In a newly built house, the builder is almost always responsible for paying to have mains supplies laid on, but you must still make an application direct to the relevant authority for the supply (gas/electricity/telephone) to be connected and for you to become responsible for payment.

You cannot make definite arrangements until contracts have been exchanged and a date fixed for completion, but, subject to this, contact the suppliers of household services well in advance of your moving out and moving in date so that you can give sufficient notice to book the work to be done on the day and at the time you want. Meters can be read at fairly short notice, but if you want a fitter to connect or disconnect appliances or turn supplies on or off at an appointed time, give at least a week's notice, preferably more. And confirm the day before that someone is coming at the right time.

If the house you are going to has been previously occupied, the owners should, on their part, tell the local gas and electricity companies that they are going and that you are moving in. But some people leave without informing the gas or electricity company and arranging for the meter to be read, so it would be best to have them read on your arrival, too.

Gas

If you are going to the area of a different gas company, ask your present supplier for the address and telephone number of your new one. Then get in touch, either personally or in writing, well in advance, so that you can sign an application form for taking over the supply, make arrangements for the meter to be read and, if necessary, have the supply turned on, on the day you move in. At the same time, you can arrange for a service engineer to call to connect any appliance and to alter the gas supply pipe to fit the incoming appliance, if necessary. The charge for connection is normally a little more than the disconnection charge.

Gas cookers can be fitted with a plug-in flexible hose instead of rigidly, so that the cooker can be easily moved for cleaning. You may want to have this fitted to your cooker when you take it to a new house.

A deposit is not usually asked for when taking over a gas supply unless a customer is known to have been a bad payer or has previously not had a gas account and cannot give an acceptable credit reference or guarantor.

Electricity

To arrange for your meter to be read on leaving, you should notify the local electricity company, giving as much notice as you can. You may be asked to fill in a form of notification of removal, giving your old and new address and details of your date of departure, and the name and address of the incoming consumer (if you know it at this stage).

Ask for a meter reader to come on the day of your move before you leave. (There is no charge for this.) Telephone the day before to confirm the time of the appointment.

You have to make formal application to the new electricity company for a supply to be made available. Write or telephone to ask for the form to be sent to you beforehand, together with details of tariffs.

The application form usually asks for the approximate total wattage you expect to use, so that the electricity company can check that the installation will be large enough to cope with your maximum demand. Ask the company for advice or put down on the form the total number of watts your appliances would use if they were all switched on full. (The wattage is usually marked on a plate somewhere on each appliance.)

The form also asks which sort of tariff you want to be on. If you are going to install storage heaters and off-peak water heating, or if you run a washing machine, tumble dryer and dishwasher in the night, you will want the Economy 7 tariff instead of the standard tariff.

You could be asked for evidence of your past record of paying, or asked for a deposit. If you have to pay a deposit, this earns interest, credited to you once a year, and will normally be refunded when you leave the company's area or have established credit-worthiness by paying bills promptly. You will not be asked for a deposit if you agree to pay a regular amount each week or month, have a slot meter put in, or give an acceptable credit reference or guarantor.

If the house is to be empty for a period, the company may ask you if the supply is to be left connected or not (there is no charge for disconnection and reconnection in these circumstances). This may depend on whether you are having any work done before you move in, when the workmen would need an electricity supply for lights, heating, electric drills or other tools. Also, if during the winter you want to keep the central heating on low, it needs electricity to run it, even if it is gas or oil-fired heating.

Lighting and sockets

Ask the present owners to show you where the electricity main switch and the consumer unit and fuses are.

You may need additional or replacement light fittings if the sellers are removing any to which they are entitled (they must not remove lamp holders or sockets or leave bare wires). There is no basis for the belief that one electric bulb must be left for the incoming owner: you should be prepared to find none and should be armed with a supply.

Compare the number of socket outlets in the house with the number of appliances you have. If you have many more appliances than there are sockets, you will need adapters to begin with but must be careful not to overload the electrical circuits and should consider installing more socket outlets. Where sockets are in places that would make it difficult to use your appliances, you may have to fit longer flexes on yours or buy an extension lead.

The heating system

Find out from the present owners as much as you can about the operation and maintenance of any central heating system and water heating, and ask them to leave you any instruction booklets.

If the system uses oil or solid fuel, check how much fuel is being left and confirm how much you will have to pay for it (if anything), and what the arrangements have been for delivery.

Ask for the name of a local plumber and electrical contractor and get details of any maintenance contract there has been, and when a service was last done. Discuss the possibility of taking over the contract.

Measuring for curtains and flooring

Check what kind of curtain rails there are (if they are being left) in case you need to change the hooks and attachments on your curtains. Have curtains cleaned before rehanging them.

When you measure for new fitted carpets so that you can give the carpet shop approximate sizes, take the measurements from skirting board to skirting board and explain to the retailer when ordering the carpet that you have not allowed for the turnings required for the edging strips now normally used for fixing fitted carpets. Do not assume that opposite walls in a room are parallel: not all corners are an accurate 90 degrees, nor is every chimney breast of the same thickness. The carpet supplier will be responsible for accurate measuring and fitting.

The kitchen, too, needs careful measuring if you intend to put down new tiles or other floor coverings. An accurate floor plan will also help you to work out where your present equipment will fit in and, if you are getting a new cooker, fridge or washing machine, what size and shape to order.

When you have measured, chosen and ordered any new curtains, carpeting, floor covering, bathroom or kitchen fitments, get them delivered, where appropriate, to the new address, on or after completion day.

Completion day

On completion day, all the weeks and months of worry and preparation will reach their climax.

The money

On the day of completion, the buyer must be able to pay the remainder of the purchase price. The money for this may come from various sources:

- anything left over after discharging your own mortgage from what your buyer (or the buyer's building society) pays for the house you are selling
- your new mortgage loan (the building society or other lender's percentage of the purchase price of the house you are buying)
- any top-up loan
- a bridging loan if you have not completed your sale or there is a temporary shortfall
- your own cash from savings.

From the total mortgage loan, the lender may deduct:

- the amount of the first premium for the buildings insurance policy
- the premium for a mortgage indemnity policy if you had to take one out
- the lender's solicitor's charges (if the same solicitor is not acting for you and the lender).

If the same solicitor is acting for you and the lender he or she may deduct from the amount of the advance his or her own fee and any disbursements – the charges paid on your behalf, such as stamp duty land tax and Land Registry fees – where applicable.

It is normally a condition of the mortgage that the solicitor should have received on completion sufficient money to pay the stamp duty land tax and Land Registry fees.

In case the remaining amount will be less than is needed to complete the purchase, ask the solicitor or conveyancer in good time what the deductions and final amount will come to, so that you can make arrangements to finance the shortfall.

You may be charged interest from the date on which the loan leaves the lender (or, with some, the following day), even if it is not used for a few days. With other lenders, interest is charged from the date of completion, which your solicitor specifies in the request for the money. Whichever procedure the lender follows, your solicitor should not get the loan money too early.

If you are getting an endowment mortgage, you may have to pay the first premium on the endowment policy. Make sure that the policy is put on risk at the right time.

If any part of the money is not coming from a mortgage, your solicitor or conveyancer will ask you either for a cheque in sufficient time to have it cleared so that he or she can draw a cheque on the firm's account for the money, or for a banker's draft. A banker's draft is a cheque signed by a bank manager, or member of the bank's staff, on behalf of the bank instead of the customer; it cannot be stopped as a cheque can be and so is treated in practice as being equivalent to cash.

Usually, on completion, your solicitor will make the final payment to the seller's solicitor by sending the money by telegraphic transfer from one bank to another. The fee for this is around £20 + VAT.

When the final payments are made, the title deeds will be handed over, including the conveyance or transfer to the buyer. You do not, however, get the title deeds of the property if you have a mortgage: the relevant documents are traditionally kept by the building society, or other lender, as security for the money being lent. If you have bought unregistered land, you will be required to register it (first registration) at the Land Registry within two months. This is compulsory. The purchaser of registered land no longer receives a land certificate. Similarly, a mortgage lender will no longer take custody of the charge certificate.

It is not usual for either the seller or the buyer to attend personally at the completion (unless they are doing their own conveyancing without a solicitor or conveyancer).

In the days leading up to completion, stay in touch with your solicitor or conveyancer, but get on with the move and let him or her take care of the rest.

Timetable and checklist for moving
(tick when done)

About four weeks to a week before

☐ Get 3 removal firms' estimates and/or quotes for d-i-y van hire charges (the earlier the better for this)

☐ Choose firm; confirm arrangements

☐ D-i-y: alert friends/family for help on the day (packing, driving, providing meals, cleaning up, being available)

Old address

- ☐ Arrange for meters to be read
- ☐ Arrange for disconnection of cooker, washing machine, dishwasher
- ☐ Arrange for carpets to be cleaned if required

New address

- ☐ Arrange for taking over gas, electricity
- ☐ Arrange for reconnection of cooker, washing machine, dishwasher
- ☐ Arrange for carpets to be laid

In general

- ☐ Notify telephone sales office of date account to be closed
- ☐ Apply to take over telephone or request new telephone to be installed at new address and extra sockets if required
- ☐ Change-of-address cards – buy, or order printing (after new telephone number known)
- ☐ Post office – apply for redirection of mail (minimum notice of 5 working days required)
- ☐ Arrange insurance of contents at new house from date of moving and during removal
- ☐ Start sorting possessions and getting rid of surplus items
- ☐ Arrange extra rubbish disposal
- ☐ Get boxes, packing material, strong string
- ☐ Buy stick-on labels
- ☐ Arrange hotel booking, if needed
- ☐ Think about what plants, shrubs, etc. you may wish to take from your garden
- ☐ Children – arrange to leave with relatives/friends
- ☐ Pets – book kennels/make other arrangements

One week before

- ☐ Prepare diagram of new house with location of furniture
- ☐ Send off change-of-address cards
- ☐ Bank etc. – arrange for transfer of account

Old address

Arrange cancellation of deliveries and settlement of accounts:

- ☐ milk
- ☐ newspapers
- ☐ laundry

New address

- ☐ Arrange deliveries, e.g. milk

In general

- ☐ Put valuables and documents in bank/safe place
- ☐ Tell police of imminent move
- ☐ Check arrangements for hiring van/borrowing car
- ☐ Get own car serviced

Confirm arrangements and timings for meter readings and disconnection/connection at old/new address:

- ☐ electricity
- ☐ gas

Arrange with seller and buyer about leaving off/on:

- ☐ electricity
- ☐ water
- ☐ heating
- ☐ Arrange to leave keys at old address
- ☐ Check arrangements for collecting keys at new address
- ☐ Finish packing and labelling
- ☐ Prepare survival kit (see page 222)

Day before

- ☐ Pack personal overnight case(s)
- ☐ Organise meals/drinks for moving day
- ☐ Switch freezer to maximum (if moving it with contents inside)
- ☐ Take children to relatives or friends to stay
- ☐ Deliver pets to kennels or elsewhere
- ☐ Get supply of cash (e.g. for tips, meals, petrol, coins for emergency telephone calls)
- ☐ Defrost refrigerator
- ☐ Go to bed early.

Chapter 9

Moving house

It is important to realise that once contracts are exchanged and you have agreed on a date for completion, you must move (or at least pay for your new house if you are not selling one) on that day, otherwise you risk having to face large claims for compensation and court proceedings.

Fixing the date of your move

Most people try to arrange for the completion of their sale and purchase to take place on the same day. This means that your old home must be vacated on the day your buyer hands over the purchase money to you, and you must be prepared to move out on that day.

When settling on a date, check the day of the week. Completions are often on Fridays at the end of the month. But Friday is not necessarily the ideal day on which to move. Even though this would give you a weekend to settle in, if you arrange delivery of goods or the connections of services – gas, electricity, for example – for Friday afternoon, if anything should go wrong with any appointments, you could find yourself without a cooker or power for three days. Similarly, if you need professional help in an emergency – a plumber, say – it is going to be more difficult (and probably more expensive) if it is a weekend. For the same reason, you should avoid bank holiday periods. (Scottish holidays do not necessarily coincide with bank holidays in England and Wales.)

If you are moving some distance away, allow for the fact that the move will have to be spread over two days, with an overnight stop somewhere. Also, if a long-distance removal is involved – say, from the south of England to Scotland – you would have to pay overtime for the remover's staff to travel back on a Saturday. Moreover, there are tight restrictions on the hours a driver of a heavy goods vehicle may legally drive in the course of a day or week, so you may have to pay for weekend accommodation.

Removal firms tend to be heavily booked at the beginning and end of the month, so you may stand a better chance of getting the firm you want on the day you want if you pick a day in the middle of the month. And if you are able to move during a period outside the peak moving periods (school holidays, especially the summer), the cost may be less.

It is not possible to predict whether the previous owners are the kind of people who will leave their home spotlessly clean on vacating it – or at least clear of unwanted rubbish. As well as allowing yourself sufficient time for clearing up your house on leaving it, you should be prepared for the probability that you will have to clean your new one before putting your possessions into it. If you move on the day of completion of your purchase, you will have no opportunity for preliminary cleaning. You could find the floors need cleaning before any carpets you have brought with you can be laid.

If you want a little time to clean up, lay the carpets, prepare the house and generally relieve the pressure, you should assess whether it would be worth completing your purchase a few days before the day of completing your sale – with a bridging loan to tide you over.

If it was your buyer who chose the date because it suited him or her to move in then and you accepted this, you may not have a new home, or at least not be able to move into it, on the day you have to vacate your old one.

Particularly where a newly built house is concerned, there is a serious risk that it will not be completed by the promised date(s) due to over-optimistic calculations by the builder.

If you cannot move straight out of the old home into the new one, it may be necessary to put your belongings into store and to find a temporary home, perhaps in rented accommodation, a hotel, or with relatives or friends. These extra expenses can add considerably to the cost of your move.

Putting furniture into store

The expense of putting furniture into store is based on:

- the cost of getting it packed up and taken to the depository
- the charge per cubic foot for the time it has to be in store

- the insurance
- the cost of getting the furniture out of storage
- the cost of delivering it to the new house.

Removal firms with storage facilities can be found in the *Yellow Pages* or similar local directory.

Storage firms accept the whole contents of a house with the exception of perishable goods such as food and plants, and of flammable goods such as matches, fuel or paint. They recommend that carpets and rugs be cleaned first and some will arrange this for you. Clothes and blankets should be treated with a moth deterrent – storage firms do not accept responsibility for moth damage.

Generally, goods are stored loose, covered but not encased, in a space allocated to you in the depository. You can inspect your goods in the warehouse (sometimes for a small charge), unless they are housed in containers.

Containerisation is now becoming the accepted method of storage: goods are packed into sealed containers at your home and these are stored untouched in a warehouse until required. The advantage is that the risk of damage by movement or careless handling during transit and warehousing is greatly reduced; also, there is much greater protection from dust and dirt and a lower possibility of loss.

You should have an inventory (and, if your goods are in containers, a note of what has been put into each one). Note the value of all items. Insurance premiums are often based on the total declared value; storage charges are more likely to be based on the space required.

Storage insurance

Insurance cover can be arranged through the storage firm, or your household insurers may give you special cover for these circumstances. Make sure it is for a sufficient sum and for 'all risks', including fire, flooding and any other loss or damage. Insurers usually charge an all-in premium covering transit from your house to the warehouse, storage for a given length of time, and transit from the warehouse to your new home. (If you later find that you need a longer period of storage, the cover can be extended by paying an additional premium.)

There may be an individual limit on specific items (of crockery, for instance), but if one item gets broken and that style is no longer made, you would have to replace the set; make sure that the insurance cover is sufficient for such a situation (the premium may be high). Check any policy carefully for exclusions and excess clauses (an excess is the amount of any claim you have to pay yourself).

Getting goods out of storage

If you think you will want to take some items away earlier than others – for example, carpets or cooker – you should advise the storage firm at the start so that these can be labelled and stored as 'keep forward' items, accessible for collection when required. If the storage firm delivers these, there will be a charge per delivery. Written authorisation is usually required if you want someone else to collect any of your goods for you.

Find out how much notice is required for getting your goods out of store when you eventually need them. If the delivery is not done by the storage firm, you may have to pay a handing-out charge.

When all your goods are delivered to you, check the inventory as soon as they arrive. Without any attempt to steal or defraud, one packing case might be left behind at the warehouse; it is easier to trace if this is notified at once, rather than some weeks later when the warehouse space may have been filled and the premises rearranged. Your insurance may stipulate that any claim must be made within a set period.

Renting storage space

In some places, there are 'self-access' facilities for storage of possessions in specially constructed steel-walled compartments or units, in a secured building or a 'mini-warehouse'. You are the only person who has a key to the compartment you rent or who is told the control code to gain entry, and you are free to go at any time within working hours to get your possessions. There is an initial refundable deposit, and you then pay monthly, according to the space taken and the period booked. You have to arrange your own insurance cover.

Arranging the move

Using a removal firm is a more expensive way of moving than borrowing or hiring a van and doing your own removal with the help of friends or relatives.

A lot will depend on how much stuff you have to move. If you have a considerable quantity of furniture or belongings, or a number which are large, heavy or awkward to move, or if there are any difficulties of access (flights of stairs or long distances to carry furniture out or in), do not do it yourself unless you are very strong and prepared for really hard work.

The preparatory work of clearing up before leaving a home, plus organising and preparing the new one, can be extremely tiring. If this is then to be followed by one or two days of hard physical work, lifting and carrying for hours on end, the effect can be cumulatively one of total exhaustion.

If you are working full-time, or if you are elderly or unfit, pregnant or have small children, you may think it worth the cost of paying for all the packing and moving to be done by experts, so that all you have to do is the supervisory work, plus transporting yourself (and your family) from one place to the other. Even with a removal firm, the actual day of the move is a tiring one.

Removal men are usually experienced, and pack and move quickly – much quicker than you could. They may not seem to be as careful with your belongings as you would be but a professional remover is used to handling articles in a way that avoids damage.

If you are moving further than a short distance, and particularly if you have a lot of furniture, using a removal firm will be more practical than hiring a self-drive van with which you would have to make several journeys (plus one more in order to return the van to its owner).

Using a removal firm

If you decide to pay for a firm to do your removal for you, you should set about choosing one well in advance. Find out the names of local firms as well as the large national firms and ask friends and neighbours for recommendations and warnings.

The British Association of Removers (BAR)* will be able to supply you with the names of three members based in your area. The National Guild of Removers and Storers Ltd* will also be able to furnish you with details of their members in your area. Unless there is no choice in the area, you should preferably get more than one estimate.

Prices vary considerably, so you should get at least two, preferably three, estimates. These are usually given free. If you are moving to a different area, consider getting a quotation from firms in the area you are moving to.

Getting an estimate

As soon as you have some idea of the date of your move, ask the removal firms to send a representative to give you an estimate. It is not wise to accept an estimate given over the telephone: you may find yourself supplied with too few men or too small a van when the day comes (or too large a van – and bill).

When the estimator arrives, he or she should inspect your whole house and garden to see the quantity and type of furniture and belongings involved. Do not forget to include the contents of any loft, garage or garden shed. Also, point out that if any items are to be left behind, have to be picked up from some other place or are being bought before the move, so that these are taken into account in the estimate.

Charges may be calculated according to the quantity and type of belongings to be packed and moved. The firm's estimator can judge how many vanloads and how many men will be needed. He or she will take into account whether the move is a local one, which can be completed in one day, or, if it is a long-distance move, the length of time it will take and how many overnight stays there may have to be.

Alternatively, charges may be estimated according to the time taken over the packing and move or may be based on an hourly rate (not suitable for a move of any distance), by half a day or a whole day. Check what the hours concerned are: when does morning/afternoon begin and end? Is a day 8 hours, 12 hours or 24 hours? Does the rate per hour vary according to the time of day? When would overtime start, and at what rate? (If you do not get access to your new home until, say, after lunch, you could be involved in overtime.)

Hourly charges are normally based on a depot-to-depot principle, but meal times are usually excluded from the charge. Charges may be more (or less) expensive for a move on certain days of the week, but this would not help you if you were committed to move on a certain day because of your completion.

If you are able to reduce the quantity to be packed by doing a lot of it yourself beforehand, you could reduce the cost. If you are moving only a short distance, and have access to your new home before the day of the move, you can transport small loads yourself in advance.

Things to discuss with the removals estimator

You may ask the firm	Pro	Con
to pack everything	important if you work full time/are elderly/unfit/have small children	more expensive
to pack only your crockery and glass for you	cheaper	needs effort and plenty of time in advance to pack contents of wardrobes, cupboards, bookcases
to provide chests, crates or purpose-made cardboard cartons for you to do packing	even cheaper	needs time in advance, effort and skill in packing breakables properly; if you pack and they carry, you may have difficulty in getting compensation for any breakage
to do the unpacking for you	important if you work full time/are elderly/unfit/have small children	more expensive; need to know at once where in new house items are to be unpacked (tiring exercise at end of moving day)
to do no unpacking and collect cases at later date (may not be possible for a move to an area some distance away)	unpacking can be done at leisure; cuts cost, especially if charge is on hourly basis (unless there is a charge for collecting later)	needs somewhere to store emptied cases to await collection; deposit payable for cases left, may be only 50% refund on collection
whether the move needs to be spread over more than one day	possibly less wear and tear/ pressure	extra expense (including overnight accommodation)

Removal firms do not generally accept responsibility for damage to any items which have not been packed by them, and nor do their insurers.

You should point out to the estimator any of your belongings that may need special packing, or may present problems in handling or transporting, such as:

- pictures
- audio equipment, records
- computer
- collections of valuable objects

- antiques, fragile items
- books, if a large quantity or of special quality
- freezer, home safe
- wine
- plants, animals
- fish tank
- any heater or appliance fuelled with LPG.

Point out any built-in cupboards or shelves that will need dismantling to get them out (but they may not be designed to be dismantled and reassembled – some of the cheaper chipboard systems will not fit together again satisfactorily).

For pictures and mirrors, there are corrugated packs which the removal firm may offer to supply; mattress sacks are also available.

Some firms offer special cardboard cartons or 'travel boxes' for use with an inner paper sack or liner (which can be filled separately) that fits into the box. The advantage is that the paper sacks can be sent by post to the client who can fill them ahead of time, and they are then left to be unpacked at leisure after the move. The cartons are less likely to snag the carpet or scratch the floor than the old-fashioned tea chests, and can be carried by one person.

Pianos Some firms have special trolleys ('shoes') and webbing for transporting pianos and are accustomed to handling them. Others sub-contract to a specialist transport firm, especially if there is any difficulty about getting the instrument in or out of a house or flat – through a window, for instance. Check with the estimator and, if your piano is a valuable one or moving it may not be straightforward, consider engaging a specialist firm. Look in the local classified telephone directory or contact any local concert hall, theatre or piano retailer for advice. (Allow the piano time to recover from its journey before having it retuned.)

Carpets If any are to be moved, discuss whether the men will lift and re-lay these, will only spread them out on delivery, or will simply unload them. Lifting and re-laying, particularly of fitted carpets, may incur extra charges.

Clothes Ask whether clothes, linen, or other contents can be left in drawers, and whether the removers can provide 'wardrobe' packing cartons to hang clothes in (these are large, collapsible cardboard cartons in which there is a clip-on plastic rail on which clothes can be hung straight from a wardrobe). Some firms will leave these for collection later, so that the cartons need not be unpacked immediately.

Access If the approach to your new home (or to the present one) is at all difficult, mention this to the removal firm's estimator. A steep drive might be too much for a large van, or a narrow entrance or approach road could mean having to use two smaller vans. Many houses do not have direct access for a van, so if belongings will have to be carried some distance from van to house, tell the removal firm's estimator.

If there are parking problems at either end – for instance, restrictions on parking during certain hours – you will be expected to make arrangements with the local police for permission to load or unload, or pay to have a parking meter suspended. The removers may ask you to reserve a parking space, if possible the night before.

Go over the layout of your new home in your mind and assess whether there could be any problems about getting any of your furniture into it. Narrow staircases or awkward corners, for example, could mean temporary removal of a window in order to improve access to a room, and the removers might need to bring special equipment to deal with this. Do not leave it until the day of the move but warn the estimator at your first meeting – otherwise, you could be faced with extra charges for difficulties in unloading.

Do not think that if you say nothing about likely difficulties they will not add to the cost. On the contrary, if there is any serious delay, you are likely to get an extra bill.

If any aspect of the move is not absolutely straightforward, confirm your requirements in writing so that the firm has no excuse to say that it was not agreed or included in the estimate.

Acceptance of the estimate

The firm's estimate is likely to be on a standard form which incorporates the terms and conditions. Study carefully the small print concerning claims, exclusion clauses about liability (even though, in law, they may not be enforceable) and insurance cover. Some firms state you are liable for any breakages during the move if you pack items yourself. If a removal firm is a member of the BAR, it will probably use a standard contract, the clauses of which have been drawn to protect the firm. You may be able to add terms of your own or ask for unacceptable ones to be deleted.

Although the terms and conditions are usually the same, prices can vary considerably from firm to firm. Many firms ask for payment to be made in advance; you may be able to arrange to pay on the day of the move. Some firms accept credit cards: this can help to spread your outgoings.

When you accept an estimate, you are expected to give a firm date for the job and, having booked a date, you would have to give reasonable notice if you want to change it – otherwise, the firm may well charge a cancellation fee.

The removal men

The estimator's principal job is to assess how much the firm should charge you, rather than make arrangements for the practical aspects and convenience of the move. The estimator will not be there on the day and should pass on any messages or warnings about what is involved and any special requirements of yours direct to the foreman of the team carrying out the removal. But do not rely on this: write down all the relevant details and send them to the firm in advance, to be given to the foreman.

Ask how many men will be provided. There should be at least three if the removers do all the packing, so that one person can be packing china, glass, kitchenware, etc. into containers while the others carry and load large items. Ring up on the day before the move to confirm the time when the men and van(s) are due to arrive.

Insurance for the move

While the contents of your home are being moved from one building to another, they may automatically remain insured by your household contents policy. (If your contents policy includes 'contents temporarily removed', do not assume that this covers a household removal: check with the insurers.) If not, most insurers will extend an existing contents policy to take in the increased risks of a removal, at an additional premium (likely to be at least £25). Insurers are unlikely to be willing to issue a separate household removal policy if you have no existing insurance with them.

Provided you are going to have the removal undertaken by a specialist firm of removers, you should have little difficulty in getting insurance. The cover offered is usually on the basis of what is called 'all-risks' insurance for loss or damage, and includes accidental breakages, but excludes scratches and dents. Very often, you are expected to pay a part (which may be £50 or more) of any claim (the excess).

Ask whether you would get the replacement value for any article lost, or the value at the time, allowing for depreciation and wear and tear. Make sure that you insure for the maximum value of your goods: if you are under-insured, you may receive only a proportion of the amount of your claim.

Watch out for the 'pairs and set clause' which means that the insurers will not pay for the cost of replacing any undamaged item forming part of a set when replacements cannot be matched – this could leave you with an odd one out.

Tell the insurers whether your removal necessitates overnight storage in the van, to make sure that the policy will cover this. A householder's policy does not cover storage at the removal firm's depot; other policies can be extended to do so.

Removals insurance generally excludes loss of or damage to bank notes, shares, bonds, deeds, stamps, securities; also, loss or damage due to atmospheric or climatic conditions, strikes, delay, the nature of the goods insured. There are likely to be other exclusions, depending on the insurers. Melamine furniture, for instance, is not likely to be covered.

Consequential loss is also excluded: removals insurance does not cover any additional expenses you may incur due to the loss of your furniture or belongings. For instance, unlike under a householder's contents policy, you cannot claim for having to stay in a hotel or for the expense of making arrangements for new furniture to be bought.

Check the time limit within which a claim must be made in writing both to the insurers and the removal firm – within three days of the delivery to the property sounds reasonable enough. But if for some reason you are delayed or arrangements have to be made for delivery in your absence, it could technically invalidate a claim later.

It is also advisable to find out whether the policy is restricted to goods that are professionally packed – which most policies are. If so, remember to allow the removers to pack everything. Do not help them do it, even if it means you have to stand around and watch all day, because if you help and something gets broken, the insurers will be able to repudiate your claim because you did not comply with the condition. Remember also that, for the same reason, the removers must themselves unpack everything.

Insurance through the removal firm

If insurance is part of the removal firm's contract, there may be a specified (low) limit on what will be paid as compensation.

Members of the BAR have to undertake to provide a specified minimum standard of insurance cover for their customers.

Ask what the payment would be for the amount you want to insure and what the maximum premium would be for any one item. Insist on seeing in writing exactly what is covered, the time limit for making a claim, how much of each claim you will be expected to bear and all the principal exclusion clauses before paying the premium and accepting the insurance.

Do-it-yourself moves

The advantage of a d-i-y move is that it is cheaper than a professional move: the basic cost is the hire of a van plus petrol, or only petrol if a van can be borrowed from a friend who owns one, or from your employer.

If you can take the opportunity to help someone else with a d-i-y move, you will learn a lot about the knack of negotiating stairs and doorways with pieces of furniture, and about packing a van to make maximum use of its capacity.

The disadvantages of a d-i-y move are that it:

- is physically very tiring
- needs strong and willing helpers who can be available on the day(s) of the move
- needs plenty of time in advance for pre-packing since the day(s) of the move will be spent carrying and loading
- is not easy if you have a lot of things or heavy equipment to move and they have to be carried up or down stairs or where there are difficulties of access – for example, where the house is in a pedestrian court
- is only practical for moves of short distances – say, not more than 50 miles; a number of journeys with a small van over a greater distance adds to the time and cost, and the hired van has to be returned to its depot at the finish
- requires providing your own packing cases and packing materials, rope or webbing to secure items in the van, blankets or other protection for polished surfaces.

Hire of a van

Before you decide on a self-drive van, you should be sure that you could cope with driving an unfamiliar vehicle. One that is larger than a private car can take some getting used to, and parking a van which has restricted rear vision may also be quite difficult. But an experienced car driver, even if unused to handling any type of van, can probably cope with a laden 18-cwt van (a Ford Transit-type van which can carry 1,000 kilos).

A self-drive van may be hired from nationwide companies specialising in this type of hire or from a local hire firm. Look in the *Yellow Pages* or the small ads columns of your local paper, or ask friends or colleagues for recommendations.

The bigger firms may have several sizes of vehicle which can be driven on an ordinary driving licence. For trucks or lorries above 7.5-tonnes laden weight, an HGV (heavy goods vehicle) category licence is necessary. You are allowed to drive small goods vehicles (up to 3.5 tonnes laden weight) from the age of 17, between 3.5 and 7.5 tonnes laden weight from the age of 18.

Hire firms may stipulate any other minimum age limit, or that a licence has been held for at least a year, and is a clean one. When you hire a self-drive van, the company will want to see your driving licence, so do not send this off to the licensing authority to notify them of your change of address until you have completed the move.

If you prefer to hire a van plus driver – which will probably cost a bit more – find out whether the driver will help you with the loading and carrying or not. Whatever the size of the van, the driver will be subject to the regulations on goods vehicle drivers' hours – he or she must not drive for more than nine hours in the course of one day and must take the stipulated rest breaks.

Size of van

The hire firm will give you the dimensions and cubic capacity of the various vehicles. It is difficult for the amateur to estimate from the capacity of a van what loads it will take and, therefore, the number of journeys that will be necessary. Because you will not be experienced in loading economically, work on the basis of needing more capacity and making more journeys than you may at first think.

The size of the door-opening of different makes of van varies, so if you have large items of furniture, measure these first and choose a van with sufficient door size. This is especially important if a fridge or freezer has to be moved because these should always be kept in an upright position.

A van with a low kerb height or a let-down tailboard can be very useful; a truck with a hydraulic tail lift is invaluable for loading and unloading cookers, wardrobes and other bulky furniture. Alternatively, see whether some form of ramp can be built up into the rear of the van. Find out about hiring or borrowing a trolley or a wheeled platform for moving the cooker, fridge, washing machine and other heavy items.

Cost of hiring a van

Charges may be either a fixed sum per day or week for unlimited mileage during the period of the hire, or a smaller fixed sum per day plus a mileage charge, or an allowance of free miles followed by a mileage charge. Ask whether VAT is included in the charge, or will be added.

Work out whether it would be cheaper to pay a higher daily rate and nothing for mileage, or a lower rate plus mileage costs. To make this comparison, you need to have some idea of how many miles you will be driving during the period of hire. Subtract the lower rental charge from the higher one and divide the answer by the charge per mile. The result will give you the break-even point: if you drive more than this number of miles, the firm offering unlimited mileage is probably cheaper; if fewer miles, the firm charging so much per mile will be cheaper.

Check the exact hours of hire and what happens if the van is returned late – there could be a penalty charge, or you may be charged for another 24 hours' hire. If you know you are going to be late, let the firm know – if only for the sake of the next hirer waiting.

Find out when a day starts and ends (24 hours, 9 a.m. to 6 p.m. or whatever). Consider whether it is worth starting the hire on the day before the move, so as to be able to get most things packed up, ready for moving off early the next morning (after a good night's sleep). But do not load the van the night before the move unless you can lock it securely and park it safely, or put it in a lock-up garage.

You will have to return the van to the hiring place, so you have to take account of the cost of the extra mileage and time. It may be more sensible to hire in the place to which you are moving, so as not to have the return drive at the end of moving day (plus an extra return journey thereafter).

Find out what insurance is included and what is excluded. There may be an excess of £200 or more which you would have to pay towards the cost of any damage to the vehicle. It may be possible to pay a small extra premium to have the excess clause waived. Some van hire firms will arrange goods-in-transit insurance cover, if required.

You will be asked for a deposit when hiring the van, but will get it back when you return the van. Some hirers ask for a deposit to cover the amount of the insurance excess.

In your calculations of the cost of petrol to cover however many journeys you think you will make, remember that an 18-cwt van does no more than about 20 mpg. Ask what the tyre pressure should be for the van when laden, so that you can check before driving with your load.

Loading a hired van

Remember that the order in which the items are put into the van will be the reverse when unloading. You will want to off-load any carpets first, so these should go in last. Also, any heavy items that will be upstairs in the new house should be loaded near the end so that, at the unloading stage, the toughest work can be done at the beginning. But keep in mind the stability of the van – heavy items should be packed low down and distributed overall.

When stacking the van, try to make flat surfaces and use rugs or blankets on top of pieces of furniture to protect them from scratches. Damage can be caused if the furniture moves about while in transit, so make certain everything is wedged firmly to prevent this. The contents of the drawer of a chest of drawers can be left inside, covered with newspaper or towels. Remove the drawers while loading the emptied chest on to the van, replace them for travelling, and reverse the process when unloading. It may be wise to code the drawers as they are not always interchangeable. Cupboards and wardrobes can be filled with small boxes when they have been loaded into the van.

There may not be enough space for your helpers to travel in the van once it is loaded, so remember to arrange separate transport for them if you want the same team to help you unload at the other end.

Preparing to move out

Allow plenty of time to sort out your possessions and, if you are going to do so yourself, to pack them. How long to allow for preliminary sorting will depend on how much you have accumulated, and this will probably be related to how long you have spent in your present home and whether or not you are moving to a smaller place. Far too many of us keep junk stored in the loft, garage or garden shed. Tackle these hoarding places as early as possible – months ahead, if you can – because they take longer to sort and clear out.

If you want to delay a decision on some things in case you would regret discarding them, ask friends or relatives if they would like to house any item while you think about it, making it clear that you might ask for it back.

It will help to draw scale plans of each room in the new house or flat, then cut out shapes to scale (as far as possible) for each piece of furniture, and see how they will fit into the room. (Remember to allow for the position of electric sockets.) This will not only enable you to see which items to keep but, when you come to the day of the move itself, you will be able to direct the operation so that no pieces of furniture finish up in the wrong room.

Once you have worked out where everything can go, list it room by room so you can direct the removal men (they come thick and fast when they are unloading). Mark the furniture with a code for each room – perhaps with coloured stickers (red for one room, green for another).

Be ruthless about parting with any surplus furniture or equipment – you will not do it once you have moved. Make each member of the family do this, particularly the squirrel-type hoarders.

Disposing of things

Sort unwanted possessions into groups of what you think are saleable items, those which could go to charities or jumble sales, and those of no value to anyone. Disposing of things takes time and can be difficult – another reason for allowing yourself plenty of time.

Selling to new owner
Do not get rid of items that the incoming buyer might want to buy at a reasonable price.

Classified advertisements

The local papers (weekly or daily) will serve as a guide to the types of things which are wanted and to current prices. Some localities have publications dealing only with articles 'For Sale' and 'Wanted'.

Find out the advertising rates for your local paper and whether there are any 'free' categories. *Exchange & Mart* and *Loot* carry ads for second-hand items.

If the article is a piece of special equipment, it might be worth advertising it in the appropriate magazine on the subject. It can take weeks to have an advertisement included in some magazines, so check this out at an early stage.

You will have to be in to answer the telephone and show the items to prospective buyers. Make sure you get paid before you let any item go.

Auctions

Some towns have permanent auction rooms where regular sales are held. Look in the *Yellow Pages* and for advertisements in the local press.

Go along to the auctioneers and explain what you want to sell. Some auctioneers divide goods offered for sale into groups according to quality, or handle only those of a certain standard. If they think your goods are not suitable for their auctions, they may refer you to a secondary, or chattel, sale room which deals in miscellaneous selections of lots.

Remember to find out what percentage commission (plus VAT) will be deducted from the sale price by the auctioneer. If any items are fairly valuable, discuss whether you should place a reserve figure on them – that is, a sum below which you do not want an item to be sold. You will have to arrange for the goods to be delivered to the sale room, and collected if not sold.

Second-hand shops and dealers

Local knowledge is probably the best way of discovering dealers. (Some removal firms are also second-hand furniture dealers.) Before approaching a dealer, try to gauge current second-hand prices by keeping an eye on advertisements or second-hand shops.

Ask a dealer (or two) to call to inspect what you wish to sell. It may be helpful to have someone with you when he or she comes, to give you moral and factual support. You may be more diffident about bargaining when you feel you are not being offered a good enough price. The dealer will probably collect the items from you if he or she agrees to buy them, and you should take this factor into consideration. If your problem is to clear your bulk, do not let the dealer pick out selected bits and pieces – insist that he or she takes the lot. Otherwise, you will be left with the unwanted residue.

Books, particularly non-fiction books, may have a saleable value to collectors or specialist second-hand dealers. You may find one through local knowledge or the *Yellow Pages*; ask the dealer to call and make you an offer.

You can organise your own sale by putting the things into the garage or on the lawn, with prices clearly marked, and advertising the fact that they are for 'Sale on Sunday between 2 p.m. and 6 p.m.', or whenever.

There may be a car-boot sale location near you, where you offer whatever you want to sell from the back of your car. You should decide beforehand what prices you will charge – and be prepared to come down (or not). It will take a day out of your pre-move weekend and timetable.

Items for charities and jumble sales

Some articles which are not worth selling, but which could not be considered rubbish – for instance, old clothing, curtains, bedding, toys etc. – can be donated to charity shops or jumble sales. Consult your local telephone directory, or ask at the Citizens Advice Bureau or council offices for voluntary services.

Local private housing associations are sometimes grateful to be given unwanted furniture, carpets or curtains. You could also try the local branch of the Salvation Army, if there is one, or your local church, social services department, British Red Cross, or other voluntary organisations. Some voluntary organisations run a 'charity auction': donated goods are auctioned in the conventional way, half the price going to the donor, half to charity.

Items of no value

If you finish with a residue of non-disposable items – rubbish – you may have to make a special arrangement with the local authority for this to be taken away. There may be a charge for a special collection of this kind. Ask your dustmen first, and if they are unable to collect it as normal domestic refuse, telephone your local council offices and ask what to do.

Some local authorities have established dumps where unwanted household waste, old appliances, mattresses or broken furniture can be taken by householders free of charge. The authority then disposes of them.

For large quantities of rubbish, and where no local authority facilities are available, it may be necessary to hire a container or skip from a commercial firm. Look in the *Yellow Pages* under 'Waste disposal services' or 'Skip hire'. Containers of varying capacity can be hired for the day or for a number of days – over a weekend, for example. It is wise to book ahead. The firm which delivers the skip also comes to collect and get rid of it. The cost varies according to how near you are to a disposal site. Payment is usually required on delivery of the container.

If the container or skip cannot be left in a garden or driveway and has to be deposited on a public highway (that is, any road), a licence is required from the local authority. It is free and should be applied for a few days ahead. Regulations govern the placing of warning cones and, if the container is parked overnight, red warning lights. The latter can be hired from a local hire shop.

A parked skip can be an invitation to two-way transactions. You may find it the next morning filled up with neighbours' junk – or that some of your discards have disappeared.

Your car

With so many additional problems to cope with at this time, the servicing of the family car may be neglected – you may have mentally added it to the list of things to be done later, but if you will be transferring goods in your car over the period of the move, or even just ferrying yourself and your family with personal luggage on the day, be sure to take precautions beforehand in order to avoid a breakdown on the way: check the oil level, battery, water and so on. The car may be carrying a lot more weight than normal, so check the brakes and, if necessary, adjust the tyre pressure. If there is anything about the car that has been worrying you, get it seen to before the move.

If you do not own a car, try to borrow one for the day of the move. It may even be worth hiring one. Find out about insurance cover.

Packing

Both sorting and packing take longer than most people estimate and they find that they have too much still to do on the actual moving day.

So start packing well in advance, particularly if you will be doing the move yourself or the firm of removers will not be packing and unpacking everything. The advantage of packing items which are not in daily use is that they can be stored in their containers somewhere until you move, and in the new home can be left to be unpacked at leisure later.

Lifting and carrying

Many a physiotherapist has patients who have come for treatment for muscular strain after a move, as a result of the unaccustomed lifting and carrying of heavy weights, often done incorrectly.

Here is some advice to help you avoid back trouble when lifting, shifting and carrying.

- You should always try to anticipate and size up the job. Think before you move: how heavy is the object? Can levers be used to reduce the stress? Is the floor space clear to move about without kicking or stumbling over an obstruction? Is the floor slippery? Where are you going to put the object? Where can you grasp it? Is it a two-person job?

- When you lift or shift an object, get as close to it as possible, with your feet around it rather than to one side or behind it. Position your feet so that you are firmly balanced, one foot ahead of the other, ready to move off in the right direction. Keep a straight back: do not tackle lifting jobs with your back rotated, twisted or bent sideways; your shoulders and pelvis should be facing the same direction. Bend the hips and knees until the object can be reached. Grasp it firmly. If there is nothing by which to hold it, use a sling or ropes.

- Lifting, heaving or carrying with arms outstretched throws needless strain on the chest, upper back and shoulders. Keep the load close to your body; the farther from the body you hold it, the greater the stress – hence the risk when lifting a box out of the car boot. Whatever you are lifting and carrying, keep its centre of gravity as near as you can over or under your own centre of gravity.

- When dealing with something large and heavy, lift it first at one end only, and get it on to a higher level before you take the full load. This halves the stress. Rather than carrying a heavy load, pull it on a trolley. If that is not possible, divide it into two smaller loads, one for each hand – or make a second journey, if need be.

- When putting things down, if you cannot safely drop the object (which is the best way), put the lifting drill into reverse. Keep the object close to your body, and put one end down first.

Packing containers

Start in good time to collect plenty of boxes, other containers and newspaper.

Chests, crates or cartons may be provided ahead of time by the removal firm. (Tea chests are becoming hard to obtain and, in any case, are heavy when full.) Some removal firms may send you a batch of paper liners for the crates and boxes they use for you to fill (with non-breakables). The paper bag is shaped to fit into the box, to be lifted into it and carried away for transporting by the removal men on moving day.

Try the local supermarket, food shop or off-licence for cardboard cartons and discarded boxes; the partitioned kind are ideal for packing food jars, bottles or breakable vases, and suchlike. Remember that cartons will get stacked on top of others, and that the bottom carton in the pile will collapse if it is not strong enough to take the weight.

For transporting larger breakables, ask electrical retailers and china shops if you can have cartons with the straw or shavings or packing materials in which goods have been delivered to them. Obviously, use all your own suitcases, trunks, holdalls, and borrow more from friends and relatives (tie on a label straight away to identify the lender – you will have to return the empties eventually).

Wearing gloves while you do the packing will protect your hands (you will be surprised to see how dirty they get).

When wrapping china and glass, it is not so much the paper that protects them as the resilience of crumpled paper. When packing china in tea chests or boxes, first put in a thick bottom layer of crumpled-up newspaper. Large plates and lids should be individually wrapped and can be packed vertically round the sides of the box or chest, or be held in place by other items. If you are packing fragile items for transporting, it is sensible to label these as 'fragile' or 'this way up'. Do not – obviously – put heavier items on top of breakable smaller ones.

Do not fill chests or boxes too full, particularly with heavy items, such as books; otherwise, they become impossible to lift or carry any distance. Instead, use a greater quantity of smaller cartons, and tie them with string to make them easier to carry.

Labelling

It is essential to label boxes and cases as you pack them, to identify the contents. You may think you will remember what each contains – you will not. Also, keep a list of the contents of boxes or containers which are not going to be unpacked straight away, identifying the room to which they belong.

People devise their own systems of labelling: per room or per type of contents or for unpacking chronologically. Choose whatever method appeals to you.

Containers which are to be emptied immediately need only be labelled or numbered to identify in which room in the new home they are to be deposited. Provided you put up a correspondingly labelled or numbered plan in a prominent position in the new house or flat, everyone should be able to see where things are to go. Some people use a colour code or a letter code – allocating a colour (or letter) to each room in the house and sticking the appropriate coloured sticker or letter on each door and on the furniture and containers.

Preferably, put the labels on the side – not the top – of boxes, so that they can be seen when stacked one on top of the other. Be careful not to put a self-adhesive label on a polished surface, or on any normally visible surface: after a day or so, the fixative may harden and then you may not be able to get it off without leaving a mark.

Some removal firms will supply labels free of charge. Stationers sell packets of adhesive labels of various sizes, also coloured stickers. Buy about twice as many as you first think you will need.

Put labels on items not to be removed from the house as well, so that they are clearly identifiable on moving day.

Keys

Sort out all the keys to rooms, windows, cupboards, garage, outhouse, as well as sets of front- and back-door keys, and label them. It will be an act of kindness to the incoming owner, and may avoid any unnecessary queries later, if you make a list of how many keys exist and which, if any, are missing. Make sure that all the keys are duly rounded up eventually – partners' sets, the children's, if applicable, and sets lent to near or distant relatives, trusted neighbours or the daily help.

Make sure you tell your buyer where you are leaving all the keys but do not let him or her have them until you know that completion has taken place.

Furniture and other items

If you have any furniture that needs renovating or re-upholstering, or you want carpets cleaned, it can be a good idea to get the firms to collect them before you move and to deliver them to the new home. This is a good time to get all these jobs done, while you are living in chaos anyway, and it means that someone else is doing some of the removing for you. It is, however, only practical if you are moving locally.

When pieces of furniture, shelving or kitchen appliances have to be dismantled, any screws and fittings should be kept with the items to save time when re-installing. Tape them to the piece of furniture, on an inside surface with adhesive tape, or ask the removers to do so.

Label all the keys to cupboards, chests of drawers, wardrobes, etc. and keep them together in a clear polythene bag; some removal firms provide key bags.

Ask the removers whether they prefer drawers to be locked or left unlocked – this could depend on the weight of the piece of furniture. Drawers can be used as packing containers: cover the contents with rugs, towels, old sheets or polythene sheeting.

Beds

Bedsteads are usually dismantled by the removers. Check whether they will also put them up again at the other end (make sure the bedstead spanner stays with it). Put identifying labels on mattresses and bedsteads or bases for matching up at the other end. Some removal firms provide special mattress sacks.

Carpets

Carpets should be rolled, not folded, to prevent creasing. Label the pieces of underlay (with a stick-on label) to identify which carpet they belong to. Some of the foam varieties of underlay may be found to have disintegrated into dust, particularly where there has been much traffic (on the stairs, for instance), so you may find nothing to take away and will need new underlays at your new home.

Valuables

If the move is a local one, valuables could be lodged with your bank for the period of the move. If you have to take them with you, consider packing jewellery and other small valuables discreetly among your clothes. But remember to make a note of where you put them.

Clocks

You will have to immobilise any clock that has a detachable pendulum or weights. If you are unsure how to do this, consult a local clock repairer before attempting to remove any weights. Some removal firms specifically exclude responsibility for any internal damage to clocks.

Flammable items

Run down or remove any fuel remaining in oil heaters, oil lamps or a lawn mower. The removers will not accept them with fuel, or half-used tins of anything volatile.

Children's toys

If you have small children, do not forget to keep out a selection of their favourite toys and games and books to have at hand over the period of the move.

Tools

Before packing up your workshop, garage or tool cupboard, prepare an emergency tool kit to take with you, readily accessible. Include such tools as screwdriver, pliers, sharp knife, adjustable spanner, nails, hammer, screws, hooks, fuses or fuse wire, adhesive, tape, rope, string, light bulbs, plugs and torch.

Dustbin

The dustbins at both houses are likely to be overflowing by the day of the move. Invest in a new dustbin, and liners, and take these – kept empty – for use as soon as you arrive at the other end.

Moving household appliances

Do not forget to check that there are sockets for portable electrical appliances and fused connection units for stationary appliances in convenient positions in your new home. There should be a socket outlet or connection unit within 1.8 metres of all likely locations of electrical appliances.

Cooker

Remember to switch off the electricity supply at the mains position before disconnecting the cooker.

Freezer

Ideally, run down stocks before moving; defrost and dry out the cabinet.

Freezers are not designed with the strength needed to be transporting containers. Some removal firms will not take a freezer with its contents, mainly because of the extra weight. The vibration during a move and weight of the contents can damage the pipework.

If you must move it with frozen food inside:

- reduce stocks to no more than 25 per cent of the freezer's capacity
- switch to 'maximum freeze' for at least 24 hours before removal
- do not open the door or lid after refrigeration is switched off.

A risk in moving frozen food is the possibility of thawing: refreezing partially defrosted food can spoil its taste and can be a health hazard if it has been left long enough for it to go off.

Even when the freezer is empty, it is vulnerable to damage during the move. If it is tipped more than about 30 degrees – to come down some steps, for instance, or when negotiating doorways – this can cause an airlock in the cooling system. A freezer that has been moved must be left to stand in its final position for a minimum of two hours before it is switched on.

Fridge

Defrost just before the move, and leave the fridge dry and empty. Pack any remaining perishables in an insulated picnic bag or wrap them in plenty of newspaper and put them into thick cartons.

Remember that fridges must be carried upright.

Dishwasher and washing machine

A plumbed-in dishwasher or washing machine with a stop valve on the supply pipe does not need a plumber to disconnect it. (Leave a label telling the new owner 'this is a water supply pipe'.) But you may need a plumber at the new house for fitting a stop valve to the supply pipe there.

If the washing machine has a revolving drum, this should be immobilised before moving it. Ideally, find the restraining bars which came with the machine when it was new. If you cannot, consult the manufacturer or a local retailer for advice. Tilting a front-loading machine can cause damage to it. Some machines have bearings or gear boxes with an open reservoir of oil – if the machine is not kept upright, you will have an indelible dribble over everything.

Home computer

Computers are vulnerable to damage – from damp, dust and magnetic waves. It is also possible to damage the recording heads by rough handling.

Ensure that your computer is sealed in a plastic bag and handled gently. You may prefer not to use the removal men for this. Disks should be kept away from sources of magnetism – such as radios, telephones and some children's toys.

Survival kit

Before packing up the contents of the kitchen, you would be wise to prepare a survival kit to be taken with you in your car, or in the van if you are travelling with it. See the box, opposite.

If you are moving over two or more days, you will also need an overnight bag of personal belongings for each member of the family.

Children on the move

Most adults find moving house a traumatic business. Children can find it disturbing, too – which, in turn, will be an added worry for the parents. So, it is important to protect the children as much as possible from the upheaval and to settle them down in the new surroundings as smoothly and as quickly as possible.

Older children should be encouraged to look forward to a move and to feel involved in it. If it can be organised, take them to see the new house beforehand. Let them have an opportunity to imagine themselves in their future surroundings, to inspect their new bedroom and perhaps to choose their own decorations for it.

Survival kit for moving day

- kettle and its flex
- can opener
- teapot
- tea and/or coffee
- milk (longlife, tin or powder)
- sugar
- soft drinks
- disposable or plastic cups/beakers, plates and cutlery
- saucepan (and camping stove if no working cooker)
- teaspoons
- washing-up liquid and brush/cloth
- rubber gloves
- vacuum cleaner
- bedding and towels
- soap
- notepad and writing implements
- any regular medication
- lavatory paper
- candles, matches
- corkscrew
- pet food, bowl and litter tray
- first aid kit, including sticking plaster, scissors, aspirin
- cash
- mobile phone, or coins and phone card for telephoning from a public call box (and the telephone numbers of the estate agents, your solicitor, the seller, your buyer, electricity and gas companies)
- cheque book, bank and credit cards
- things to amuse the children
- clean clothes (and slippers)
- plugs and adapters
- self-sealing plugs for sinks and basins
- hot water bottle
- basic tool kit
- torch
- driving licence, motor insurance document
- removal contract
- champagne, G&T etc.

Even if the children are very young, talk to them well in advance about what is to happen; they may not fully understand what it is all about, but they will be getting some warning of what is to come.

A baby in a carry-cot can be less trouble than an older child, provided you take with you enough milk, baby food, drink and nappies.

If it is practical, it may be better to 'farm out' a toddler or small child with relatives or a neighbouring family with children over the day or days of the move.

When the time comes to collect the children from relatives or friends for their first night in the new home, arrange this so that they have sufficient time to find their way round it, and to explore a little, before bedtime. If there is any spare time or energy left, use this to make their bedroom as familiar as possible by putting out their toys, clothes, and so on. They are at first going to feel insecure in the strange new surroundings, so anything which can be done to reduce this – such as providing them with their favourite toys – will help.

As soon as possible after the arrival in a new area, make it a priority to locate any neighbouring children of the same age for yours to play with. Your children will miss their friends, and will need new ones quickly if they are to enjoy the change.

Moving pets

The societies for the prevention of cruelty to animals are ready to give advice on any problem to do with animals.

Dogs

Whether you would be wiser to put the animal into kennels or not depends on the kind of move, the distance, the duration of the changeover – and on your dog. A good guard dog might find the comings and goings of workmen or removal men a strain, in which case it would be less harassing for dog – and owner – if it were not about the house. And if there is any chance that your dog might escape and run off while doors are left open during loadings of the furniture van, or that it would continually get under everyone's feet, it would be kinder and safer to board it out for this stage of the move or to ask a neighbour to have it for the day.

If you can leave the dog for the day with a relative or friend, so much the better, but it may be necessary to put it into kennels for a day or so if you are involved in a lengthier operation. If you do not know of a local kennels, consult your vet or look in the *Yellow Pages*. If you are moving some distance away, it would be more practical to find kennels near your new home if arrangements can be made for the dog to be delivered there beforehand. Good kennels get booked up in the holiday season so make your booking as soon as you know the date of the move and get any required injections done; a recent certificate of vaccination will almost certainly be required.

Do not forget to check the new garden (if there is one) to make sure that it is dog-proof before releasing your dog into it.

Cats

A cat can be more of a problem, particularly in terms of settling into the new home. It is probably best to take your cat with you in the car in its travelling basket or carrier; some removal firms provide cardboard pet-carrying cartons.

If your journey is to be a long one – say, over four hours – or a disturbing one, ask your local vet whether he or she would consider prescribing a tranquilliser. This would depend on the age, size and fitness of your cat, and how accustomed it is to travelling.

Immediately on arrival, choose one of the rooms as the cat's temporary quarters and release it in it, keeping the windows and door shut. Warn everyone, or even lock the door, to avoid the cat being released accidentally, and leave it there with food, water and a litter tray (and perhaps its favourite chair or cushion) while the unloading goes on. At the end of the day, close all the windows and doors and then allow the cat the run of the rest of the house. (It may take refuge in a safe corner – under a stack of packing cases, perhaps – and may need to be coaxed out.) Do not let it out for at least three weeks after the move, in order to allow time for it to become accustomed to its new home. When you do let it out, only do this just before its feeding time.

For the first few weeks, just to be on the safe side, put a collar on the cat, with a tag giving your name, address and telephone number.

Small caged birds

Birds should be no problem because they can be transported in their cage covered with a cloth. Make sure that there is adequate ventilation and remove any loose articles that could move around inside the cage. Birds are susceptible to changes in temperature, so be careful not to leave the cage in a draughty spot during transit or in the new house while everyone is occupied with moving in. Empty the water and seed containers and remember to fill them again after you arrive. Alternatively, use non-spill containers.

Other small pets

Mice, guinea pigs, gerbils, hamsters and rabbits should be transported in 'chew-proof' well-ventilated containers. Water should be provided in a securely fixed inverted bottle with a drip tube, making sure that the end of the tube is at a convenient height for the animal to drink. Some food and bedding (not the synthetic variety) should be provided in the container.

Fish

For fish being moved from a pool you need a non-spillable, well-oxygenated container: for instance, a large polythene bag quarter-filled with pool water, placed in a bucket for protection and support during transit. Polystyrene chips can be used to cushion the bag and will also help maintain the temperature of the water.

For tropical fish, get the advice of the local aquarium expert or pet shop about maintaining the correct water temperature, and tell the removers.

Plants from the garden

Plants in the garden are legally part of the fixtures and fittings of the house and what you take with you will need to be agreed upon before you remove them. Plants in containers are considered your property and can be treated like the rest of your furniture.

The best time to move plants is in spring or autumn when the plants are dormant and the soil easy to work. Carefully dig around the rootball, removing as much as possible and plant up into containers. Plastic pots or bags are lighter and easier to handle. Do not water on the day of the move as this also makes the plants heavier.

If you are moving in summer and digging is difficult because the soil is dry and hard, water the plant first to loosen the soil and help you remove the rootball.

As long as they have adequate drainage and water, these plants will live happily in containers until you find a space for them in your new garden. Stand them together in a sheltered area to give them some protection over winter and shade in summer.

Larger plants, such as shrubs and climbers, will be easier to move as cuttings – consult *The Gardening Which? Guide to Successful Propagation*, available from Which? Books★. Remember to tell the removers about the plants as they should not be stacked in the removal van.

On the day of the move stake plants securely so they are supported and tie any delicate branches up with sacking or netting to prevent them bending or breaking.

The day of the move

Have a good night's rest and start the day with a proper breakfast, since the next meals may not materialise when most needed. You could try enlisting the help of one very good friend to be responsible for making the innumerable cups of tea or helping with last-minute packing or cleaning and generally giving moral support.

Last-minute jobs will be the stripping of beds, and the final clearing and packing of foodstuffs in the kitchen. Prepare any packs of sandwiches or snacks you have planned, and fill a vacuum flask (or two) with soup, hot drinks or hot water for making drinks.

Wear sensible clothes, with large pockets (tuck a notebook into one of them) and comfortable shoes: you will be doing a lot of running about and standing around. Keep out a stool or folding chair to sit on during the day whenever you can.

Arrange to keep to one side the vacuum cleaner or a broom and dustpan and brush, and any other basic cleaning equipment, to be loaded among the last lot, so that they can be used for a final clean-up if needed, and will be readily available at the other end.

Collect your survival kit to go with you in the car (do not let it go with the removal van in case it does not reach your destination as quickly as you do). Decide where you will put any documents you may need on the day, and your valuables. Do not leave cash or jewellery around on moving day. There is no need for absurd security, but it is always best to take common-sense precautions.

You may need to get some cash unexpectedly during the move (to have the money for tips, for instance, or to buy fish and chips or a dozen light bulbs) so keep your bank card handy.

If arrangements go according to plan, the engineers from the electricity and gas companies will call early in the day to read any meters and disconnect any appliances you are taking with you. (This may mean no more hot water or hot food for you there.) You can also telephone through your meter readings at both properties.

When the removal men arrive, show the foreman round, not forgetting any loft, garage or outhouse. Explain the labelling system you have adopted and indicate which items are not to be removed. Check whether the requests you made to the estimator have been passed on to the foreman. If they have not, telephone the management right away, or get the foreman to, so that it can be sorted out as soon as possible.

Carpets in the entrance hall should be protected with druggets, plastic or dust sheets, especially if it is a wet day. Be prepared to provide these coverings in case the removal men do not bring their own. See that they are brought away in the van.

If the removal men are to do all the packing and loading, leave them to it at this stage. As far as possible, keep out of their way, and give any further instructions only to the foreman. Cups of tea or coffee will be welcome several times.

When everything has been loaded on to the van, make a final tour of inspection of the house both inside and out, to check that nothing has been left behind (look into built-in cupboards and drawers), but that all items included in the sale have been left.

Check that you have left the heating system on or off according to the arrangement made with the new owner, and turn off the mains water if this has been agreed. This could be important if the house is to stand empty and unheated for any time in winter. Close and lock all windows and doors, and leave the keys wherever you have arranged with the new owner.

Before the removal men leave with the van, check that they have the new address, and give clear instructions how to find the house if it is at all difficult. Make sure you have made arrangements about what they should do if they should arrive first – you could be delayed en route for some reason. (An emergency contact telephone number might also be useful.) But try as far as possible to be at the new house in time to supervise the unloading, or arrange to have a reliable friend or relative there to do so.

Completion and handover of keys

While you are moving out, your solicitor or conveyancer should be dealing with the legal (and financial) side of completion. Unless you are doing your own conveyancing, neither the buyer nor the seller is there. The crucial factor of completion is the handover of all the money.

Normally, the keys of a house are not released until the purchase money has reached the seller's solicitor. Strictly, the seller should get a set of keys to the solicitor, who will hand them over to the buyer's solicitor, and the buyer then gets them from him or her. This can be physically difficult, and complicated by the venue where completion takes place.

It may be more convenient for the keys to be handed over by the estate agent. The seller's solicitor will then authorise the estate agents to hand over the keys as soon as completion has taken place. In practice, the buyer and seller often make their own arrangements for the handing over of the keys.

Delays in the money reaching the solicitor or in the estate agent being notified of completion will delay the buyer being able to get hold of the keys and can cause a hiatus in the moving-in operation. Waiting outside your new home for some time before you are able to start unloading could prove expensive if your removal is being charged on a time basis.

At the new home

Before any furniture is unloaded, see that the carpets in the entrance, hall, or stairs are protected with coverings of some kind. These can get very dirty, especially on a wet day or in a house on a new estate where there is still a lot of mud on the site.

If you have adopted the method of labelling each item with a colour or number corresponding to the room in which it is to be put, label the rooms accordingly and stick the plan in a prominent place by the front door. Or, you may prefer to position yourself there and to indicate the correct room as each item is unloaded. Remember, with the heavier pieces of furniture you should specify exactly where in the room each should be put – you should have worked this out beforehand – to avoid finding yourself having to heave them about later.

When the foreman tells you they are ready to go, have a look inside the van, just to make sure that nothing has inadvertently been left there.

The removal men will expect a tip. If you feel they deserve one, you can give a sum to the foreman for distribution or give individually to each man (and the driver). But if you are not satisfied, say so. If you give a tip without comment, it can sometimes lead the removers to suspect that any claim you may subsequently make is exaggerated or even false.

You may be asked to sign a discharge document that the job is completed. (It may incorporate a receipt for payment, if you pay at the end of the moving operation, not ahead of time.) This is the document on which to record any reservations about how the work has been carried out. If you have not yet inspected your belongings, sign as 'unexamined'.

Switch on the water heating. Make up the beds as soon as they are unloaded, so that they are ready to be collapsed into when needed. If it is possible to hang curtains in the bedrooms, do this as well.

Unpack only essentials – not only because you may want to clean any fitted cupboards and shelves before putting your belongings into them, but because you should not tire yourself out on jobs that can wait. Also, the more items that can remain packed in boxes or containers, the less chaos. But, you will have to empty the chests or containers that the removal men will want to take away.

Be prepared for:

- a lot of discarded packing materials
- emptied containers waiting for collection/disposal
- piles of books unloaded but not put on to shelves
- pots, pans, crockery everywhere on the wrong surfaces
- débris and dirt.

Do not expect to be fully organised at your new house straight away. If you try to be, you could be heading for a nervous breakdown.

There may be a kind friend or neighbour who will feed you. But if you are planning to prepare some sort of meal the first evening, you will have to locate crockery and food. If you find you are too exhausted to want to prepare a meal at this stage, find a café, take-away or fish-and-chip shop.

Claiming for damage or loss

If anything gets broken or damaged, try to make a written note of it at the time, and ask the removers' foreman to sign or initial it. Such an *aide-mémoire* should not be altered or amended after signature. Keep your copy carefully, to support any claim.

You may not spot deficiencies, loss or damage in all the hurly-burly straight away. Make a list of anything that has been broken or damaged as soon as possible, and notify the insurers and the removal firm's head office that there is a likelihood of a claim on the removal insurance policy.

If something prevented you from being present when the goods were unloaded, or everything is not being unpacked immediately, tell the insurers (and the removers) at once that you are unable to comply with a claims time limit.

If damage is caused to your goods as a result of negligence on the part of the removers, they should, as far as possible, put it right by repairing or replacing it or compensating you financially. Take the advice of your solicitor. Many solicitors will not charge extra for sorting out the odd problem after completion if you have to claim on your insurance.

The claim form you receive will not have been designed specifically for this type of insurance: many questions may be irrelevant – or missing. Describe the circumstances as precisely as possible in the blank space provided. If only a few articles have been damaged, you should list each item. Depending on the extent of the loss, the insurers will either ask you for further details before taking up the matter with the removers or send you a cheque rather than waste time and money with enquiries about a small sum. Keep any bills or receipts for repairs or replacements to produce in support of your claim.

If a lot has been destroyed (by fire or a major accident perhaps), the insurers will arrange for a representative to call to formulate some idea of what has been lost and what can be salvaged, and the value. Do not agree to a figure if you think it is too low.

After the move

Security

It is wise to have the locks of the outer doors changed. There may be unaccounted-for keys: you never know who else had keys from the previous owners.

Consider fitting door and window locks, an alarm system or security lights. You can get advice from the crime prevention officer at the local police station.

Safety

Consider also the safety of your new home, particularly if there are young children or elderly people involved.

Safety checklist

- Are there any holes or worn places in the carpets or other floor coverings. Are any not fixed securely (especially stair carpets)?
- Are there adequate smoke alarms positioned in the right place? Do they work and are their batteries in good condition? Consider getting interconnectable alarms.
- Are there fire extinguishers – appropriately located?
- Are safety gates (top and bottom) needed on the stairs?
- Are there any locking cupboards which cannot be opened from the inside?
- Are there any stoves or open fires which need guards?

Documents

You should keep safely in one place all the documents, certificates, policies, guarantees, and other paperwork connected with your purchase. Although you may feel that you will never move again, some of these papers would be required if you did so at any time in the future. If any papers are being kept by your solicitor, bank or mortgagee, make a note of this in the file.

Chapter 10

Conveyancing

'Conveyancing' is the popular word for all the legal and administrative procedures involved in transferring the ownership of a house. The system's checks and balances are designed to ensure that the buyer gets a 'good title' (i.e. the legal right to possession) to the house with all the rights that go with it – and none that should not. Pitfalls for the unwary can range from undisclosed mortgages, the seller's bankruptcy, or Granny refusing to move on completion day, to difficulties over rights of drainage, disputes over fences or ancient common rights. The conveyancing process should unearth and resolve such problems.

Legal background

Historically, ownership of property has been divided into two groups: real property and personal property. Real property is confined to freehold ownership of land (hence the American expression 'real estate') and everything else is personal property (including leases). The distinction between the two types of property is less than it used to be, but it still has some relevance when property is being bought and sold.

What makes buying a house unlike buying a car or washing machine is that you are acquiring something which is permanent – built on land which has always existed and may be affected by things which happened years ago. For instance, any land can be subject to easements or common rights or even to ancient ecclesiastical rights. 'Land' includes all the buildings on it and, in theory at least, everything below it to the centre of the earth and everything above it. It is not enough just to check that the house has the right number of bedrooms and no rising damp.

The law treats land transactions differently from consumer transactions. Every contract to buy land has to be in writing and contain essential details: the price, who is buying and selling, and a description of the property. But even though a large amount of money is at stake you have in many ways much less legal protection than if you are buying a washing machine from a shop. There is no guarantee that a house is in good order, or even that the person who lives there has the right to sell it. That is why the legal side of house buying involves so much detective work. Your solicitor's job will be to find out if there are problems before you commit yourself to going ahead. Your best chance of making sure there are no nasty surprises is to work together with the person you appoint. Pass on any information which you think might be relevant and ask about things that seem odd or trouble you.

The two main stages of conveyancing

Up to exchange of contracts

Buying a house involves two main stages: firstly the contract to buy, and secondly the deed (called a 'transfer') required to actually transfer

---

e-Conveyancing

The government anticipates that in the next ten years or so all conveyancing will become electronically based, which will be compulsory. The key features of the scheme are that:

- the conveyancing documentation will be in electronic form. This is known as 'dematerialisation'
- most conveyancing steps, and communications between the parties, will occur online
- there will be simultaneous completion and registration of title. At the moment, there is a 'registration gap' (of up to two months) between these stages
- the payment of fees and balance transfers will be coordinated electronically
- there will be increased up-to-date information and transparency as to chain transactions
- mortgages will be the subject of immediate e-discharge on redemption – in other words the mortgage will be paid off and discharged by electronic transfer of funds and extinguishment of the debt.

---

ownership of that house. 'Exchange of contracts' is the legal term applied to the process by which the contract to buy and sell becomes binding. Unlike sales of other kinds of property, the contract for the sale of land is usually drawn up in two identical copies. The buyer signs one copy and the seller the other, but the agreement does not become binding unless and until contracts are 'exchanged'. This consists of the buyer and seller swapping the contracts they have signed, so the buyer ends up with the copy signed by the seller and vice versa. Exchanges can be by fax, telephone, email, post or by physically swapping documents.

Until contracts are exchanged either side is legally free to change his or her mind. It is the investigative period, when the buyer finds out as much as possible about the property; when the local and other pre-contract searches are carried out and preliminary enquiries are raised; when the documents are examined in great detail and if necessary the contract changed to suit circumstances. At this stage the buyer will check to ensure that the seller does indeed have the right to sell the property and that no one else has any rights over it. Once contracts are exchanged, the buyer and seller are committed and cannot pull out.

The delay before either party is bound can cause problems. Many weeks can elapse between a buyer saying he or she wants to buy a house and contracts being exchanged. During this time a transaction may appear to proceed smoothly, but there is always the risk – even at the last minute before exchange of contracts – that one party may decide not to go ahead after all. Or the seller may say that he or she has received a higher offer and will proceed only if the buyer meets that offer, which means that the buyer has been gazumped.

The government is keen to reduce the time taken by the buyer to make all the necessary searches and enquiries which delay exchange taking place. This is why the 'home information pack' is to be introduced (see page 144). With this system, the seller will provide all this information at the time the house is placed on the market. Procedures to enable buyers to access the results of searches through the Internet by means of the National Land Information Service (NLIS)★ are now in place, although it may well be several years before all information is obtainable this way. The NLIS brings together different agencies involved in a conveyance and allows the buyer easily to access a wide range of land and property information.

From exchange of contracts to completion

This stage involves the preparation of the transfer and mortgage documentation.

The buyer's goal

This is to become the legal owner of the house, free from the claims of other people, and free from legal and other problems. Try to imagine the house and garden as your territory. You want to make sure that everything within that territory becomes yours and that no one else has any rights over it (or at least none that you do not know about – like shared driveways, drains etc.). Your territory must also have access to the outside world, which means that you must have the right for pipes, wires, drains etc. to be connected to the mains – and to be able legally to get to and from the property.

From the seller's point of view

Here the role is more passive. Questions are asked about the property, and what is included in the price. The seller must answer these truthfully, and not in a way that will lead to civil claims after completion. The seller (or his or her solicitor) has to ensure that all liabilities charged on the property (mortgages, hire purchase and the like) are cleared on completion and that the property is handed over, empty, and in accordance with the contract on completion day.

Calculating the cost of conveyancing

See Chapter 2, noting in particular the advice to obtain a written quotation from the solicitor or licensed conveyancer before giving instructions to start work.

Ask at an early stage how much the other fees will be, such as search fees and the Land Registry fee and stamp duty on the transfer. (These amounts depend on the price being paid for the property.)

Who will do the work?

As soon as you decide to sell or start hunting seriously for a new home, decide who you want to do the conveyancing work for you. The choice you have in England and Wales is to:

- appoint a solicitor
- appoint a licensed conveyancer, or
- do it yourself.

The advantage of d-i-y conveyancing is that you can save on solicitors' or conveyancers' fees (and VAT). Also, you are largely in control of events. It does away with the frustration of chasing up your solicitor/conveyancer to get him or her to chase up the seller's solicitor. To some extent you can dictate the pace and possibly eliminate delays. An outline of the procedures is given in Chapter 11 but you will need to know not only what to do but how to do it before embarking on doing it yourself.

D-i-y conveyancing has become less popular in recent years partly because in real terms the fees charged by solicitors and licensed conveyancers have reduced dramatically and so, therefore, have the potential savings to be made. It will become even more unpopular once electronic conveyancing is introduced. The parties will then have to travel to their nearest Land Registry in order to access a secure terminal.

Solicitors

Traditionally, solicitors have carried out the legal work on house-buying and -selling. Since the creation of licensed conveyancers they no longer have a monopoly on this work.

Solicitors (and licensed conveyancers, see below) are required by law to be on guard against money-laundering and other types of fraud. Do not take it amiss if you are asked to produce proof of your identity and your address, especially if you have not used the firm before or for some years.

Conveyancers

It is unlawful for unqualified conveyancers (those who are not solicitors or licensed conveyancers) to draft conveyancing documents or contracts for a fee.

The Council for Licensed Conveyancers (CLC)★ can verify the name of any local licensed conveyancers in an area and, for a fee, can provide a list of all licensed conveyancers in England and Wales.

The Council deals with the licensing and supervision of non-solicitor conveyancers. It regulates the conduct of licence holders and

has disciplinary machinery to deal with complaints against li
conveyancers. It has set up a master policy to provide ind
insurance and has established a compensation fund.

Choosing a solicitor or conveyancer

The choice is not so much between a solicitor and conveyancer (both
of whom are qualified to do the work); rather, it is the choice of the
best person to work with you. Price is not the only consideration: if
you get a very low quotation, the solicitor/conveyancer may have had
to take on a huge workload to make ends meet, and may have little
time to give you personal attention. Worse than that, corners may be
cut and the job could be done inadequately. On the other hand, the
most expensive may not give the best service. House-buying and
-selling is a stressful experience. It may be worth paying a little extra
for a good service. The best indication of choice will come from
someone who has used a particular licensed conveyancer or solicitor
and still thinks that he or she is wonderful when it is all over.

If you have successfully used a firm of solicitors for any legal business
in the past, you could start by asking to be put in touch with a member
of the firm who specialises in conveyancing, or you could ask for a
recommendation from a relative, friend, colleague at work, bank
manager, building society manager or estate agent; or consult the Law
Society's★ website (which lets you search for a solicitor in your area
who specialises in property) or their regional directory in the local
reference library. Many solicitors' firms have their own websites; some
allow you to check on the progress of your sale or purchase by logging
on to the site. Alternatively you could simply look for an advertisement
in the local paper or *Yellow Pages*.

If you rely on personal recommendation, make sure that the
professional you have chosen is recommended for skill in property
transactions. A criminal lawyer may not appreciate the difference
between a restrictive covenant and a mortgage!

If you found the house you want to buy through a multi-firm
solicitor's property centre, one of the other firms (not the one involved
with the seller of your property) can be used. One solicitor can act for
you in both transactions if you are buying and selling at the same time
(and usually also deal with your mortgage). Except in very few cases,
the same solicitor cannot act for both buyer and seller at the same time

but two members of the same firm may act for the buyer and seller where both are already established clients of the firm, so long as there is no clash of interests between the buyer and seller. This is more likely to happen in a small rural town than in an urban area. However, where a newly built or converted house is being sold, a firm of solicitors can never act for both the builder/developer and the buyer, even if both are long-established clients.

It is not necessary for the solicitor to be local to the property being bought, although it can help, particularly if you are moving to another part of the country. Try to find someone you feel you will get on with, and who gives you confidence that matters are being well handled.

Do not expect a solicitor to be able to tell you precisely how long your transaction will take – but the reply may give you some impression of his or her tempo.

Delays that are not the making of your solicitor/conveyancer can include the time it takes to obtain a mortgage offer and the time it takes to get the result of local searches – some local authorities take many weeks to deal with local searches, although the NLIS system should speed this up. These details will in future be included in the home information pack (see page 144). A good solicitor/conveyancer should advise a client about how long the procedure is likely to take, judging from experience of local conditions, and warn that there may be periods when nothing seems to be happening. In practice, however, it is difficult to estimate the exact time a transaction will take: a chain of buyers and sellers can proceed only at the pace of the slowest party in the chain.

You should ask your solicitor or conveyancer whether he or she uses the NLIS system – not all do – as this should result in a quicker return of searches. Those solicitors and conveyancers using the planned system of electronic conveyancing (see box on page 233), when it becomes available, should be able to offer a faster service.

When to appoint your solicitor or conveyancer

Consult your solicitor or conveyancer at as early a stage as possible, so that he or she can be ready when you decide to make an offer and advise you on any legal snags before you become too involved, such as:

- local restrictions (perhaps preventing or limiting extensions or alterations)
- the possibility of undesirable development in the neighbourhood.

Teamwork

The transaction is most likely to go smoothly if you work together with your solicitor/conveyancer. If you spend your time laying traps, and telephoning at three minutes past nine to say that there was a spelling mistake in the previous letter, you will only cause irritation. Work in tandem and the stress will be much less.

On the other hand, if you feel from the very start that you are just not going to get on, or that you do not have confidence in the person, consider changing to another straight away. Your solicitor/conveyancer will probably not see the house: all he or she will have to work from will be the draft contract, the agent's particulars and information from the title deeds or the Land Registry. So, if you know of or can guess at any peculiarities about the property or if you have any proposals for using or changing the property in any particular way, pass on the details, in case they could create a legal problem.

The sort of items to be alert about include:

- the boundaries of a property (see below)
- any shared rights of access: for example, a drive shared with another property, and whether there is any obligation to contribute towards its upkeep
- a separate access to the back garden: you may need a right of way to it
- other 'easements': for example, a short-cut through your property, or the way a neighbour's drains join yours
- any structural additions or alterations carried out by previous owners, such as an extension or a garage: these might have required planning permission or building regulation consent which may never have been obtained
- any remedial treatment for damp or woodworm or any re-roofing or double glazing for which guarantees still operate
- any reason for the sale which may give rise to problems over possession – e. g. matrimonial or relationship difficulties. If the seller's house is not jointly owned by a couple, it is important to get written consent for the house to be sold from the partner who is not the owner in case of domestic dispute before completion; the solicitor/conveyancer can check whether that party has registered a claim

- any indication that the seller may be badly in debt. Your solicitor should know this at an early stage because he or she can then make preliminary searches and avoid trouble and delay later
- whether any part of the property is let or occupied.

Points like these will normally be dealt with in the contract, or cleared between the two parties before signing, but this can only be done if the points come to light. Do not assume that your solicitor/ conveyancer is a clairvoyant or knows the property personally. Draw attention at an early stage to any features about the house, the neighbourhood or the sellers. Check the estate agent's particulars against what is in the house and what is stated in the contract. Tell the solicitor about anything which is shown up by the structural survey.

Some practical matters

The deposit

On exchange of contracts, a deposit has to be paid by the buyer to the seller. Traditionally, the deposit is 10 per cent of the purchase price but a lower figure (say, 5 per cent) can usually be negotiated. This deposit (unlike any preliminary deposit paid to an estate agent) is non-refundable and is used as security for the performance of the contract. The amount will be deducted from the balance that has to be paid at completion.

Normally, the seller's solicitor will hold on to the deposit until completion when it will be handed over to the seller. However, the contract will usually permit the seller to use this money towards the deposit on any house that he or she may be buying. Indeed, the sum the seller receives may be derived from a deposit the buyer has in turn acquired on a house he or she is selling. Ultimately the money will be held by a solicitor, so you can be sure of getting your money back should someone in the chain default and refuse to proceed with their sale or purchase.

If you do not have the ready money for a deposit, you may have to arrange a bridging loan (see page 178), which will be paid off when you receive the mortgage loan or the money from the sale of the home.

The chain situation

Unless you are a first-time buyer, you are likely to be selling your existing house as well as buying a new one, and will be trying to time the two operations to run as closely together as possible. The buyer of your present home might be in a similar situation. This is how a chain of buyer and seller, buyer and seller is created. Where there is a chain of transactions, each dependent upon the other, the pace of the slowest can dictate the speed of the whole transaction. When a problem occurs along the chain, it affects all those in it. Obviously, the longer the chain, the greater the risk that one of the 'links' will collapse.

Buying a newly built house

Your solicitor or conveyancer must check:

- that the contract provides for the house to be properly built to specification with appropriate services laid on
- that the boundaries of the property are as shown on the plan
- that you are granted all necessary rights, such as rights of way and drainage
- that the builder has made an agreement with the appropriate local authority to construct the roads and that, when they are built, the authority will take them over and maintain them
- that the builder has a similar agreement to deal with drainage and sewerage
- what restrictions operate: these are often connected with the appearance of the estate – for example, no parked caravans in front gardens, no cutting down of trees, no swimming-pools; there may be rules about keeping animals: e.g. forbidding the keeping of chickens or a pig. You may have to get the developer's approval before building an extension – even long after the estate has been finished
- whether the original planning permission for the estate contained conditions which restrict or remove the normal permitted development rights.

Registered or unregistered property

Where the property is 'registered', the details of the ownership of the land and most of the burdens affecting it are kept at the Land Registry.

(A 'burden' is an obligation affecting land or buildings, usually restricting the way they can be used.) The information is divided into three parts: the property register, the proprietorship register and the charges register. There will also be an official site plan of the property, known as 'the filed plan'. Until 13 October 2003, the owner was provided with a land certificate containing an exact copy of the entries on the register. (If the property was subject to a mortgage, the mortgage lender was provided with a charge certificate instead.) Since 13 October 2003, land and charge certificates have been abolished and existing ones no longer have any significance. A buyer becoming registered after that date will instead receive a title information document, which will also contain details of the register entries. It used to be necessary on the completion of a purchase for the land or charge certificate to be handed over to the buyer. This is no longer the case, nor is it necessary for the title information document to be handed over. However, these may be offered to the buyer on completion as they are of no further use to the seller.

A buyer can get the information about ownership of the property (and matters such as other people's rights over it) from the Land Registry. This information is now publicly available. You do not need the seller's permission. If you do not know the registered title number, send the appropriate application for a search of the index (formerly called an index map search) to the relevant office of the Land Registry. There is no fee for this. Once you know the title number, send the appropriate application for official copies to the Land Registry (fee £4) and you will be sent details of everything that is registered against the property, along with (for a further £4) a plan showing its location. This could well be useful if you want to find out more about the property before you make an offer. The relevant form can be downloaded from the Land Registry website at *www.landreg.gov.uk*. If you just want to look at the details of ownership, this can be done online (on payment of a fee of £2 per title) using Land Registry Online at *www.landregistryonline.gov.uk*.

Transferring registered property is easier than unregistered – some people do it themselves without a solicitor or licensed conveyancer. Not all the land in England and Wales is yet registered, but in all areas registration is now compulsory. This means that a property either has a registered title or, when the house is next sold, leased (for over seven years) or inherited under a will the title has to be registered by the new owner (known as 'first registration'). (In Scotland, registration started during 1980.)

If the house you are buying does not yet have a registered title, ownership is proved by production of a copy of the title deeds going back at least 15 years. This will have to be checked by your solicitor/conveyancer, who will deal with it as a purchase of unregistered property and, when you become the new owner, will register your ownership at the Land Registry. There is a two-month time limit for lodging the documents at the Land Registry after completion. The Registry may take longer than you would wish – or expect – to record the change (often many weeks).

A fee is charged by the Land Registry for registration, based on the price paid for the house – see page 23. These Land Registry fees are always payable by the buyer.

Joint ownership

Where two or more people buy a house together – for example, husband and wife, or brother and sister – they should consult with their solicitor/conveyancer as early as possible as to which of the two kinds of joint ownership is more appropriate.

- **Joint tenancy** (the word 'tenancy' has nothing to do with rented property in this context) – under this arrangement there exists a 'right of survivorship'. When one dies, the survivor will automatically inherit the other's share. This may be a suitable arrangement for husband and wife, but may often not suit other kinds of shared ownership – e.g. two couples buying a house together.
- **Tenancy in common** – here, each joint owner is able to dispose of his or her share as he or she wishes by will. This form of joint ownership is generally chosen by co-owners who are not married and who prefer to retain this independence. Joint tenants always hold the property in equal shares but tenants in common can have unequal shares in the property – for example, to reflect their different contributions to the price.

It is easy for a joint tenancy to be converted into a tenancy in common at any time – simply by one co-owner giving written notice to the other – but the reverse is more complicated and would need a lawyer.

Buying extra items

Your solicitor/conveyancer needs to know the details of any items in the house which you have agreed to buy as an extra, as well as what fixtures and fittings you have agreed with the seller are to be included in the sale.

If the TransAction Protocol (see page 247) procedures are being used you will be provided with a comprehensive fixtures, fittings and contents form. This will set out in detail which items are and are not included in the sale. This should avoid any misunderstanding as to whether items such as light fittings and curtain rails are included in the sale. If TransAction is not being used, your conveyancer should still ensure that clarification is obtained. This topic is covered in detail in Chapter 4.

Boundary walls and fences

It is most important to know where the boundaries lie before you commit yourself to buying a property. Boundary disputes are difficult to resolve and generate great animosity between neighbours.

Boundary hints

- A line of trees or a hedge at the side or far end of the garden does not necessarily indicate the limit of the property: it could be within or beyond that line.
- Ask to see the plan. Check (or ask your surveyor to investigate) exactly where the boundaries lie. If necessary, measure on the ground and compare the results with any dimensions given in the title documents or plan.
- The deeds are not always a help. Some deeds have no plan at all or are imprecise about where the boundaries actually are. Sometimes, the boundary is not where the deeds say it should be.
- Even established boundaries may not be accurate. Mistakes can be carried forward. Neighbours sometimes make their own adjustments without regularising the position in their deeds.
- Traditionally, 'T' marks on a boundary line drawn on an original site plan indicate that that particular wall or fence belongs to the owner of the property inside which the 'T' mark appears.
- The deeds may say, or there may be other evidence, that a fence or wall on the boundary is on your land – in which case, you own it.

- If the house is registered at the Land Registry there will always be a plan but even this is not guaranteed to be accurate: it is still important to check for discrepancies.

Responsibility for boundaries

- Some deeds specify clearly what your obligations are as far as fencing is concerned (the type, or minimum or maximum height).
- If nothing is stated, you may not need to have a fence at all (unless one would be necessary to prevent damage or injury to others).
- Walls dividing semi-detached or terraced properties with supports on both sides are generally regarded as belonging to both, with repairs being a joint expense.
- Where there is a fence which you are not obliged to have, you generally cannot be made to repair it, but if it is likely to fall on your neighbour's land it is up to you to make it safe or remove it.
- If you have to go on to a neighbour's land to repair a fence or wall, you will normally need permission unless the right is granted to you in your or his/her deeds.
- Sometimes you are not allowed to fence. Some new estates, for example, impose restrictions against front gardens being divided, and the original planning permission may have been granted on this basis. Corner properties may have special provisions about 'line(s) of sight' for traffic.
- Under general planning law, you may not erect a fence more than one metre high in front of a house, nor over two metres high at the rear or side.

If there are doubts about the position of boundaries or the obligation to repair them it may be necessary to investigate further and obtain additional evidence, such as a sworn statement from someone familiar with the property. When boundaries are unclear, you can get the seller to pay for insurance in case of future disputes – ask your solicitor. Issues should be dealt with before contracts are exchanged. It is the seller's responsibility. Buyers should not be involved in the expense of sorting out these matters.

The Access to Neighbouring Land Act 1992

This Act gives the courts power to award access for certain necessary repairs and other works. An access order will be made only if it is impossible – or extremely difficult – to carry out the works without gaining access on to neighbouring land. The new legal provisions are extremely complex and would undoubtedly be costly to invoke. It is therefore sensible to ensure that you buy a house which either already has rights of access over the neighbouring property to carry out repairs, or does not need them.

The conveyancing procedure: buying

The draft contract

It is the seller's solicitor/conveyancer who prepares a draft contract. He or she will produce this from the information to hand about the transaction (price, names of the parties and so on) and from the seller's title deeds. With the draft contract there will also be sent a 'package' consisting of a copy of the title deeds (or entries on the Land Register if the ownership is registered). If the solicitors are operating the TransAction Protocol (see page 247) the seller's solicitor will also send various other documents.

The job of the buyer's solicitor/conveyancer is to make whatever searches and enquiries may be necessary to ensure that there are no points which might affect your decision to buy, or your later enjoyment of the property. One of the main things that has to be done when you buy a house is to make sure that the seller really owns it and has the right to sell it.

With unregistered land, the solicitor/conveyancer has to check on all previous transactions which affect the title every time property changes hands – matters such as sales, mortgages, the granting of rights over the property, rights of way, drainage. This is done by investigating a copy (prepared by the seller or his or her solicitor/conveyancer) of the title deeds covering at least the previous 15 years (and often much longer). If the property is registered, it is a more simple matter of examining the registered details (office copy entries).

Ask your solicitor/conveyancer to send you a copy of the draft contract if it has not been sent to you. If the seller has agreed to pay for remedial work, or to undertake any other obligations to you, make sure it gets put into the contract. Do not leave anything to chance. Human nature being what it is, people forget their promises once they achieve what they want! At this stage, the contract is only a draft because your solicitor/conveyancer has to be given the opportunity to check, change or add anything as a result of the enquiries and searches made, plus anything you may have told him or her.

Local searches

These are standard forms of questions; enquiries (called local searches) are sent off to the local authority, the answers to which may show, for example, whether there are any plans to build a trunk road nearby, or whether there are any serious defects which the local authority would require to be put right.

Note that these searches are mainly against the house itself. They do not show up information about nearby property (except matters like road proposals). If there is a derelict building or any vacant land nearby ask your solicitor/conveyancer to make a search on that too or go to the local authority and find out if anything is registered against it (such as planning permission for development or compulsory purchase).

Water and other searches

A separate set of standard questions is sent to the water authority dealing with ownership of drains, etc.

Your solicitor/conveyancer should consider carrying out other searches and enquiries if appropriate (there are many to choose from,

---

The Law Society's TransAction Protocol

This Law Society scheme is used by many solicitors. The seller's solicitor determines whether it is used. If it is used, the seller's solicitor provides a package containing the following:

- the draft contract
- copies of earlier title deeds (if unregistered) or official copies of the entries in the register (if registered)
- a special form of preliminary enquiries called the property information form
- a fixtures, fittings and contents form, listing all the fixtures and fittings which are included in the price and those which will be removed by the seller. The idea behind the scheme is to get the paperwork under way quickly at the beginning of the transaction.

---

such as coal mining, commons searches etc.). These will depend on the location of the house.

Preliminary enquiries

Another set of standard questions, known as 'preliminary enquiries' or 'enquiries before contract', concerns the property itself, boundaries, whether there are any neighbour disputes, restrictions and so on. These are sent to the seller's solicitor/conveyancer with such additional questions as the buyer's solicitor/conveyancer thinks appropriate for the particular transaction, so as to get as much information about the property as possible before exchanging contracts. If the TransAction protocol is being used, the seller will normally supply answers to similar questions using a 'Property Information Form'.

Finalising the draft contract

It is essential that the contract contains everything that has been agreed between buyer and seller. Make sure you tell your solicitor/conveyancer about all agreements you have made with the seller.

Agreeing amendments to a draft contract can take time if the contract goes back and forth between the two professionals. Rather than sit at home fretting, ask what is going on if delays or silences are occurring. But do not telephone daily – that would not help matters and you may find yourself paying for the time you take up.

Exchange of contracts

Exchange of contracts means that the documents are physically (or are deemed to be) swapped over. If you are buying, a contract with your signature goes to the seller's solicitor/conveyancer, who sends an identical contract signed by the seller to your solicitor/conveyancer.

Once contracts are exchanged, you (and the people selling to or buying from you) are locked into a legal agreement from which neither side can withdraw, unless exceptional circumstances apply.

Exchange is therefore a crucial point in the proceedings. A good solicitor/conveyancer will take time before you reach the stage of exchange of contracts to see you at the office and go through all the paperwork with you. Do not be afraid to ask questions on any points that are still unclear. It is important to make sure that everything is right now. It will be too late to change things after exchange of contracts.

Contracts should not be exchanged until:

- preliminary enquiries and local searches are completed
- any surveyor's report has been made and the facts accepted
- the source of funding is settled: a mortgage loan is offered in writing (and all conditions can be complied with)
- the deposit of 10 per cent of the purchase price (or less, by agreement) is available
- all terms are agreed between the parties. If there are matters which still have not been agreed it is not wise to leave matters to chance or goodwill. In a dispute, the contract will be relied on. If terms are missed out they cannot be put back once contracts are exchanged.
- the date for completion (i.e. the date to finalise the deal) has been agreed. (Completion day is often about two weeks from exchange of contracts, but this period can be longer or shorter, depending on the wishes of the people concerned.)

Buyer's exchange of contracts checklist

- Survey report received and in order?
- Mortgage offer received and in order?
- Other finances calculated and in place?
- Deposit amount agreed and available?
- Removers lined up?
- Insurance (life and property) arranged and ready to be put in force?
- Completion date agreed with seller/own buyer/lender/all parties in chain?
- Terms of contract finalised and checked?

Contracts are then exchanged. There are two identical copies of the contract – one signed by the seller and one by the buyer. It is only when these documents have been exchanged that the two parties become legally bound to the transaction. Exchange of contracts now usually takes place between the seller's solicitor/conveyancer and yours by telephone, using procedures laid down by the Law Society.

After exchange of contracts, a buyer no longer needs to worry about gazumping or a seller whether the buyer really will go through with the deal. But it also means that you cannot change your mind. You have to buy (or sell) even if you lose your job or you discover some dreadful defect in the house you are buying.

Between exchange of contracts and completion

After exchange of contracts considerable activity takes place between solicitors. It is the time when the transfer document is prepared. If the land is already registered this will be called a 'transfer', but if the land is not yet registered your solicitor/conveyancer may prepare a 'conveyance' or a special form of transfer.

The transfer must be signed by the seller and almost always by the buyer. This time will also be used to finalise the mortgage arrangements. Your solicitor/conveyancer (or that of the lender, if separate) will prepare the mortgage documents and arrange for the loan to be available on completion. If you are having an endowment mortgage, the life insurance policy must be in force by the completion date (it is best to put this on risk as soon as contracts are exchanged).

Final searches and enquiries will be carried out. Your solicitor/conveyancer will check whether anything is registered against the seller at the Land Registry (if the house is registered) or at the Land Charges Registry (if the house is not yet registered). The sort of things which might show up are undisclosed mortgages or disputes.

If you are buying from a company, your solicitor/conveyancer will make a company search. This will ensure that the company is still legally in existence and that there are no loans secured against the property. The solicitor/conveyancer will also finalise the arrangements for completion. Nowadays, completion normally takes place through the post to save time (and money). The arrangements for this will be put in place, backed up by Law Society rules to ensure all goes well.

Just prior to completion

Make sure you remain available to your solicitor/conveyancer in the weeks leading up to completion. There will be documents to sign and last-minute matters to arrange. You will not have to do any of the legal work but you will be needed to pay any sums due in sufficient time for cheques to clear before completion. This will include not only the balance of the money needed to buy, but also Land Registry fees and stamp duty. Most solicitors/conveyancers ask to be paid their own fee before completion.

It is most important to make sure before completion that outstanding obligations (e.g. remedial work) have been carried out in accordance with the contract. If not, you may have considerable difficulty in enforcing the contract once completion has taken place.

You should now be dealing with the logistics of moving. See Chapter 9.

Completion

This is the day when:

- the buyer pays the seller the balance of the price for the house (usually through solicitors or conveyancers)
- the deeds transferring ownership are handed over to the buyer (through solicitors or conveyancers) and arrangements are made to pay off outstanding mortgages owed by the seller
- the seller *must* move out
- the keys are handed over to the buyer.

After completion

A lot of tidying up has to be done by the buyer's solicitor/conveyancer after completion, including:

- notifying the lender that completion has taken place
- giving other notifications (where appropriate) that completion has happened – such as to life insurance companies (where there is an endowment mortgage) or to the freeholder (where a leasehold has been transferred)
- the Land Transaction Return, giving details of the financial side of the transaction, is submitted to the Inland Revenue together with any stamp duty payable
- registering the change of ownership at the Land Registry
- sending you a 'completion statement', giving a complete financial summary of the transaction
- (and finally) sending you the bill if this was not done earlier.

The conveyancing procedure: selling

The same procedure takes place as under 'Buying' but from a different perspective.

Contract

The seller's solicitor/conveyancer will obtain the title deeds from the current lender (if the house is mortgaged) and from these prepare the draft contract. If the TransAction procedures are being used, together with the contract will be sent the answers to standard questions on the property and a detailed list of items to be included or excluded. Your solicitor/conveyancer will contact you and check that all information given is accurate. Make sure you give full and correct information. If in doubt, take advice at this stage. If difficulties appear only at a late stage (for instance, because your solicitor/conveyancer did not know that there was a domestic dispute in your family), you could be liable for compensation if completion is delayed. If you have relevant documents (such as planning permissions, or treatment guarantees) these should be sent on to your solicitor/conveyancer.

Once the contract is sent out there may be further queries.

Negative equity

If there is any doubt that the price you sell at will cover the cost of repaying existing mortgages, ask your solicitor/conveyancer to obtain settlement figures (redemption statements) before contracts are exchanged.

Exchange

You may also be buying. It is essential that your transactions tie in. Make sure that the completion date is agreed all round. Make sure too that your finances are in order before you exchange contracts.

Completion

You must move all your possessions out of the house (except those which you have agreed to leave). It is a courtesy to clean the house before you go. Your solicitor/conveyancer will receive the purchase money, pay off existing mortgages and account to you for the balance after paying all expenses (or put the balance to your new house if you are buying another).

When things go wrong

Tens of thousands of house sales take place each year. Most of them go virtually without a hitch, but problems can occur very occasionally. These can range from minor irritations to major crises. The following are some of the things that go wrong and how they might be put right.

The seller fails to move out on completion day
If you get any warning that this might happen, instruct your solicitor/conveyancer immediately to hold up the transfer of the money. He or she will take steps to enforce the contract. A 'notice to complete' will be served. This will 'make time of the essence' and legally require the seller to complete the sale within ten working days. If he or she does not, you will be within your rights to withdraw from the transaction. Your solicitor/conveyancer may also advise you on the question of issuing legal proceedings.

You can claim compensation if you are put to extra expense (e.g. hotel bills) if your move is delayed.

The buyer fails to pay the money due on completion
It goes without saying that you should not let the buyer move in. Once again, a notice to complete will be served, and other legal steps may be necessary to enforce the contract.

The money fails to get through
Much of the conveyancing process relies on high technology. It has been known for the computers operated by banks or building societies to fail, locking millions of pounds into the system while the problems are sorted out. There is very little that can be done in this situation, except to do the British thing and have a cup of tea while the problems are sorted out. Solicitors/conveyancers can often rely on local goodwill to get clients moved, and then pick up the financial pieces later.

The seller has taken away things which were included in the contract
Depending on what these are, a claim for the return of the original items (and the costs of re-installing them) can be made or the seller can be sued for compensation.

You find that you have not got what you bargained for

If the property is in worse condition than you expected, or there is a major defect in it, your remedy will depend on the circumstances:

- if it is something which should have been revealed in your survey, you could have a claim against your surveyor
- if it is a new property with a Zurich Municipal or NHBC guarantee, follow the claims procedures available under these schemes
- if the problem is the result of false information, you may have a claim against the estate agent (under the Property Misdescriptions Act) or against the seller.

But, except in the cases of new houses, there is generally no guarantee about the state and condition of a house. This underlines the need to have proper checks carried out before you exchange contracts.

You find that there are legal problems

It must be stressed that the conveyancing procedure cannot be certain to unearth all problems, but it should protect you against most.

If you have received poor service but have not suffered financially you may have a right of complaint either to the Office for the Supervision of Solicitors (OSS)★ (complaints against solicitors) or to the Council for Licensed Conveyancers (CLC)★ (complaints against licensed conveyancers). Both have disciplinary powers. The OSS can order a refund of fees and/or compensation. If you are not satisfied with the way in which the OSS has handled your complaint you may complain further to the Legal Services Ombudsman★.

If your solicitor or licensed conveyancer has not delivered the required level of service, and you have suffered financially as a result, you will have a compensation claim. This could happen, for instance, if steps are not taken to ensure that the seller's mortgage is repaid on completion, or if the solicitor/conveyancer fails to find out about (or tell you about) a restriction which prevents you using the house as a home.

Solicitors and licensed conveyancers are required by law to be covered by negligence insurance. Neither the OSS nor the CLC will handle negligence claims. In such circumstances, seek advice from an independent solicitor. The Law Society★ has a 'negligence panel' of solicitors prepared to take on cases against other solicitors. They will offer a free preliminary consultation of one hour, after which normal solicitors' rates apply. Contact them through the OSS.

The solicitor/conveyancer defaults and keeps your money

This is fortunately very rare. If it happens, take immediate steps to contact an independent solicitor. The Law Society administers a fund (paid for by solicitors) to compensate clients who have lost out in these circumstances. The CLC operates a similar scheme.

Other legal matters

Your will

If you have become a property owner for the first time, it is important to make a will or amend an existing one, making clear what you wish to be done with your estate after your death. It is not too difficult for a person with straightforward affairs to draw up a will but it is essential that this is done correctly. *Wills and Probate* (published by Which? Books*) explains how to draw up your own will.

If you think your case is at all complicated, it would be worth consulting a solicitor (also if you have moved to or from Scotland). Some solicitors will make a deal with you over fees if you make a will at the same time as you move if the firm is handling the conveyancing.

Keep your will in a safe place – and tell your executors where this is.

Tax

Capital gains tax

Normally, you do not have to worry about capital gains tax (CGT) when you are selling your home. So long as you have lived in the house throughout your ownership and have lived in (or owned) no other house as your principal residence, no tax will be payable. But tax might be payable if, for instance, you have spent time abroad and let the home to tenants, or if you have not actually occupied the home (even if you owned no other). You might also have to pay tax if part of the house was used for business purposes, you have more than one lodger or the house and the land sold with it was more than an acre and a quarter (about the size of a football pitch).

Capital gains tax is payable only on the net profit on the sale (after knocking off the costs of buying and selling and improvements – other than things such as redecoration). And you may be able to deduct various allowances and reliefs (e.g. indexation allowances for gains due to inflation and taper relief which rewards you for holding on to assets for a long time). In addition, the first £7,900 (in 2003-04) of taxable gains is exempt. Tax is payable at your income tax rate on remaining gain.

There are specific exemptions to having to pay CGT. For instance, you can overlap two houses if you buy your new home before selling your old one but for no more than two years.

Inheritance tax

Buying a home can have a big impact on your estate (i.e. what you own less what you owe), so this is a good time to review the inheritance tax position in the event of your death. Once the value of your estate, plus certain gifts made in the seven years before death, exceeds the tax-free limit (£255,000 in 2003-04), inheritance tax at 40 per cent is payable on the excess. Some bequests and lifetime gifts – e.g. those between husband and wife (but not unmarried partners) – are always tax-free.

Often, husband and wife leave everything to each other. But, although this avoids tax when the first of the couple dies, there could be a big bill when the second dies. One solution is to spread assets between husband and wife so each can make maximum use of their tax-free slice when leaving assets to other people – e.g. children.

Make sure that any life insurance policies you arrange at this time are written 'in trust' so that they do not form part of your estate. If the value of your estate is up against the inheritance tax threshold, it would be worth getting advice from a solicitor or accountant.

Credit blacklisting

In the past, home buyers have found that they are unable to obtain credit because of debts run up by previous owners or occupiers of the property. When a potential lender checked with a credit reference agency, details of everyone who had lived in the property in recent years and their bad debts would show up. Since 1993 this has no longer been the case because only information about the person applying for credit and people in the house closely associated with him or her can be given. However, this will not protect new owners from being harassed by debt collectors trying to obtain payment of bills left unpaid by previous owners or occupiers.

Normally, a credit reference agency will not give you information about an individual or an address, unless you live at the address. If you are worried that there may be a problem with the seller, tell your solicitor. You have no right to be given credit, but if you are refused a loan you are entitled to know which credit reference agency has been used by your lender, as long as you request the information within 28 days of the decision. Once you have the details of the credit reference agency you can (on payment of a small fee) request details of the information it holds on you. If any of it is incorrect, you have a right to have it corrected.

Another source of information about credit is the Registry of County Court Judgments★. For a small fee you can check against any name and address.

Chapter 11

Doing your own conveyancing

You would be unwise to attempt to do your own conveyancing if the property you are buying or selling is:

- not freehold or not registered
- not in England or Wales
- not a house
- part of a property. Special considerations apply where part of a garden or house is sold, or where part of the property is let to tenants. In such situations, always use a solicitor
- sold at auction
- not wholly occupied by the seller
- being sold to you as new by a builder or developer
- a 'hybrid transaction' – housing associations and other bodies have developed schemes to help first-time buyers get a foot on the house-owning ladder. These usually involve complex documentation which is part freehold and part leasehold
- being sold by a divorcing or separating couple. Buying or selling a house in these circumstances requires specialist skill and knowledge
- not through a solicitor or licensed conveyancer. You should be very careful if you are dealing with either an unlicensed conveyancer or a private individual acting for him/herself. There is nothing wrong with two unqualified people handling their own transactions, but the scope for problems does increase greatly.

If you are getting a mortgage, the cost saving may not be great: you will still have to pay the lender's solicitor's charge. However, there may be a saving in the time the transaction takes.

Usually, your own solicitor will do the lender's work as well and charge an all-in fee. If you do your own conveyancing, you will be charged at a higher rate for the lender's solicitor's work. Once e-conveyancing becomes possible (see page 233), d-i-y conveyancing will involve trekking backwards and forwards to the District Land Registry in order to access the secure Internet service. This will make d-i-y conveyancing more unpopular and less common.

Getting started

To have a chance of doing your own conveyancing successfully you must acquire as much knowledge as you can about what you are doing. You will need to have knowledge of the law and the procedures and will have to be able to devote time to the exercise. You will need to be on hand during the working day and will probably have to travel around quite a bit. The protocols which are available to solicitors and licensed conveyancers (such as exchange of contracts by telephone, completion through the post) will not be available to you.

You should have access to a daytime telephone or a mobile phone and preferably also a fax machine and computer – most solicitors and licensed conveyancers are on email. You should also adopt basic office techniques – have your letters typed (and keep copies), keep a file, and so on.

This book contains background information about house transactions. Read it and become familiar with it. *The Which? Guide to Doing Your Own Conveyancing* (Which? Books*) contains full details of the process and legal principles.

You will need to get hold of some forms from law stationers (such as Oyez). These can be ordered by telephone or over the Internet.

In each section of this chapter you will be told what forms you need.

The steps to take

The stages have been outlined earlier in the book. In practice this converts into the following action. **This is not a detailed guide to doing it yourself and you should not use it as such**. It is simply a checklist of the steps that are taken in a normal, straightforward transaction, where the land is already registered.

Buying

The forms you will need are:

- CON 29 (local search) (2 copies)
- LLC1 (1 copy)
- Water search CON 29DW
- Preliminary enquiries (2 copies)
- Land Registry search form OS1
- Land Registry application to register AP1 (for registered land) or FR1 (for unregistered)
- Requisitions on title (2 copies)
- Land Registry transfer form TR1 (3 copies) (mandatory for registered land, optional for unregistered)
- Inland Revenue form SDLT1.

Step 1
Once terms have been agreed, the legal side of house buying begins in earnest. Your first step is to write to the seller's solicitor asking to be sent a draft contract.

Step 2
Make the mortgage application. Tell the lender that you will be doing it yourself and ask what the requirements will be.

Step 3
Arrange survey.

Step 4
The seller's solicitors will send you:

- copies of the draft contract
- official copies of Land Registry entries.

As part of the TransAction procedure you may also receive the following:

- property information form
- copies of relevant documents such as NHBC★ (National House Building Council) guarantee, planning permissions etc.
- fixtures, fittings and contents form.

Step 5
Acknowledge them. Send in your local and other searches as soon as possible.

You should already have been told either by the estate agents or the solicitors for the seller which is the relevant local authority. In London, it will be one of the London boroughs. Outside London it will be a council of District Council status.

Step 6
Carry out water search.

Step 7
Decide whether you want to make other searches or enquiries; if so, get them under way.

Step 8
Check all the documents. Go through every detail of and approve (or make changes to) the contract and send one copy back to the seller's solicitor. At the same time make preliminary enquiries (or extra preliminary enquiries if you have already received the answers to the standard questions on the property information form).

Step 9
Check the plan with the contract or official copy entries against the property itself.

Step 10
Check very thoroughly each of the following as they come in: the result of your local searches, the answers to preliminary enquiries and all other searches and enquiries you make. Query and resolve any problems that arise.

Step 11
Deal with the requirements of your lender's solicitors.

Step 12
Discuss and agree a completion date with your seller.

Step 13
Agree the amount of deposit you will pay on exchange of contracts.

Step 14
Check survey result and, if appropriate, have the contract amended to deal with any problems.

Step 15
Make sure that: your survey is satisfactory; your mortgage offer is received and has no conditions which would cause problems (including insurance conditions if you are having an endowment mortgage: you will need to have received acceptance terms for any new endowment policies required for the mortgage); your searches disclose no problems; your answers to preliminary enquiries are full, detailed and accurate; the amount of deposit you can pay is acceptable.

Step 16
Make sure that the terms of the contract are agreed, with all detail completed. Both parts of the contract must be identically worded.

Step 17
All buyers sign the contract. Agree with the seller's solicitor how contracts are to be exchanged, either through the post or in person. Exchange contracts, sending (or taking) the signed contract together with the agreed deposit to the seller's solicitor.

Step 18
Put property insurance (and life insurance if applicable) on cover.

Step 19
After exchange of contracts you will receive the contract signed by the seller.

Step 20
Confirm your removal arrangements.

Step 21
Notify the lender's solicitor of exchange of contracts and remind him or her of the completion date. Deal with all requirements as soon as possible.

Step 22
Prepare the transfer and send two copies to the seller's solicitor for

approval. At the same time send two copies of requisitions on title to confirm the arrangements for completion.

Step 23
Carry out final searches at Land Registry (£4) using form OS1 (free from the Land Registry).

Step 24
Receive back transfer from the seller's solicitor approved/amended. If you agree to the amendments, prepare fair copy (engrossment – see Glossary). In most cases the buyer needs to sign and have his or her signature witnessed.

Step 25
Send signed transfer back to the seller's solicitor and ask the seller to sign in readiness for completion.

Step 26
Check the result of final searches and ask the seller's solicitors to clear off any entries revealed (not previously disclosed).

Step 27
A few days before completion date, make final arrangements for the finances. If you are having a mortgage, the lender's solicitor will attend on completion and will need to be assured that you will pay the necessary balance plus all expenses (such as stamp duty and Land Registry fees).

If you are not having a mortgage, arrange for a bank draft to be issued (a personal cheque will not be acceptable). Check that even a bank draft will be accepted by the seller's solicitor. A bank draft represents guaranteed funds but these still take several days to reach the solicitor's bank account. The solicitor will need to have 'cleared funds' in his or her account so that he or she can account to the client for the money – or pay it on for a connected transaction. In order to achieve this, you may be asked to arrange for your bank to transfer the money to the solicitor's bank account by the computerised system (known as CHAPS) for transferring funds. It will cost you approximately £30 + VAT. You would have to obtain from the solicitor an undertaking not to account to his or her client for the money until completion had taken place. If you do use a bank draft, keep it safe. It is virtually impossible to 'stop' a bank draft.

Step 28
The day before completion make an appointment with the seller's solicitor to complete the purchase.

Step 29
On completion day (if not having a mortgage), attend in good time for the appointment. **Receive:** the title deeds and other documents (e.g. the originals of all guarantees, certificates, planning permissions, building control consents etc.) in accordance with details previously supplied to you; the transfer (check that it is signed by the sellers) which should be dated the day of completion; an undertaking from the solicitor to pay off all outstanding mortgages (or form DS1 discharges in respect of them all); the keys. Note that until 13 October 2003, the owner of land registered at the Land Registry was provided with a land certificate containing an exact copy of the entries on the register. (If the property was subject to a mortgage, the mortgage lender was provided with a charge certificate instead.) Since 13 October 2003, land and charge certificates have been abolished and existing ones no longer have any significance. A buyer becoming registered after that date will instead receive a title information document, which will also contain details of the register entries. It used to be necessary on the completion of a purchase for the land or charge certificate to be handed over to the buyer. This is no longer the case, nor is it necessary for the title information document to be handed over. However, it may be that these are offered to you on completion, as they are of no further use to the seller. **Hand over**: a bank draft for the balance of the money (if not transferring under the CHAPS system – see Step 27).

If having a mortgage you may still need to attend to provide the balance of the money, collect the keys etc.

Step 30
Move in!

Step 31
If stamp duty is payable, you will need to send the Land Transaction Return, giving details of the financial side of the transaction, to the

Inland Revenue together with any stamp duty payable. Note that it is no longer necessary to send the transfer deed to the Revenue. The Revenue will in return send you a certificate to show that you have paid the appropriate duty. You should send this to the Land Registry (Step 32). Without it the transaction cannot be registered and you will not become the owner of the property.

Step 32

Before the expiry date of the priority period shown in your Land Registry search (and allowing for delays in the post), complete AP1 application to register and send off with the appropriate documents (the land or charge certificate, form DS1, if applicable, the result of your Land Registry search, the Inland Revenue certificate, the transfer and correct fee) to the Land Registry office which covers the property.

Step 33

Deal with any queries raised by the Land Registry within the time limit set.

Step 34

If there is no mortgage, receive back from the Land Registry the title information document, showing you to be the registered proprietor – check it very carefully.

Selling

The forms you will need are:

- Contract (2 copies)
- Application for Land Registry official copy entries form OC1
- Form DS1 discharge if you have a mortgage.

Step 1

Send off for official copy entries (form OC1 + fee of £4) to the relevant Land Registry.

Step 2

If you have a mortgage, find out from your lender what procedure will be required for releasing the title deeds on completion (if you are selling unregistered land).

Step 3

On receipt of official copy entries, prepare contract and send two copies to buyer's solicitors, along with office copy entries and copy documents referred to in these entries. Once the sellers' packs become compulsory, all the necessary information should be contained within the pack, which will have to be prepared by the seller at this stage – see page 144.

Step 4

Answer the preliminary enquiries raised by the buyer's solicitors and send copies of accompanying documentation.

Step 5

Deal with the amendments to the contract suggested by the buyer's solicitors and agree its terms. All sellers must sign the contract.

Step 6

Agree method of holding the deposit. The buyer's solicitor will not agree that you hold it. There are three possibilities: open an account in the joint names of yourself and the buyer's solicitor; or allow the buyer's solicitor to hold it as a stakeholder; if you are buying a house simultaneously, the buyer's solicitor may agree to pay the deposit direct to the solicitor acting for your seller.

Step 7

Agree a completion date (which may need to tie in with your purchase).

Step 8

If you have a mortgage, find out from your lenders what their requirements will be for the repayment of the mortgage and release of the deeds to your buyer. Communicate these to the buyer's solicitor.

Step 9

Exchange contracts.

Step 10

The buyer's solicitor will send you a draft transfer and requisitions on title in duplicate.

Step 11

Approve (or amend) and return to the buyer's solicitor the draft transfer, along with answers to the requisitions on title.

Step 12

When the engrossment copy of the transfer is sent to you, all sellers must sign it in the presence of an independent witness in readiness for completion. Do not date it yet.

Step 13

Make arrangements for completion. **Hand over** to the buyer's solicitor the transfer, all other relevant deeds and documents and, of course, the keys. If you have a mortgage, you should complete a form DS1 discharge. Completion will either have to take place at the lender's office or will have to be attended by the lender's solicitor. Receive from the buyer's solicitor the balance of the purchase money.

Step 14

Move out.

Chapter 12

Auctions

An estate agent may advertise or give you details of a house which is going to be sold by auction. The method of sale in this case differs fundamentally from a sale 'by private treaty' in that when the house is 'knocked down' to a bidder, he or she exchanges contracts there and then with the auctioneer and cannot back out of the purchase later. The buyer is legally bound to it, even if he or she were to flee from the sale room without signing anything.

Buying a house at auction

Before the day of the auction, the would-be buyer needs to have taken all the steps which are normally taken before exchange of contracts: made the preliminary enquiries and local searches, checked the title documents, had a survey carried out, and completed the organisation of his or her finances.

Because an auction is likely to attract a number of interested house-buyers all needing the answers to a number of questions about the property, a set of particulars more detailed than usual is prepared by the agent. This normally takes the form of a brochure, sometimes with photographs, containing full details of the house itself, with additional facts about the tenure, possession, fixtures and fittings, council tax band, and Special Conditions of Sale. These, along with the Memorandum of Agreement (contained in the brochure) are the equivalent of a contract for sale by private treaty. The problem is that there is no scope for negotiating its terms.

The price of the property

Check whether one of the conditions of sale is that the seller is selling 'subject to reserve price' – this figure is not usually disclosed, although the agent may be able to give you a guideline figure. The auctioneer may, during the bidding, use a phrase like 'I'm going to sell this property', as an indication that the reserve price has been reached. If the bidding does not reach the reserve, the auctioneer withdraws the property. If you were among the last bidders for a property that is withdrawn, tell the agent afterwards at what figure you are prepared to buy – the seller may accept your offer.

The publicity for the auction may contain the proviso 'unless previously sold'. In this case, the seller's agent is open to offers and is prepared to negotiate a sale by private treaty before, and instead of, the auction. The seller will still, however, expect to sell on the auction contract so you may have only a few days (or hours) in which to make enquiries and raise funds.

Check straight away whether the intention really is to go to auction; it may be more of an incentive for offers than an intention to go to auction and you may lose your chance by waiting for auction day.

Some properties have to go to auction for legal reasons connected with proving that a proper price has been obtained when it is sold by executors or creditors. If the property is one of these, you will see a phrase such as 'sold by order of executors or trustees'. Do not make a prior offer as this may colour the reserve price.

Before and at the auction (buying)

- Study the agent's brochure extremely carefully, reading all the small print. There may be conditions or disclaimers which would make the property unsuitable. Look for mention of any planning restrictions or refusals, in case you would want to make any alterations or improvements.
- View the house in the normal way and be sure that it is what you want. Remember that you cannot back out after the auction.
- As early as possible, send to your solicitor or conveyancer the brochure with all the details, and arrange for him or her to carry out the usual enquiries and searches and check the title before the day of the auction. Sometimes the seller's solicitor will carry out the searches and send a copy to yours. Arrange to have a survey and a valuation done and to get the results before the auction.
- Fix your price limit, and complete arrangements for the necessary finance for the purchase before the day of the auction. A building

society or other lender will have to inspect and value the property in the usual way before making an offer of a mortgage.

Resolve not to get carried away during the bidding and so exceed your price limit. If you have doubts about this, appoint someone else to bid for you – such as your solicitor (who will charge for his or her time).

If you are outbid, you lose not only the house but the expenses of a survey and solicitor, just as you do if you fail to buy by private treaty.

If you are successful, you will have to pay 10 per cent of your bid to the auctioneer straight away. The Memorandum of Agreement is countersigned by the seller's agent as confirmation of the sale and acknowledgement of receipt of the 10 per cent deposit. The rest of the transaction then follows in the same way as with a sale by private treaty arrangement. Completion usually takes place 28 days after the auction, and the balance of the purchase money has to be paid then.

If you cannot complete, the seller can sue you for the difference between your agreed bid and what he or she realises on a subsequent sale if this is less, and for any expenses incurred.

Sale by tender

An alternative to an auction is a tender, which invites buyers to put their offer, together with a 10 per cent deposit, in a sealed envelope and return it to the agent by a specified date. A 'Form of Tender' is included in the sale particulars. Check whether the terms of the tender include a contract, in which case you may be bound to the purchase. In other cases, you may still be able to back out after your tender has been accepted.

This method is not normally used for sales of private houses, although a simplified version of it may be, in cases where two or three offers have been made near to or at the asking price.

Selling a house by auction

Having assessed your property in the light of prevailing market conditions, the estate agent may recommend that you should not sell by private treaty (the most usual method) but by auction. Holding an auction creates a situation where the price may be forced upwards by a number of keen bidders.

An agent may find a house difficult to put a price on because of its unusual nature – a converted mill, chapel or barn, for instance – and if it is the only one of its kind in the district, he or she may have no precedent for an accurate valuation. The agent may, therefore, suggest that an auction would be the best way of ensuring that the seller gets a good price for it. Most firms of estate agents are also property auctioneers.

The seller has to pay the auctioneer a percentage of the price reached (2.5 per cent is usual). You should agree beforehand what this will be and whether it will be the same if the property is sold before the auction.

Before the auction (selling)

A brochure, sometimes with a photograph, describing the house in detail and containing the particulars, is prepared and printed.

The estate agent arranges for extensive advertising (for which the seller pays) in order to get the widest possible coverage for the auction. Posters and advertisements in specialist magazines add to the cost.

Discuss what the expenses may amount to (not forgetting photographs for the brochure: a professional photographer may be expensive) and try to agree on limits. You can either agree to pay all the publicity expenses incurred, or fix a set sum for them. Some agents require a lump sum in advance for advertising purposes.

The brochure will include the Special Conditions of Sale (which should be drawn up by your solicitor). It should also include the auction contract with blank spaces for the buyer's name and the purchase price to be inserted.

Some auctions are advertised for three or four weeks, others for two or three months, depending on the kind of property involved. Top-of-the-market houses or investment properties usually attract cash buyers rather than buyers needing a mortgage (which takes time to arrange), so the period leading up to the auction can be shorter.

A good auctioneer/estate agent will consult the client half-way to the auction date on whether further expenditure on advertising is justified in view of the response to date.

If, during the period before the auction, a number of would-be buyers emerge, they will want to have surveys and valuations carried out, and you must be prepared to accommodate these. You will probably also have a larger proportion of 'just curious' viewers as well as genuine potential buyers.

The auctioneer's terms may be that you give his or her firm sole selling rights up to the date of auction and for some specified period afterwards. This means that you would have to pay the commission even if you found a private buyer yourself.

Ask the agent to include in the brochure and advertisement that the auction will take place 'unless previously sold'. This gives you the option of accepting an offer from a private buyer. Many people who would make satisfactory buyers will not come to buy at an auction. The idea of bidding at an auction is a daunting prospect, and a keen purchaser may be induced to make an attractive offer beforehand. Whether or not you decide to let the property 'go to the room' a buyer will, in any case, have to sign the auction contract. A great advantage of this is that it avoids the pre-contract stress of a sale by private treaty.

But consider carefully before agreeing to accept an offer: the auction may still be the best conclusion.

The agent should help you decide what the reserve price should be. This is usually not revealed to bidders: the sale particulars just state 'subject to reserve price'. If the figure is not reached, the auctioneer withdraws the house. A fee may be payable to the auctioneer in place of commission: this should be part of the agreement made between seller and auctioneer.

At the auction

Public auctions are held on a specified day in a particular auction room, hotel or rented hall. A number of properties may be being sold at the same time.

Bidding takes place along similar lines to the auctioning of goods such as antiques or second-hand furniture. The prospective buyers will be people prepared to go through the preliminaries (including the expenses) without any guarantee of getting the house, or people who have enough cash and confidence to risk bidding without prior investigation.

The reserve price not being revealed, it cannot be leaked beforehand. Also, if you think the signs are propitious (lots of enquiries and a rising market), you can lift it a bit. If, on the contrary, signs are bad, you can pare it down a shade.

When the bidding has reached the reserve, it is usual for the auctioneer to let the audience know, particularly if it seems that competition is flagging. This tends to sharpen things up a bit. On the other hand, if it is rolling along in a lively style, he or she will not let on that the reserve has been passed, so that it does not take the steam out of things.

At the fall of the hammer, the successful bidder is committed to buy. He or she has to sign the auction contract and pay 10 per cent of the price there and then to the auctioneer. This should be held by the auctioneer as stakeholder.

The advantage of selling by auction is that there is an immediate binding contract without the uncertainty of the 'subject to contract, subject to survey' stage. The buyer cannot be gazumped and the seller cannot be let down. Completion is usually within four weeks of the auction.

Drawbacks when selling by auction are:

- the cost to the seller is more, sometimes considerably more, than a sale by private treaty – although this may be offset by a better sale price
- the house may be sold before auction (hence, some of the extra cost will have been unnecessary)
- the seller has no choice over who is to be the next owner
- the house could fail to sell if the reserve price is not reached
- the seller must be prepared to get out of the house and give vacant possession 28 days after the auction.

Chapter 13

Buying and selling in Scotland

There are major differences between Scottish and English law, particularly in the law relating to the purchase and sale of houses and flats. If you are moving from England to Scotland, while the practical aspects of the move are much the same as they would be in England, you will find that the legal aspects are very different.

You are strongly advised not to do your own conveyancing or missives, but to employ a solicitor (or a licensed conveyancer, though these are rare in Scotland, where they are known as 'independent qualified conveyancers').

Prices of houses outside the main cities and suburbs in Scotland are generally slightly below the United Kingdom average. Properties in outlying rural areas are relatively inexpensive, less so when they are within easy commuting distance of a major city. But properties in the most sought-after residential areas command high prices.

The inner areas of the major Scottish cities have many good residential areas, where there are many purpose-built old stone tenements (or blocks of flats) and terraced houses.

Virtually all this chapter applies to flats in the same way that it applies to detached, semi-detached or terraced houses. However, in considering whether to buy a flat you would need to look at the condition of the whole tenement, as well as the flat itself, and make sure that the cost of repairing the structure and common parts of the tenement is shared on some equitable basis amongst the proprietors. The word 'house' is used to include a flat unless the text states otherwise.

Tenure

The term freehold is not used in Scotland. Most houses and flats, and indeed most other kinds of heritable property (land and buildings), are owned on 'feudal tenure'. For practical purposes, this means that they are owned absolutely and can be disposed of freely in the same way as freehold land and property in England. The property offered for sale is sometimes referred to in Scotland as 'the feu', pronounced 'few'.

The main distinguishing feature of feudal tenure is that the original developer of the land or estate owner, who is known as the superior, can impose conditions on its future use – for instance, by prohibiting commercial use, extensions or alterations without his or her consent. It is also usual for the superior to require the maintenance of the property in good condition and reinstatement following damage or destruction.

Once feuing conditions have been imposed, they remain in force in perpetuity unless the superior agrees to waive or modify them. Any purchaser will be bound by the feuing conditions, but it may be possible, once he or she has bought the property, to negotiate with the superior for a waiver. Normally, the superior charges a capital payment for agreeing to waive feuing conditions. If a superior refuses to vary unreasonable conditions, or if the existence of a condition impedes some reasonable use of land, the owner (or 'feuar') can apply to the Lands Tribunal for Scotland★ for an order to vary them. A leaflet on land obligations and how they may be varied or discharged, and the fees payable, is obtainable from the Lands Tribunal for Scotland. If you think that you may be justified in seeking such an order, consult your solicitor in the first instance.

In the past, the feuar paid an annual cash sum or 'feuduty' to the superior. Since 1974, the creation of new feuduties has been prohibited, and the feuar is obliged to redeem the feuduty when he or she sells the property. This means that the majority of feuduties have ceased to exist. The feuing conditions, however, still apply even if the feuduty has been redeemed.

The Scottish Parliament enacted the Abolition of Feudal Tenure, etc. (Scotland) Act in 2000. However, this does not come into effect in its entirety until 28 November 2004. Under the new legislation there is a system of outright ownership. Burdens affecting properties in some instances will cease to be enforceable by superiors, who will disappear, but neighbouring proprietors may be able to enforce burdens in some instances. (A burden is an obligation affecting land or buildings, generally restricting the way they can be used.) In addition, the Title Conditions (Scotland) Act 2003, which will also come into effect on 28 November 2004, will modernise and simplify the law relating to burdens affecting property and who can enforce them. The provisions in both these Acts are complex and it will be for your solicitor to advise you as to whether they have any impact on the property you are seeking to buy or sell. These changes in the legislation will not, however, fundamentally change your role in the purchase and sale of your house.

Flats

Flats are owned absolutely on feudal tenure, in the same way as houses, rather than on long leases as is the practice in England; long leases of residential property in Scotland are rare. In the case of flats, the *solum* (the ground on which the block of flats is built), the roof, stairs and common services are normally owned by the proprietors in the block equally or on some other equitable basis. The external walls bounding each flat are owned by the proprietor of it but all the proprietors have an interest to see that they are properly maintained. The title deeds normally set out the basis on which the costs of repairs and maintenance are shared between the various owners.

The Scottish Parliament is at the time of writing considering the terms of a new piece of legislation called the Tenements (Scotland) Bill. This will modernise the law relating to ownership and liability for common parts in a tenement or flatted development, and will also bring in to these developments a proper management system. It is hoped that when the legislation comes into force it will make the law less complex and more fair for home owners.

Solicitors, their role and charges

You will probably need a solicitor as there are very few practising independent qualified conveyancers (the Scottish equivalent of licensed conveyancers). In theory you could do all the legal work yourself, but it is not usually considered practicable to do so, particularly if you need a mortgage.

If you do not know a solicitor, the best recommendation may be that of a friend or colleague who has used one for this type of work and who can give you a personal introduction. English solicitors are not permitted to practise in Scotland, but if you are moving from England, your English solicitor may have a Scottish solicitor with whom he or she deals regularly. The Law Society of Scotland★ publishes a directory of solicitors' names, addresses and telephone numbers which is available at Citizens Advice Bureaux and libraries. Leaflets explaining the role of solicitors in buying and selling houses can be obtained from most solicitors' offices; the Society also publishes leaflets explaining the role of solicitors. You will find a full list of solicitors in the *Yellow Pages* or on the Society's website at *www.lawscot.org.uk*

You should ask your solicitor, at the outset, to give you an estimate of the fees involved and the outlays (disbursements) he or she will have to make. There are no set fees, so you can shop around for competitive estimates. The outlays are substantial and should be budgeted for.

Property pricing

The general practice in Scotland is that houses are offered for sale at 'offers over' a stated figure, sometimes referred to as the 'upset price'. The quoted figure may be the minimum which the seller will consider accepting, but it may have been set low in order to attract purchasers and encourage competitive bidding. Purchasers will generally have to pay more than the upset but much depends on the demand, the condition of the property and market conditions. Houses in modern estates or blocks of flats where there are many similar properties tend to sell for close to the upset. On the other hand, older and more individual properties in sought-after residential areas tend to go for considerably more than the upset.

Sometimes houses are offered for sale at a fixed price. This may be because a quick sale is sought or because earlier attempts to sell it at an 'offers over' price have proved to be unsuccessful. If you want to buy a house which is offered for sale at a fixed price, you should be ready to proceed very quickly, since the first acceptable offer at the stated price will secure the house. Builders and developers invariably sell at fixed prices.

Buying a house

The main steps involved are:

- finding a suitable house
- arranging a loan and having the house surveyed
- making an offer
- obtaining a legal title to the house.

It is advisable to see your solicitor as early on in the procedure as possible. Things can move very fast and if you have not made contact you may miss your chance to make an offer for the house you have decided on. Solicitors can also give useful general advice about buying and assist you in obtaining a loan.

Finding a suitable house

The three main sources of information about houses for sale in Scotland are solicitors' property centres or offices, newspapers and estate agents.

If you are thinking about a new house, you could contact the sales departments of building firms in the area or go to see the various developments.

A quarterly list of buildings of historic or architectural interest for sale in Scotland is available from the Scottish Civic Trust*.

Newspapers

The English national daily and Sunday newspapers tend to advertise only a limited selection of Scottish houses and do not reflect the range of properties on the market. However, many more are advertised in the principal Scottish 'quality' daily newspapers and each has its main property day – *The Scotsman* (Edinburgh and the Lothians) on Thursdays; *The Herald* (Glasgow and Strathclyde) on Wednesdays; the *Press and Journal* (Aberdeen and Grampian) on Tuesdays; and the *Courier and Advertiser* (Dundee, Perth and Tayside) on Thursdays. A good range of properties for sale is also advertised in the smaller local newspapers circulating in various districts.

Solicitors' property centres and solicitors' offices

More properties in Scotland are sold by solicitors than by estate agents. This is particularly so in the Edinburgh, Aberdeen and Dundee areas (and to a lesser extent Glasgow) and in many large towns, where the vast majority of houses are sold by solicitors and where solicitors' property centres have become established. These are run by solicitors on a co-operative basis and are situated in shopping areas. They provide details of all properties being sold by solicitors in the area. There is a solicitors' property centre in Berwick-upon-Tweed, unique in that it deals with properties for sale on both sides of the border – England and Scotland.

Most solicitors' property centres operate only as information centres and not as selling agents – the solicitors themselves retain the selling role. The staff at a centre are conversant with house purchase and sale procedures and will give general advice and information but will direct a customer who is interested in a property to the solicitor actually selling it. All properties are displayed (most with photographs) and full estate agency-type particulars are available for each property, including the name of the solicitor handling the sale. The biggest centres, in Edinburgh and Aberdeen, each have several thousand properties on display at any one time, and Glasgow is rapidly catching up. The service is free to people looking for property to buy.

All solicitors' property centres publish regular property lists, most of them weekly, with full listings of all properties registered at the centre in question. Copies can be mailed to prospective purchasers if requested and are available from the particular centre and from all the solicitors practising in the area.

A list of solicitors' property centres with addresses and telephone numbers is available from the Law Society of Scotland★. The centres also have their own websites and these can be found via the links section on the Society's website.

Solicitors are allowed to call themselves 'Solicitors and Estate Agents' and often do so. Some firms of solicitors have their own property department where details of available properties are displayed and from whom you can obtain particulars of properties for sale. Many firms of solicitors employ specialist sales staff who deal with the non-legal aspects of buying and selling property.

Estate agents

There are many estate agents in Scotland. Many are part of chains owned by UK insurers or building societies, others are local firms.

The larger estate agencies issue regular property lists and most estate agents maintain mailing lists. Estate agents in Edinburgh have grouped together to publish a fortnightly property list, *Real Homes*, which is available through offices of its member firms.

Generally, estate agents in Scotland operate in the same way as those in England and Wales, and the points to bear in mind when dealing with an estate agent in Scotland are the same.

When you have found a house you want

When you have found a house that you would like to buy, tell your solicitor immediately. You can discuss with the seller the date of entry and what contents, such as carpets, curtains, light fittings etc., are included, although these should be in the particulars of sale. You can try to negotiate a price, but many sellers will simply ask you to put in a formal offer via your solicitor. An oral agreement for the sale of land or a house cannot create a binding contract and can be repudiated by either party without any consequences. You should never write letters or sign any documents relating to a sale or purchase without consulting your solicitor. Developers usually have their own documents for intending purchasers to sign and it is very difficult to negotiate different terms. Even so, you should show the document to your solicitor before signing it so that he or she can explain the terms and effect of the document to you.

When you tell your solicitor that you are interested in buying a particular property, the first thing he or she will do is to telephone the seller's solicitor or estate agent to notify him or her of your interest. The seller's solicitor or estate agent will generally give you a chance to offer, once your interest has been notified, although this is not a legal obligation.

Mortgage loan

If you have not already made your loan arrangements, the next thing to do is to arrange with a building society, bank or other source of finance to lend you the money you need to borrow. If you have difficulty in finding a loan, your solicitor will probably be able to help you.

It is wise to make sure at an early stage that the necessary loan finance will be available when it is needed. Most of the leading English building societies and banks, and all the Scottish banks and building societies, will lend on the security of Scottish properties.

Even before you have a specific house in mind, you should establish that the amount you require will be available on the type of property which you are seeking and that it will be available when you want it – subject always to a satisfactory survey report on the chosen house. See also Chapter 6.

Survey

Building societies and banks require the property to be surveyed before committing themselves to making you a loan. Even if you are paying for the house without a loan you are strongly advised to have the property surveyed before making an offer. In Scotland it is customary to have a mortgage valuation inspection or a more detailed homebuyer's survey and valuation carried out before you make an offer for a property. An offer made 'subject to survey' may be rejected by the seller unless the property requires expensive specialist surveys, but this will depend on the property market.

The mortgage valuation inspection or survey is usually instructed by your solicitor or independent financial adviser once he or she is informed that you are interested and wish to go ahead. If your offer is unsuccessful you will still have to pay the fee for the survey or valuation that you have had done, but some firms of surveyors may offer a discount on further surveys.

The range of types of survey is similar to that in England. The briefest and cheapest is the mortgage valuation instruction for a building society or bank. The home-buyer's report and valuation gives a wider range of standard information, while a building survey normally costs much more and gives very detailed information about the condition of the property. RICS Scotland★ publish a helpful leaflet which explains the different types of survey, entitled *Buying Property? Then you need a survey*. In April 2004 the Scottish Executive will pilot in some areas of Scotland a new survey, called the Single Survey. This survey aims to provide more information to house purchasers and sellers. If you are in a pilot area your solicitor or surveyor will be able to tell you about the pilot project.

A building society valuation is undertaken merely for the purpose of satisfying the building society that the house or flat will provide suitable security for its loan to you. The inspection is commissioned by the building society which is making the loan, although it is you who pays the surveyor's fee. The surveyor or building society will tell your solicitor whether the property in question is suitable for the loan which you require, the valuation placed on it, and any significant matters about the condition of the property which may affect value. Many building societies now make a practice of giving the borrower a copy of the surveyor's brief written report.

Making an offer

If the survey report is favourable, the next thing to do is to make an offer to buy the property. An offer is a formal document, usually a letter running to several pages, or sometimes a shorter letter with a schedule of conditions attached. It specifies all the conditions on which you are willing to buy the property. You are strongly advised not to make an offer yourself. Your solicitor will prepare it and send it to the seller's solicitor or estate agent.

In making the offer, you will have to decide, with guidance from your solicitor, how much to pay. You should also be clear when you want to move in and what extras you want to buy. If you are the only person interested in the property, your solicitor may be able to find this out from the seller's solicitor or estate agent and may be able to negotiate an acceptable price.

If more than one person is interested in buying the same property, the seller's solicitor or estate agent will normally fix a closing date, intimating to each person interested that offers must be submitted by a stated time on a stated date. You will have to offer 'blind', without knowing how much other people will offer. There may be quite a large gap between the highest and the next highest offers. It is not possible to get round this by making a bid of '£100 more than the highest offer you receive'.

Your solicitor will normally help you decide how much over the upset price you should offer (he or she probably has access to information about prices achieved for similar properties to guide you in making your decision; the solicitor's knowledge of the market locally is important and usually helpful to you). But the final decision about what to offer is yours.

Date of entry

Stating the date on which you want to move in is part of your formal offer. Whether this is acceptable is largely governed by when the seller wants to move out. The date of entry is a matter for negotiation between you and the seller. If there are no compelling reasons on either side for a very early or very far-off date of entry, the period between making the offer and moving in is typically between six and eight weeks. This gives you a reasonable period in which to sell your house and have all the legal work completed, if you have not already done so.

Extras

What extras, such as carpets, curtains, kitchen equipment, etc., you wish to purchase may be relevant if there is competition for the house and one prospective purchaser is offering a better price than another for the contents. Sale particulars normally specify what is, and what is not, included in the price and your offer will normally be drawn up accordingly.

If the extra items included in your price are valuable, you may want to allocate part of the price on them – for example, house £75,000, moveable property £3,000 – as this will give you a small saving in stamp duty. For stamp duty to be saved, the items must be moveable. Heritable fittings and fixtures (fitted kitchens, built-in bedroom furniture etc.) are transferred by the disposition (title deeds). The offer will therefore contain a statement of the value of the building including heritable fittings and fixtures.

The remaining conditions of the offer are taken up with technical legal matters such as ensuring that you will receive a good marketable title, that the property is not adversely affected by planning proposals, that structural alterations/extensions have received local authority approval and that you can withdraw from the contract if the house and contents included in the sale are not in substantially the same condition when you move in as when you offered for them.

If there is some special use to which you want to put the property, such as using part of it as an office or as a guest house, or if you plan to make major alterations, you must tell your solicitor so that he or she can include conditions in the offer to make sure that there are no relevant prohibitions in the title. If you are planning alterations or a change of use, you may have to make the offer conditional upon obtaining planning and/or building control permission. Sellers are not very keen on such offers but sometimes they are unavoidable.

Concluding the contract

If a closing date has been fixed and there is more than one offer, the seller and the solicitor or estate agent will consider all the offers made and decide which one, if any, to accept. Although the highest offer is normally the one accepted, the seller can, and sometimes does, take other factors into consideration, such as the date of entry proposed and the extras to be included in the sale.

Your solicitor will usually be informed by the seller's solicitor or estate agent, by telephone, within an hour or so after the closing time, whether your offer has been successful.

Your offer will stipulate that the property is not subject to any local authority proposals, notices or orders which might adversely affect it and oblige the seller to obtain and exhibit local authority certificates to this effect. Should the certificates disclose any adverse matter, you are permitted to withdraw from the purchase or you could renegotiate the price. You should ask your solicitor to explain the legal and practical effects of any matters disclosed, such as the building being listed as being of architectural or historic interest.

An oral acceptance is not legally binding; usually the selling solicitor will deliver an acceptance modifying or adjusting some of the terms of your offer, such as the date of entry, or making provision for payment of interest on the price of the house if settlement of the price on the date of entry is delayed through no fault of the seller, and to what extent (if any) the contract to be concluded will form a continuing contract after the date of entry. This is called a qualified acceptance and is often delivered within a day or so of receipt of the offer. If the modifications are acceptable to you (your solicitor will advise you on this), your solicitor sends a letter to the selling solicitor confirming that a binding contract is concluded. This can be done within a day or so of receipt of the qualified acceptance, after which the contract can be concluded within a few days of making the offer. However, the current trend in Scotland is that the conclusion of the contract takes longer than was previously the case.

The written offer and subsequent letters between the buyer's and seller's solicitors relating to it are known as 'the missives'. Once they are concluded, missives constitute a binding legal contract and neither the buyer nor the seller can withdraw without liability to pay damages. Missives are concluded by the solicitors; there is nothing for the buyer or seller to sign.

Insurance

At common law in Scotland the purchaser becomes responsible for the property from the date when missives are concluded. However, it is now usual for the missives to provide that the seller will remain liable for any damage to the property until the date of entry, and for its insurance until that date, and that the purchaser can withdraw from the purchase without penalty if the house and any extras included in the sale are seriously damaged or destroyed before the date of entry.

Completing the purchase

Once missives have been concluded, your solicitor will put in hand examination of the title and the conveyancing procedures to ensure that the disposition (the legal document transferring the house to you) in your favour is ready for delivery by the date of entry in exchange for payment of the price.

If you are buying the house together with your husband or wife or some other person, you will need to think about how the title is to be taken. The terms of the title will regulate the ownership, the respective shares of the co-owners and what happens to their shares on their death. You should discuss these matters with your co-owners and your solicitor before the disposition is prepared.

A title simply in the names of two people gives each of them a separate and distinct equal share in the property. If you and your co-owner are to have unequal shares (say one-third to you and two-thirds to your brother) the title must state this. During life, each co-owner can dispose of his or her share (by sale or gift) or can demand that the whole property be sold and his or her share of the proceeds paid over. It is possible for co-owners to agree not to demand a sale. Where the co-owners are a married couple the Matrimonial Homes (Family Protection) (Scotland) Act 1981 requires both spouses (or the court) to agree to any sale of the whole property or any disposal by one spouse of his or her separate share.

Two co-owners, particularly spouses, often take the title in name of each of them and the survivor. Then the survivor automatically becomes entitled to the whole property. Such a survivorship title cannot usually be altered without the agreement of both co-owners and it will in general prevail over any will made by either of the co-owners. It is very important to take advice from your solicitor about these matters.

Mortgage

As soon as the missives have been concluded, complete your loan application papers if you have not already done so.

If you are borrowing from a building society, bank or other lender, your solicitor normally acts for the lender as well as for you. He or she will report to the lender on the title and prepare the necessary mortgage document, called a 'standard security'. Sometimes there is additional security by way of assignation of a life policy or pension plan. He or she will also arrange for the loan money to be available in time for the date of entry, and will ask you to sign the standard security and other documents by that date.

If you are in any doubt about the terms of the mortgage documents, ask your solicitor to explain them to you before you sign them. Almost all such documents prohibit letting of the property without the lender's consent. They also set out detailed conditions about maintenance, insurance, and so on, and give the lender a wide range of remedies, including the right to sell the house if you fail to maintain your payments or otherwise fail to observe the loan conditions.

The building society's or other lender's cheque will be sent to your solicitor before the date of entry and he or she will ask you to pay the difference between the price and your mortgage loan. If you are selling another house, and you are relying on the money from the sale, which will not be available by the date of entry, you should make bridging loan arrangements at an early stage and tell your solicitor.

Documents

On the date of settlement, your solicitor will arrange with the seller's solicitor to hand over a cheque for the full price in return for the title deeds, including the disposition in your favour. This may be done by sending someone along or by post. The keys are usually handed over at settlement unless other arrangements have been agreed.

Your solicitor will register the disposition and the standard security in the Land Register of Scotland. In a couple of months the documents will be returned to your solicitor. If you had a loan, the solicitor will send the documents to the building society or other lender. If there is no loan, your solicitor will hand the title deeds over to you once the registration process has been completed. He or she may offer to hold them in safe custody for you.

Solicitors' charges

After completing the purchase (or sometimes before doing so) your solicitor will send you the account for his or her fees and outlays (disbursements). Solicitors in Scotland do not charge according to fixed scales.

In addition to the solicitors' fees for the preliminary work leading up to and including missives, the conveyancing and the mortgage (on all of which you will have to pay VAT), there will be registration dues for recording the documents in the Land Register, as well as stamp duty: nothing for a property costing up to £60,000; one per cent for properties costing between £60,001 and £250,000; three per cent for properties costing between £250,001 and £500,000; and four per cent above that. (Note that, though correct at the time of writing, these fees may be subject to change.) Exemptions apply to properties under £150,000 in certain disadvantaged areas – see page 23.

Outlays must be paid by the date of entry; the solicitor may agree to accept payments of fees a month later or to have payment by instalments, but is not obliged to do so.

Succession

If you buy a house in Scotland intending it as your residence or principal residence, you will acquire Scottish domicile. This may affect, amongst other things, the way your property is inherited on your death.

If you die without a will, Scottish law will regulate the distribution of your heritable property (that is, land and buildings) in Scotland and moveable property (all property other than 'heritable') in Scotland and elsewhere.

If you die leaving a will, it regulates the distribution of your estate, but the provisions of your will are subject to Scottish rules of succession, which differ in a number of important respects from English law. The most important difference is that a spouse and children cannot be cut out of the succession to the moveable estate, no matter what the will may say. They are always entitled to their 'legal rights', which, depending on the circumstances, may be either one-third or one-half of the net moveable estate.

With heritable property, regardless of the domicile of the owner, succession is governed by the law of the country in which the property is situated. Even if only a holiday home is bought in Scotland, with no question of the buyer thereby acquiring Scottish domicile, the succession to heritable property in Scotland is governed by Scottish law.

In Scotland, a will is not automatically revoked if the person making it subsequently marries, nor are provisions in favour of a spouse automatically revoked on divorce.

Selling your house

If you are selling in Scotland, you are likely to have been a purchaser already and thus familiar with the Scottish system. Many matters dealt with in the previous section, 'Buying a house', will be of interest to you as a seller.

The main steps involved in selling a house in Scotland are:

- advertising and showing your house
- dealing with offers
- transferring title to the seller and repaying any loan.

You should alert your solicitor, before putting it on the market, to the fact that you are about to sell your house. This is because a binding contract for the sale can be concluded within a few days of a purchaser making a formal offer and your solicitor will need an opportunity to:

- look over your title deeds to ensure they are in order and that you have good title to the property. (He or she will borrow them from your building society or other lender if you have an outstanding loan over the property)
- check the amount of any outstanding loan
- order local authority searches to make sure that the property is not affected by any outstanding local authority notices, orders or proposals.

Someone who has been used to the English method of sale, where the solicitor becomes involved at only a relatively late stage, should be aware of the need to bring a solicitor into the picture early in Scotland.

Consent to sale

Where a house is owned by two or more people, all of them must consent to its sale, although a sale can be forced by the court. Try to get agreement – legal proceedings are expensive.

The Matrimonial Homes (Family Protection) (Scotland) Act 1981 makes it imperative for a married seller whose spouse is not a co-owner to obtain the spouse's consent to a sale at the earliest opportunity and certainly before missives are concluded. Failure to do so may mean that the seller finds he or she cannot give the purchaser possession of the property as provided for in the missives. This is especially important where the couple are separated or estranged.

Advertising and showing your house

The three most common ways of marketing your house are to employ a solicitor, employ an estate agent or do it yourself.

Even if you employ a solicitor or an estate agent you will probably be showing prospective purchasers round the house yourself. As the owner, you will show the property to its best advantage and know the answers to all the questions people are likely to ask. Moreover, solicitors and estate agents will generally charge extra for showing prospective purchasers round property.

Selling through a solicitor

If you ask your solicitor to sell your house, you should expect him or her to provide a full estate agency service.

Your solicitor may register your property in the local solicitors' property centre, for which a charge of approximately £200 including VAT (may be less in some centres) is made. This covers display of the house in the solicitors' property centre for six months, and insertion in the property centre's regular property listing or mailing where there is one.

Although solicitors are entitled to charge a sales commission of 2.5 per cent, it is recommended that no more than 1.5 per cent is charged where the solicitor is also able to charge fees for legal work, and many charge 1 per cent or slightly less. Legal fees for conveyancing are in addition to the commission. It is quite common for a solicitor to charge a single percentage fee (usually 1.5 per cent) to cover both the selling and the conveyancing. VAT is due on commission and fees. Ask your solicitor for an estimate of charges before instructing him or her to act for you, and if you are not satisfied with the estimate, discuss it with the solicitor, or seek an alternative estimate from a different one.

If you decide to handle the sale yourself and need your solicitor to attend only to certain specific items, make sure that the basis of the charge is agreed in advance.

Selling through an estate agent

Generally speaking, estate agents' terms of business are similar in Scotland to those in England. Commissions are generally 1.5 per cent of the achieved selling price, although lower charges may be negotiated, and higher charges normally apply in the case of large country houses or other specialised properties. Ask the estate agent for an estimate and make sure you understand what is included in the charge, whether VAT is included and whether advertising costs are extra; you may be charged for the insertion of the property in the estate agent's house magazine.

Even if you instruct an estate agent to sell your house for you, he or she will normally pass to your solicitor any formal offers which are made. It is important to realise that as well as the estate agent's commission you will have to pay the solicitor's fee for concluding missives and the conveyancing fees.

Selling the house yourself

This entails advertising the property, showing people round it, letting surveyors inspect it, answering questions about room sizes, the price and what items are and are not included in the sale. You should prepare written particulars similar to those issued by solicitors and estate agents, but stress to people viewing the house that these are provided only as a guide and are not to form part of any contract.

If you decide to sell your house yourself, the only costs which you need incur are those for advertising. Advertising can be expensive, since if you are selling the property without the help of a solicitor you will not be able to register it with one of the solicitors' property centres, and it is probably not sensible to 'go it alone' the first time you sell. However, if you have been through the process of buying and selling before, and if you have a readily saleable house in which a large number of people are likely to be interested, you may feel that the saving in sales commission is justified.

If you decide to sell your house yourself, you will still need a solicitor to do the conveyancing and should tell him or her in advance, and tell prospective buyers that formal written offers are to be submitted to your solicitor.

The advertisement

If you are selling through a solicitor or an estate agent, he or she will prepare the advertisement for you and agree its terms with you, and will also advise you on the upset price and the price you should expect to achieve.

Arrangements for viewing are normally stated in the advertisement. There may be fixed viewing times or viewing by telephone appointment, or a mixture of both. Remember that the easier you make it for people to view a house, the more people are likely to do so and the quicker you may find a buyer. Evenings and weekend afternoons are popular viewing times.

The advertisement also normally states an upset price and invites offers over that price. The upset is generally fixed below the actual price that a seller hopes to obtain in order to attract purchasers and encourage competition. You should be able to judge what upset to put on your house if selling it yourself by looking at advertisements for comparable houses in the neighbourhood. A surveyor could carry out a quick pre-sale valuation on your behalf. The cost will vary according to the type of property: expect to pay about £100–£120 + VAT for a house worth £75,000–£100,000. A detailed survey (see page 281) would be considerably more expensive.

After the advertisement

You may gain an impression of whether people are seriously interested or not when they come to view, particularly if they return a second time. However, this is not always so and the first sign that you may be going to receive an offer is often when a solicitor telephones your solicitor or estate agent to say that he or she has a client interested in your property. You should then not sell to anyone without giving everyone who has notified an interest to you or your solicitor or estate agent an opportunity of offering.

Noting interest is usually followed by a visit from a surveyor. If the survey is favourable, it is likely to be followed by an offer.

If you are doing the selling of your house yourself, ask purchasers to lodge formal offers with your solicitor. Never sign a written acceptance of an offer or exchange letters with a prospective purchaser without consulting your solicitor.

Receiving offers

If several people have expressed an interest in your house, it is usual to fix a closing date for offers – that is, a date and time at which you will consider all offers which have been lodged. All those people whose interest has been noted will be asked to submit formal written offers through their solicitor by the date and time fixed. Your solicitor or estate agent will advise you whether to fix a closing date or not, and will suggest when it should be. Where there is competition, a higher price may be achieved if you do not rush the sale, but this may be nerve-racking for the seller.

On the closing date, you and your solicitor or estate agent will have to decide which offer to accept. You are not under an obligation to accept the highest offer or any offer. If offers are close, you may take into account other factors such as the proposed date of entry, what extras are included in the price, or even whether or not you liked the highest offeror. If the price is acceptable but other conditions of the offer are not, your solicitor or estate agent can negotiate these other conditions with the offeror or his or her solicitor. If the top offer is too low, you may have to re-advertise. It is unethical to try to get the top offeror to pay more without giving the other offerors a chance to re-offer.

Concluding the missives

If you are selling through an estate agent, he or she will normally pass the offers, or at least the offer which is to be accepted, to your solicitor. Once you have received an offer which you want to accept, or identified which of competing offers is to be accepted, your solicitor will adjust points of details with the solicitor acting for the successful offeror. When these adjustments have been made, they are confirmed in writing: this exchange of letters is referred to as the 'missives'. This process may take just a few days although there are signs that this stage of conveyancing is taking longer to complete. As with buying a house, the conclusion of missives constitutes a binding contract from which neither party can withdraw. The solicitor will accept the offer and conduct the bargain on your behalf. Make sure therefore that you understand exactly what you are agreeing to.

In theory, it would be possible for 'gazumping' to take place between the date when an acceptable offer is received and the date when missives are concluded, but it would be unethical for a solicitor acting for a seller to negotiate with a third party during this period. If in such circumstances you decided to withdraw from negotiations with the successful offerors and to negotiate with someone else, your solicitor would have to stop acting for you and you would have to appoint another solicitor. The absence of gazumping, and the short time between offers being made and becoming binding, are advantages of the Scottish system.

Completing the sale

Once the missives have been concluded, your solicitor will send the title deeds of the property to the purchaser's solicitor so that he or she can examine them and prepare the disposition (the document transferring title to the purchaser) in favour of the purchaser. He or she will also inform your building society, bank or other lender that missives have been concluded and obtain a redemption statement to show the amount of loan to be repaid on completion of the sale. He or she will prepare the discharge document and have it signed by the lender before the date of entry.

Your solicitor will instruct searches in the Registers to demonstrate to the purchaser that there are no adverse entries in respect of the property or against you as seller. He or she answers any questions raised by the purchaser's solicitor, adjusting the terms of the disposition with him or her. You have to sign it before the date of entry. The date of entry is the date on which settlement of the sale takes place and the disposition is handed over in exchange for the price and the keys. It is also the date on which the purchaser is entitled to take possession of the property, although he or she may choose not to move in on the same day.

Immediately prior to the date of entry, your solicitor will agree with you what arrangements are to be made about handing over the keys (often it is best to deliver these to your solicitor on the date of entry).

The disposition in favour of the purchaser is handed over in return for the purchaser's solicitor's cheque for the full purchase price. Out of that amount, your solicitor repays your outstanding mortgage loan, and any bridging loan, in accordance with instructions received from you or your bank and will then let you have a cheque for the balance of the price payable to you, after deducting fees and outlays. He or she should provide you with a detailed statement showing all the financial details; if not, make sure you ask for one. You should normally expect your solicitor to send you the balance of the price and his or her statement on the day after the sale is completed, or on the following day.

Epilogue

If moving has turned out to be particularly complicated or strenuous in spite of your endeavours to foresee all the hazards, try to get away, even if only for a couple of days. A break at this point from the physical and mental effort can make all the difference. You should find that you return eagerly to your new home, ready to enjoy it in a new period of your life.

Glossary

Here are some terms you may come across in connection with conveyancing, insurance, or arranging a mortgage.

Advance The mortgage loan (also capital sum, principal sum).

All-risks insurance Insurance that covers all happenings that are not specifically excluded in the policy (as opposed to a policy of specified perils, which covers only the happenings that are listed).

APR Annual percentage rates of the total charge for credit: standard way (laid down by the Consumer Credit Act 1974) of working out the true interest rate; by law, the APR has to be shown by banks and building societies alongside their quoted rates for each mortgage term, to enable potential borrowers to compare equally what is being offered.

Assignment The transfer of ownership to another person of some kinds of property, such as an insurance policy in the case of an endowment mortgage, or a lease.

Balance outstanding The amount of loan owed at any one time.

Bonus Additional amounts paid on with-profits policies – periodically (reversionary) or at the end of the policy term.

Bridging loan A loan, usually from a bank, to tide a person over between the time when he or she has to pay the purchase price of one house and the time when the proceeds of sale of another and/or mortgage funds become available.

Capital The mortgage loan (also called the advance, or principal).

Capital-reducing mortgage Repayment mortgage.

Cash-in value see *surrender value*

Charge Any right or interest, subject to which freehold or leasehold property may be held, especially a mortgage; also used to denote a debit, or a claim for payment.

Charges Register One of the three registers maintained by the Land Registry for a property. It records interests adverse to the owner.

Completion date The finalisation of a transaction. The day when the money is paid, the deeds are handed over, the keys are released and you can move into the house.

Conditions of sale The detailed standard terms which govern the rights and duties of the buyer and the seller of a house, as laid down in the contract which they sign; these may be the National, Standard, or the Law Society's conditions of sale.

Contract The agreement to sell the property. Not binding until exchange of contracts.

Conveyance A written document transferring unregistered land from the seller to the buyer.

Conveyancing The legal and administrative process involved in transferring the ownership of land or any buildings on it from one owner to another.

Covenant A promise in a deed to undertake (if covenant is positive) or to abstain from doing (if restrictive covenant) specified things.

Creditor Someone owed money; the lender.

Deeds see *title deeds*

Differentials When a lender operates a 'banding system' under which extra interest is charged on larger loans; the 'bands' are known as differentials.

Early redemption Paying off a loan before the end of the mortgage term.

Early redemption charge The sum charged by a lender to cover administration costs in the event of a loan being repaid before the end of the mortgage term (usually in the first three to five years).

Easement The legal right of a property owner to use the facilities of another's land – for example, a right of way.

Endowment policy Investment including life insurance which can be linked to a mortgage loan to pay off the capital at the end of the term (or on death, if sooner).

Endowment mortgage A loan on which only interest is paid throughout the term; linked to an endowment policy.

Engrossment Effectively, the top or final copy of a legal document.

Exchange of contracts The process of making an agreement to buy and sell a house legally binding.

Freehold Property held absolutely (that is, until the end of time). Also known as 'fee simple'.

Indemnity covenant A clause in the transfer in which the buyer undertakes to indemnify the seller in respect of breaches in any of the restrictions in the title deeds which affect the property.

Index map search A search to find out if ownership of a property is registered at the Land Registry.

Joint tenants Two or more people holding property as co-owners; when one dies, his or her share of the property automatically passes to the survivor(s).

Land Certificate The certificate, akin to a log book, issued by the Land Registry to confirm the ownership of a house.

Land Registry A government department (head office in London and district registries in various other places in England and Wales) responsible for opening, maintaining and amending the registers of all properties in England and Wales which have registered titles.

Leasehold Ownership of property for a fixed number of years granted by a lease which sets out the obligations of the lessee (or tenant), for example, regarding payment of rent to the landlord, repairs and insurance; as opposed to freehold property, where ownership is absolute.

Legal charge To all intents and purposes the same as a mortgage.

Lessee A person who takes a lease (i.e. the tenant).

Lessor A person who grants a lease (i.e. the landlord).

Local search certificate An application made to the local authority for a certificate providing certain information about a property and the surrounding area.

Low-cost endowment mortgage A mortgage secured by an endowment policy that does not guarantee to pay out enough to repay the mortgage at maturity but includes life insurance that guarantees to pay off the loan in full at death.

Low-start mortgage A loan for which premiums start low and increase by a certain percentage each year until the full level premium is reached.

Making time of the essence If either party is late for completion, the contract can be enforced only by serving a notice to complete setting a time limit to finalise the transaction. This step has serious legal consequences.

Mortgage A loan (usually for house purchase) for which a house is the security or collateral. It gives to the lender (usually a building society or bank) certain rights in the property, including the power to sell if the mortgage payments are not made. These rights are cancelled when the money advanced is repaid with interest, in accordance with the agreed terms.

Mortgage deed The document enshrining the conditions of a loan secured on a property (also called a legal charge).

Mortgagee The lender.

Mortgage indemnity guarantee Compulsory insurance required by a lender for a loan which is above the percentage of the valuation of the property at which the society will normally lend (also called high-lending fee).

Mortgage protection policy Life insurance taken out by borrower which would pay off the outstanding mortgage loan in case of borrower's death, usually taken out with a repayment mortgage.

Mortgagor The borrower (whose property is security for the loan).

Office copy (entries) A copy (officially prepared by the Land Registry) of the entries on a Land Register. The term also applies to other official copies – such as probates or letters of administration.

Preliminary enquiries The questions asked about a property before exchange of contracts.

Premium Payment (one-off or periodical) for an insurance policy, the amount depending on the sum insured and the type and degree of risk to the insurer.

Principal The amount of money that has been borrowed and on which interest is calculated.

Property Register One of the three parts of a Land or Charge Certificate. It describes the property and rights that go with it.

Proprietorship Register Another of the parts of a Land or Charge Certificate. It records the names of the owners and any restrictions on their right to sell.

Redemption Paying off a loan; the final payment of principal, interest and costs of the mortgage; if all or part of the loan is repaid early, an additional charge may be payable.

Registered land Land (including buildings, houses on it), the title to which is registered at the Land Registry, with the result that ownership is guaranteed fully or to some degree by the state; in all parts of England and Wales, registration of title is compulsory.

Repayment mortgage Loan on which the capital as well as interest is paid back throughout the period of the loan.

Requisitions on title The questions asked about the seller's title to land, and the matters raised before completion.

Retention The withholding of part of a mortgage loan, should structural defects need to be repaired on the property in question; the amount is normally the sum required to carry out the repairs, and it will be withheld until the work has been completed satisfactorily.

Right(s) This is an interest protected by law (as opposed to mere permission or licence, which can always be terminated). In house-buying it often amounts to a right for the benefit of one property over another (an easement). There are many types of rights, such as rights of light, air, way and drainage. Rights for the benefit of the property appear in the property register and rights adverse to the property show in the charges register.

Stakeholder One who holds a deposit as an intermediary between the buyer and seller, so that the deposit may only be passed on to the seller with the permission of the buyer, or returned to the buyer with the permission of the seller.

'Subject to contract' These words should appear in every letter to the seller, his or her solicitor or agent before contracts are exchanged. It is an accepted formula to stop a contract being created in correspondence. (Since September 1989 this procedure has not been strictly necessary. However, it does no harm and might still provide protection in rare cases.)

Sum insured The amount that will be paid out when a term insurance policy matures or the event insured for happens (such as, for life insurance, the death of the policyholder; for household insurance, loss of or damage to property).

Surrender value The amount of money a policyholder receives if a life insurance policy is terminated before the expiry date (other than on death), for instance, when the endowment mortgage is paid off early.

Tenants in common Two (or more) people who together hold property in such a way that, when one dies, his or her share does not pass automatically to the survivor but forms part of his or her own property and passes under his or her will or intestacy (in contrast to what happens in the case of joint tenants).

Term insurance A life insurance contract which pays out only on death within a specified period (also known as temporary insurance); it is used to cover the period of a mortgage.

Term of mortgage The number of years at the end of which the loan is to be repaid; the shorter the term, the higher the monthly repayments (and the APR).

Title The right to ownership of property.

Title deeds The documents conferring and evidencing ownership of land. In registered land transactions the 'title deeds' are the Land Certificate or the Charge Certificate.

Title number The unique number allocated to each property by the Land Registry (and an essential reference number in any correspondence with the Land Registry).

Top-up mortgage Additional mortgage from another lender when the first lender does not provide enough finance to purchase a house.

Transfer The Land Registry document transferring the ownership of the property from the seller to the buyer.

Vendor The seller.

With-profits policy A life insurance policy in which bonuses (varying according to the company's profits) are added regularly to the original sum assured paid when the policy matures; the type of policy often used for an endowment mortgage.

Unit-linked policy A life insurance policy under which the premiums buy units in an investment fund.

Addresses

**Advisory Centre for Education
(ACE Ltd)**
Unit 1c Aberdeen Studios
22 Highbury Grove
London N5 2DQ
Business line: 020-7354 8318
Freephone advice line:
(0808) 8005793
Fax: 020-7354 9069
Website: www.ace-ed.org.uk

Architectural Association
34-36 Bedford Square
London WC1B 3ES
Tel: 020-7887 4000
Fax: 020-7414 0782
Email: arch-assoc@aaschool.ac.uk
Website: www.aaschool.ac.uk

Association of British Insurers (ABI)
51 Gresham Street
London EC2V 7HQ
Tel: 020-7600 3333
Fax: 020-7696 8999
Email: info@abi.org.uk
Website: www.abi.org.uk

**Association of Building
Engineers (ABE)**
Lutyens House
Billing Brook Road
Northampton NN3 8NW
Tel: (01604) 404121
Fax: (01604) 784220
Email: building.engineers@abe.org.uk
Website: www.abe.org.uk

**Association of Plumbing and Heating
Contractors (APHC)**
14 Ensign House
Ensign Business Centre
Westwood Way
Coventry CV4 8JA
Tel: 024-7647 0626
Fax: 024-7647 0942
Email: aphcuk@aol.com
Website: www.aphc.co.uk

**Association of Relocation
Agents (ARA)**
PO Box 189
Diss
Norfolk IP22 1PE
Tel: (08700) 737475
Fax: (08700) 718719
Email: info@relocationagents.com
Website: www.relocationagents.com

British Association of Removers (BAR)
3 Churchill Court
58 Station Road
North Harrow
Middlesex HA2 7SA
Tel: 020-8861 3331
Fax: 020-8861 3332
Email: info@bar.co.uk
Website: www.bar.co.uk

British Telecom (BT)
81 Newgate Street
London EC1A 7AJ
Tel: (0800) 328 9654
Fax: 020-8810 9192
Website: www.bt.com

British Wood Preserving and Damp-proofing Association (BWPDA)
1 Gleneagles House
Vernon Gate
Derby DE1 1UP
Tel: (01332) 225100
Fax: (01332) 225101
Email: info@bwpda.co.uk
Website: www.bwpda.co.uk

Council for Licensed Conveyancers (CLC)
16 Glebe Road
Chelmsford
Essex CM1 1QG
Tel: (01245) 349599
Fax: (01245) 341300
Email: clc@theclc.gov.uk
Website: www.theclc.gov.uk

Council of Mortgage Lenders (CML)
3 Savile Row
London W1S 3PB
Tel: 020-7437 0075
Leaflet line: 020-7440 2255
Fax: 020-7434 3791
Email: info@cml.org.uk
Website: www.cml.org.uk
Contact the CML for leaflets and copies of the Mortgage Code

Council for Registered Gas Installers (CORGI)
Unit 1
Elmwood
Chineham Business Park
Chineham
Basingstoke
Hampshire RG24 8WG
Tel: (01256) 372200
Fax: (01256) 708144
Email: enquiries@corgi-group.com
Website: www.corgi-group.com

Department for Work and Pensions
Correspondence Unit
Room 540
The Adelphi
1-11 John Adam Street
London WC2N 6HT
Tel: 020-7712 2171
Fax: 020-7712 2386
Website: www.dwp.gov.uk

Electrical Contractors' Association (ECA)
ESCA House
34 Palace Court
London W2 4JG
Tel: 020-7313 4800
Fax: 020-7221 7344
Email:
electricalcontractors@eca.co.uk
Website: www.eca.co.uk

English Heritage
23 Savile Row
London W1S 2ET
Tel: 020-7973 3000
Fax: 020-7973 3001
Website: www.english-heritage.org.uk

Federation of Master Builders (FMB)
14-15 Great James Street
London WC1N 3DP
Tel: 020-7242 7583
Fax: 020-7404 0296
Email: central@fmb.org.uk
Website: www.fmb.org.uk

Financial Services Authority (FSA)
25 The North Colonnade
Canary Wharf
London E14 5HS
Tel: 020-7066 1000
Helpline: (0845) 606 1234
Fax: 020-7066 1099
Email: consumerhelp@fsa.gov.uk
Website: www.fsa.gov.uk

Forestry Commission
231 Corstorphine Road
Edinburgh
EH12 7AT
Tel: 0131-334 0303
Fax: 0131-334 3047
Email: enquiries@forestry.gsi.gov.uk
Website: www.forestry.gov.uk

*Guarantee Protection Insurance
Company Ltd (GPI)*
27 London Road
High Wycombe
Buckinghamshire
HP11 1BW
Tel: (01494) 447049
Fax: (01494) 465194
Email: shirley@gptprotection.co.uk
Website: www.gptprotection.co.uk

*Heating and Ventilating Contractors'
Association (HVCA)*
ESCA House
34 Palace Court
London W2 4JG
Tel: 020-7313 4900
Fax: 020-7727 9268
Email: contact@hvca.org.uk
Website: www.hvca.org.uk

Housing Corporation
Maple House
149 Tottenham Court Road
London W1T 7BN
Tel: 020-7393 2000
Publications dept: 020-7393 2228
Fax: 020-7393 2099
Email:
enquiries@housingcorp.gsx.gov.uk
Website: www.housingcorp.gov.uk

*Independent Schools Council
Information Service (ISCis)*
Grosvenor Gardens House
35-37 Grosvenor Gardens
London SW1W 0BS
Tel: 020-7798 1500
Fax: 020-7798 1531
Email: info@iscis.uk.net
Website: www.iscis.uk.net

Institute of Plumbing
64 Station Lane
Hornchurch
Essex RM12 6NB
Tel: (01708) 472791
Fax: (01708) 448987
Email: info@plumbers.org.uk
Website: www.plumbers.org.uk

Lands Tribunal for Scotland
1 Grosvenor Crescent
Edinburgh EH12 5ER
Tel: 0131-225 7996
Fax: 0131-226 4812

Law Commission
Conquest House
37-38 John Street
Theobalds Road
London WC1N 2BQ
Tel: 020-7453 1220
Fax: 020-7453 1297
Email:
secretary.lawcomm@gsi.gov.uk
Website: www.lawcom.gov.uk

Law Society of England and Wales
113 Chancery Lane
London WC2A 1PL
Tel: 020-7242 1222
Fax: 020-7831 0344
Email:
info.services@lawsociety.org.uk
Website: www.lawsociety.org.uk

Law Society of Scotland
26 Drumsheugh Gardens
Edinburgh EH3 7YR
Tel: 0131-226 7411
Helpline: 0131-476 8137
Fax: 0131-225 2934
Email: lawscot@lawscot.org.uk
Website: www.lawscot.org.uk

Legal Services Ombudsman
3rd Floor
Sunlight House
Quay Street
Manchester M3 3JZ
Tel: 0161-839 7262
Fax: 0161-832 5446
Email: lso@olso.gsi.gov.uk
Website: www.olso.org

Mortgage Code Compliance Board
University Court
Stafford ST18 0GN
Helpline: (01785) 218200
Fax: (01785) 218249
Email:
enquiries@mortgagecode.org.uk
Website: www.mortgagecode.org.uk

National Association of Estate Agents (NAEA)
Arbon House
21 Jury Street
Warwick
Warwickshire CV34 4EH
Tel: (01926) 496800
Or call the Homelink Hotline direct on
(01926) 417792
Fax: (01926) 400953
Email: info@naea.co.uk
Website: www.naea.co.uk

National Debtline
Tel: (0808) 808 4000
Website:
www.nationaldebtline.co.uk

National Federation of Builders (NFB)
56–64 Leonard Street
London EC2A 4JX
Tel: 020-7608 5150
Fax: 020-7608 5151
Email: info@builders.org.uk
Website: www.builders.org.uk

National Guild of Removers and Storers Ltd
3 High Street
Chesham
Buckinghamshire HP5 1BG
Tel: (01494) 792279
Fax: (01494) 792111
Email: info@ngrs.co.uk
Website: www.ngrs.co.uk

**National Inspection Council for
Electrical Installation Contracting
(NICEIC)**
Vintage House
37 Albert Embankment
London SE1 7UJ
Tel: 020-7564 2323
Fax: 020-7564 2370
Email: enquiries@niceic.org.uk
Website: www.niceic.org.uk

**National Land Information Service
(NLIS)**
Local Government Information
House
Layden House
76–86 Turnmill Street
London EC1M 5LG
Tel: (0870) 240 6760
Email: dorothypugh@cix.co.uk
Website: www.nlis.org.uk

NHBC
Buildmark House
Chiltern Avenue
Amersham
Buckinghamshire HP6 5AP
Tel: (0870) 241 4302
Customer Service: (01494) 735363
Fax: (01494) 723530
Email: cssupport@nhbc.co.uk
Website: www.nhbc.co.uk

**Office of the Deputy Prime Minister
(ODPM)**
26 Whitehall
London SW1A 2WH
Tel: 020-7944 4400
Website: www.odpm.gov.uk

ODPM Planning Inspectorate
Temple Quay House
2 The Square
Temple Quay
Bristol BS1 6PN
Tel: 0117-372 6372
Fax: 0117-372 8139
Email: enquiries@planning-
insp.gsi.gov.uk
Website:
www.planning-inspectorate.gov.uk

**Office for the Supervision of Solicitors
(OSS)**
Victoria Court
8 Dormer Place
Leamington Spa
Warwickshire CV32 5AE
Tel: (01926) 820082
Fax: (01926) 431435
Website: www.lawsociety.org.uk

Ombudsman for Estate Agents (OEA)
Beckett House
4 Bridge Street
Salisbury
Wiltshire SP1 2LX
Tel: (01722) 333306
Fax: (01722) 332296
Email: admin@oea.co.uk
Website: www.oea.co.uk

The Pension Service
Ground Floor
Trevelyan House
30 Great Peter Street
London SW1P 2BY
Tel: (0845) 60 60 265
Helpline: 0113-232 4143
Textphone: 0113-232 4342
Fax: 0113-232 4476
Website: www.thepensionservice.gov.uk

Pre-school Learning Alliance (PLA)
69 King's Cross Road
London WC1X 9LL
Tel: 020-7833 0991
Fax: 020-7837 4942
Email: pla@preschool.org.uk
Website: www.preschool.org.uk

The Publications Centre
PO Box 236
Wetherby LS23 7NB
Tel: (0870) 122 6236
Fax: (0870) 122 6237
Email: odpm@twoten.press.net
dft@twoten.press.net
Website: www.odpm.gov.uk
www.dft.gov.uk
For publications produced by the ODPM,
the DFT and the Planning Inspectorate

Registry of County Court Judgments
Registry Trust Ltd
173-175 Cleveland Street
London W1T 6QR
Tel: 020-7380 0133
Website: www.registry-trust.org.uk

Royal Incorporation of Architects in
Scotland (RIA Scotland)
15 Rutland Square
Edinburgh EH1 2BE
Tel: 0131-229 7545
Fax: 0131-228 2188
Website: www.rias.org.uk

Royal Institute of British Architects
(RIBA)
Clients' Services
66 Portland Place
London W1B 1AD
Tel: 020-7307 3700
Fax: 020-7255 1541
Email: cs@inst.riba.org
Website: www.architecture.com

Royal Institution of Chartered
Surveyors (RICS)
Parliament Square
12 Great George Street
London SW1P 3AD
Tel: 020-7222 7000
Fax: 020-7222 9430
Email: info@rics.org
Website: www.rics.org

Royal Institution of Chartered
Surveyors in Scotland (RICS Scotland)
9 Manor Place
Edinburgh
EH3 7DN
Tel: 0131-225 7078
Fax: 0131-240 0830
Email: scotland@rics.org.uk
Website: www.rics-scotland.org.uk

Royal Society of Architects in Wales
Bute Building
King Edward VII Avenue
Cathays Park
Cardiff CF10 3NB
Tel: 029-2087 4753
Fax: 029-2087 4926
Email: rsaw@inst.riba.org
Website: www.architecture-wales.com

Royal Society of Ulster Architects
(RSUA)
2 Mount Charles
Belfast BT7 1NZ
Tel: 028-9032 3760
Fax: 028-9023 7313
Email: info@rsua.org.uk
Website: www.rsua.org.uk

Royal Town Planning Institute (RTPI)
41 Botolph Lane
London EC3R 8DL
Tel: 020-7929 9494
Fax: 020-7929 9490
Email: online@rtpi.org.uk
Website: www.rtpi.org.uk

School Government Publishing
Company (SGPC)
Darby House
Merstham
Redhill
Surrey RH1 3DN
Tel: (01737) 642223
Fax: (01737) 644283
Email: info@schoolgovernment.co.uk
Website: www.schoolgovernment.co.uk

Scottish Building Employers
Federation (SBEF)
Carron Grange
Carrongrange Avenue
Stenhousemuir FK5 3BQ
Tel: (01324) 555550
Fax: (01324) 555551
Email: info@scottish-building.co.uk
Website: www.scottish-building.co.uk

Scottish Civic Trust
The Tobacco Merchant's House
42 Miller Street
Glasgow G1 1DT
Tel: 0141-221 1466
Fax: 0141-248 6952
Email: sct@scottishcivictrust.org.uk
Website: www.buildingsatrisk.org.uk

Scottish Council of Independent
Schools (SCIS)
21 Melville Street
Edinburgh EH3 7PE
Tel: 0131-220 2106
Fax: 0131-225 8594
Email: information@scis.org.uk
Website: www.scis.org.uk

SELECT
The Walled Garden
Bush House
Bush Estate
Midlothian EH26 0SB
Tel: 0131-445 5577
Fax: 0131-445 5548
Email: admin@select.org.uk
Website: www.select.org.uk

Society for the Protection of Ancient
Buildings (SPAB)
37 Spital Square
London E1 6DY
Tel: 020-7377 1644
Fax: 020-7247 5296
Email: info@spab.org.uk
Website: www.spab.org.uk

Solicitors Property Group
c/o Funnell and Perring
192-193 Queens Road
Hastings TN34 1RG
Tel: (01424) 426287
Fax: (01424) 434372
Website:
www.solicitorspropertygroup.co.uk

Spacia
Network Rail
26 Southwark Street
London SE1 1TU
Tel: 020-7645 3000
Fax: 020-7645 3001
Website: www.networkrail.co.uk

Stationery Office Publications Centre
PO Box 29
Norwich NR3 1GN
Tel: (08706) 005522
Fax: (08706) 005533
Email: book.enquiries@theso.co.uk
Website: www.tso.com

Telecommunications Industry
Association
Douglas House
32–34 Simpson Road
Fenny Stratford
Bletchley
Milton Keynes
Buckinghamshire MK1 1BA
Tel: (01908) 645000
Fax: (01908) 632263
Email: info@tia.org.uk
Website: www.tia.org.uk

UK Timber Frame Association
(UKTFA)
The E Centre
Cooperage Way
Business Village
Alloa FK10 3LP
Tel: (01259) 272140
Fax: (01259) 272141
Email: office@timber-frame.org
Website: www.timber-frame.org

Which? Books
PO Box 44
Hertford X
SG14 1LH
Tel: (0800) 252100
Fax: (0800) 533053
Website: www.which.net

Zurich Insurance
Galaxy House
Southwood Crescent
Farnborough
Hampshire GU14 0NJ
Tel: (0870) 241 8050
Website:
www.zurichmunicipal.com

Property websites
www.easier.co.uk
www.fish4homes.co.uk
www.findaproperty.co.uk
www.homes-on-line.com
www.homepages.co.uk
www.propertyfinder.co.uk
www.propertylive.co.uk
www.propertyworld.com
www.rightmove.co.uk

Index

access, shared, and rights of 239, 245–6
Access to Neighbouring Land Act 1992 245–6
accommodation and layout 60–2
  bathroom(s) 62
  bedrooms 61–2
  hall 60
  kitchen 60–1, 62
  living room(s) 60, 62
  staircase 61
  storage space 60
  utility room 61
adjacent land and buildings, ownership of 65
advertisements 48, 153–7
  cards in local shops 154
  company notice boards and email 155
  drafting 156–7
  estate agents 48, 166–7
  'For Sale' signs 40–1, 154, 162, 167
  house-hunter's advertisements 48
  on the Internet 48
  new house developments 34–5
  newspapers 35, 48, 155–6, 212, 278
  private advertisements 48
  property shops 41, 154–5
  videos 157–8
appliance connection/disconnection 188, 189

APR (annual percentage rate) 119–20
architects 100–2
armed forces members' removal expenses 26
asphalt roofs 68
Association of Building Engineers 85, 102, 162
Association of Relocation Agents 44–5
auction
  buying a house at 268–70
  commission and fees 271
  reserve prices 268–9, 272
  selling goods by 212
  selling a house by 270–3

bank drafts 193, 263, 264
bank transfer fees 23–4
banks
  accounts, transferring 183
  mortgage loans 129
bathrooms 62
  fittings 77
bedrooms 61–2
beds 218
bookshelves 76
boundary walls and fences 70, 244–6
bridging loans 19, 40, 82, 138–9, 178–9, 192
  charges 24, 138, 179
  for the deposit 22, 240
  from your employer 27

interest rates 179
open-ended 19, 82, 179
British Wood Preserving and
Damp-proofing Association
(BWPDA) 88–9, 106
builders 102–4
builder bankruptcy 31, 34, 37
mortgage schemes 130
rogue traders 103–4
warranty scheme 103
see also newly built houses
building or design consultants 102
building regulations 51, 73, 98–9
building societies 129
building surveyors
building work 97–112
building regulations 51, 73, 98–9
burglar alarm 109–10
damp, rot and woodworm 105–6
dirt and débris 104–5
doing your own 110–11
electrical wiring and installations
106–8, 111
estimates 103
finding a builder 102–3
floors 108–9
heating and insulation 105
hiring equipment 111
house cleaning and decoration
110
house improvement grants 49–50
listed buildings and conservation
areas 50, 51, 99–100
organising 104–10
planning permission 49, 50–1, 73,
97–100
plumbing 108
professional advice 100–4
programme/timetable 104
restrictions 99–100
roof repairs 106
telephone installation 109
timber-frame houses 99
warranties 103
buildings insurance 15, 25, 179–81,
192
flats 14
index-linked policies 181

mortgage lender's chosen policies
180
premiums added to mortgage
loan 181
reinstatement cost 15, 179
sum insured 179
bungalows 15
burglar alarms 109–10
business use 73, 98, 119
buyer's market 19
buying a house 9–19
at auction 268–70
buying from a housing association
54–5
buying from a local authority
52–4
costs and fees 23–7
financing the move 20–2
fixtures and fittings 26, 75–9, 82,
150
items offered separately 77, 80,
244
leaseholder's right to buy 55
maximum price, calculating 20
mobile homes 55–6
repossessed houses 56–7
in Scotland 277–88
see also conveyancing; house
hunting; newly built houses;
old houses
buying items from the seller 77, 80,
244, 253
buying and selling at the same time
18–19, 172–3, 177–8, 196

capital gains tax (CGT) 255–6
car 16, 214
insurance 16, 182
carpets 76, 109, 150
cleaning 110
lifting and re-laying 203, 218
measuring for 191
protecting 227, 228
ceilings 67
chain situation 174, 241
chain-linking schemes 174
change of address notification 26,
184–6

charge and budget accounts 183
charities and jumble sales 213
chattels 75
checklists
  change of address notification
    184–6
  exchange of contracts 249
  home safety 231
  house viewing 58
  items included/excluded from
    sale 78–9
  moving: basic expenses 28–9
  removals process 193–5
  survival kit for the move 222
children
  moving with 219, 221, 223
  new schools 186–7
  playgroups and nurseries 187
chimney stacks 68, 106
chimneys and flues 87, 106
church buildings, redundant 52
civil servants' removal expenses 26
clocks, moving 219
clothes 16, 203–4
coal authority searches 23
coal and heating oil 80
Common Parts Grant 50
Commonhold and Leasehold
  Reform Act 2002 55
commons 23, 74
company searches 23, 250
completion
  balance of purchase price 192–3
  completion date 173, 177–8,
    191–3, 196, 249
  handover of keys 218, 228
  on newly built houses 34, 40,
    197
  notice to complete 253
  practical matters before 178–91
  procedures after 251
  transfer of deeds 193
computers, moving 221
conservation areas 50, 51, 99
contaminated land 74
contents insurance 16, 112, 172,
  181, 205
contingency fund 26

contract race 10, 57, 92–3, 174
conveyancing 232–67
  aims of buyer 235
  chain situation 174, 241
  complaints concerning 253–5
  costs 235
  d-i-y conveyancing 236, 258–61
  delays 238
  e-conveyancing 233, 236, 238,
    259
  fixtures, fittings and contents
    form 77, 247
  legal background to 232–3
  legal language 17–18
  main stages 233–5
  newly built houses 241
  potential problems 238, 253–5
  practical matters 339–46
  role of seller 235
  solicitor or licensed conveyancer?
    236–7
  term explained 232
  TransAction Protocol 77, 175,
    179, 244, 246, 247
  working with your
    solicitor/conveyancer 239–40
conveyancing procedure (buying)
  246–51
  completion and after 251
  draft contract 246–7, 248
  exchange of contracts 174, 234,
    248–9
  local searches 247
  preliminary enquiries 248
  preparation for completion 250–1
  transfer document 250
  water and other searches 247–8
conveyancing procedure (d-i-y) 236,
  258–67
  buying 260–5
  potential problems 258
  preparation for 259
  selling 265–7
conveyancing procedure (selling)
  251–2
  completion 251
  draft contract 252
  exchange of contracts 252

Conveyancing Standing Committee 94
cookers 220
costs and fees
    architects and building surveyors 101
    bridging loans 24, 138, 179
    building regulations 99
    buildings insurance 25
    contingency fund 26
    estate agents 22, 165, 166–7
    expenses checklist 28–9
    furniture storage 197–8
    help with moving expenses 26–7
    house hunting expenses 25
    incidental expenses 26
    Land Registry fees 23, 192, 243
    lender's legal fees 24, 138, 192, 259
    local authority searches 23
    mains services 25
    mortgage arrangement fee 24, 238
    mortgage indemnity guarantee 24
    mortgage intermediaries 131
    mortgage redemption fees 22–3, 116, 125, 175
    mortgages 138–41
    relocation services 45
    removal expenses 25
    searches 23–4
    solicitors/conveyancers 22, 24, 138, 250
    stamp duty land tax 23, 82, 192
    surveys 24–5, 86
    valuation fee 83, 138
Council of Mortgage Lenders 117, 134
council tax 16, 74, 112, 182
    apportionment 182
    refunds 112
council tenants 52
country, moving to the 11–13
covenants 73, 100
cracked or bulging ceilings and walls 67, 68, 87
credit blacklisting 137, 256–7

curtain rails, tracks, rods and pelmets 76
curtains 76, 150, 191

daily life and outgoings, changing patterns of 15–16
damp-proof courses 68, 89, 105–6
debt counselling 142
demolition 99–100
deposits 21–2, 177, 240
    on exchange of contracts 21–2, 240
    initial deposits 82–3, 169
    newly built houses 31, 33
    pre-contract deposit agreements 94
    using a bridging loan for 22, 240
derelict property 52
Disabled Facilities Grant 50
dishwashers 220–1
doctors' removal expenses 26
door furniture and door chimes 77
doors and windows 69, 87
draft contract 246–7, 248
drains 37, 66, 87
dry and wet rot 67, 90, 106
dustbins 219

e-conveyancing 233, 236, 238, 259
easements 232, 239
electric heating systems 66, 77, 191
electrical wiring and installations 25, 66, 87, 106–8, 111, 190
electricity supply 189–90, 227
employers
    assistance with costs of moving 26–7
    bridging loans from 27
    mortgages for employees 129–30
empty houses
    building work 112
    council tax 112
    insurance 112
    maintaining 168–9
    security 112
    selling 168–9
endowment mortgages 122–3, 193
endowment policies

low-cost policies 122
mis-selling 123
shortfalls 122
English Heritage 51
entrance halls 60
environmental matters 74
estate agents 41–3, 144, 161–9
    chain-linking schemes 174
    choosing 162–3
    Code of Practice 163–4
    complaints against 163
    dealing with 42–3
    euphemisms 47
    fees and costs 22, 165, 166–7
    and initial deposits 82–3
    key-handling policy 167, 168
    listings 41
    mortgage arrangements 131
    multi-listing services 44, 162
    National Homelink Service 43–4
    Ombudsman scheme 41, 163
    particulars 45–7, 75
    'personal interest' statements 46
    professional associations 41, 162
    referral services 43–4
    in Scotland 279–80, 290
    selling through 144, 161–9,
        173–4
    sole agency 165–6
    valuation of the house 149, 164
    websites 43, 48
estate roads 34, 37
exchange of contracts 174, 234,
    248–9, 252
    checklist 249
    legal work after 250
    preparation for 173–4, 177–8
extensions 15, 98, 99, 239

faxes 18
Federation of Master Builders
    (FMB) 103
felt roofs 68
feudal tenure (Scotland) 275, 278
financial planning
    checklist of expenses 28–9
    contingency fund 26
    costs of buying 23–7

costs of selling 22–3
house hunting expenses 25
incidental expenses 26
insurance 25
mains services 25
raising purchase price 20–1
removal expenses 25
Financial Services Authority (FSA)
    133
Financial Services and Markets Act
    2002 116
first-time buyers 171
fixtures and fittings 26, 75–9, 82,
    150
fixtures, fittings and contents form
    77, 247
flammable items, moving 219
flat roofs 68
flats
    buildings insurance 14
    conversions 15
    moving from 14–15
    in Scotland 276
flight paths 74
flooding 63, 67
floors 67–8, 87, 108–9
'For Sale' signs 40–1, 154, 162, 167
Forestry Commission 52
foundations 87
freehold property 72
fridges and freezers 220
fuel consumption and costs 16
furniture
    built-in 77
    moving 218–19
    storage 197–9

garage sales and car-boot sales 213
garages and car space 14, 37, 71
gardens 16, 69–70, 87, 146
    garden furniture 76, 77
    moving plants 225–6
    newly built houses 34
    sheds and greenhouses 76
    trees, shrubs and plants 70, 76
gas appliances 66, 111, 189
gas supply 25, 188–9, 227
gas-fired heating systems 66

gazumping 93
    avoiding 94–5
gazundering 93
grants 49–50
    Common Parts Grant 50
    damp-proof courses 106
    Disabled Facilities Grant 50
    discretionary criteria 49
    heating installation and insulation
        105
    HMO Grant 50
    house improvement grants
        49–50
    House Renovation Grants
        49–50
    listed building repairs 51
    means-testing 50
green belt areas 12
ground rents 72
Guarantee Protection Insurance
    Company 88, 90, 106
guaranteed treatments 88–9, 106
    existing guarantees 90
guttering 69, 106

heating and insulation 65–6, 105
helpers, thank-you presents for 26
HMO Grant 50
home information pack 7, 85, 91,
    95, 144, 238
home security
    burglar alarm 109–10
    free advice 109–10
    locks 26, 230, 231
    unoccupied property 112
    while selling your house 160, 167
homefinders 44
house buyer's report 24, 85
house cleaning 110, 197
house hunting 30–71
    advertising for a house 48
    estate agents see estate agents
    expenses 25
    homefinders 44
    on the Internet 43
    methods and opportunities 40–1
    in a new area 43–5
    new houses 30–40

property shops/centres 41, 278–9
    relocation services 44–5
    viewing houses see viewing
        houses
house improvement grants
    Common Parts Grant 50
    Disabled Facilities Grant 50
    HMO grant 50
    House Renovation Grant 49
    listed buildings 51
house prices 6, 7
    inflation 7
House Renovation Grant 49
household appliances, moving
    219–21
    cooker 220
    dishwasher and washing machine
        220–1
    freezer 220
    fridge 220
    home computer 221
housing associations 54–5
Housing Corporation 54, 55
Housing Defects Act 1984 69

Index Map Search 23
inheritance tax 256
insurance
    buildings 15, 25, 172, 179–81, 192
    car 16, 182
    combined (buildings and
        contents) policies 181
    contents 16, 112, 172, 181, 205
    deposit guarantee scheme 240
    furniture storage 198–9
    life insurance 122
    mortgage indemnity guarantee
        24, 118, 138, 192
    mortgage payment protection
        insurance 139–40
    mortgage protection insurance
        121
    for periods of illness or
        unemployment 139–40
    professional indemnity insurance
        102
    removals 205–7
    unoccupied properties 112

Internet
  e-conveyancing 233, 236, 238, 259
  Internet searches 234
  mortgage information online 134
  product comparison sites 134, 135
  property websites 41, 43
ISA mortgages 120, 124

joint ownership 243
joint tenancy 243

'key worker' housing 8, 54
keys 167, 168, 175–6, 217–18, 228, 230
kitchen units and appliances
  built-in 77
  free-standing 76
kitchens 60–1, 62, 109, 150

lamp shades 76
land certificate 193
Land Charges Registry 250
Land Registry 193, 241, 242, 243, 245
Land Registry fees 23, 192, 243
Land Registry title search 242
Land Transaction Return 251
land use 73, 98
Law Society 22, 237, 254
leasehold properties 55, 72, 100
  ground rent 72
  maintenance charges 72, 118
  mortgages 118–19
  right to buy 55
licensed conveyancers 17–18, 236–40, 274
  complaints against 254–5
  fees 22, 250
life insurance 16
light bulbs 76
light fittings 76
listed buildings 51, 99–100
living rooms 60, 62
loans see bridging loans; mortgages
local authorities
  buying from 52–4

house improvement grants 49–50
  mortgages 129
  'right to buy' 52–3, 129
  searches 23, 173
lockout agreements 93
locks 26, 230, 231
loft conversions 99
loft insulation 66
London Plan 7–8

mail redirection service 25, 184
mains services see electricity supply; gas supply
maintenance, property 14, 16, 69
manholes 66
matrimonial disputes 239, 258
meter readings 188, 189, 227
mining activities 74
Ministry of Defence activities 74
mobile homes 55–6
mortgage 16, 21, 113–43, 170
  affordability 115, 137
  application refused 137
  applications 135–7
  arrangement fees 24, 138
  cashbacks 126–7
  conditions 136
  costs 138–41
  earnings multiples 113–14
  high lending fee 24, 118, 138
  illness and unemployment 139–40
  income for mortgage purposes 114
  information and advice 131–5
  insurance requirements 122, 137, 180
  interest rates 119–20, 125–6, 126
  joint mortgages 114
  on leasehold property 118–19
  loan to value (LTV) 115–16, 118
  low offers 137
  maximum loan 113–14, 116
  mortgage certificate 135
  mortgage indemnity guarantee 24, 118, 138, 192
  mortgage intermediaries 130–1
  mortgage payment protection insurance 139–40

mortgage protection insurance 121
negative equity 142–3, 252
newly built houses 139
non–status mortgage 135
online information 134
paying off 174–5
payment difficulties/arrears 117, 142–3
percentage of price loaned 115–16, 137
redemption penalties 22–3, 116, 125, 175
regulation of mortgage advice 133–4
released in instalments 39, 139
retentions 84, 137, 138
Scotland 280–1, 285–6
and the self-employed 114–15, 130, 135
shopping around for 128–31
Social Security benefits and 140–1
term of the loan 119
through estate agents 131
top-up loan 24, 138
unmarried couples 114
valuation for mortgage purposes 24, 83–4, 136, 168
Mortgage Code of Practice 131, 132, 133, 134, 142
mortgage lenders 7
  approval for structural alterations 100
  banks 129
  builders 130
  building societies 129
  centralised lenders 130
  direct lenders 129
  employers 129–30
  finance houses and credit companies 130
  insurance companies 129
  legal fees 24, 138, 192, 259
  local authorities 129
  private lenders 130
  and repossessed houses 57
  responsible lending 116–17

mortgage types
  base rate trackers 126
  capped rate deals 126, 138
  discounted-rate mortgages 22, 125–6, 127
  endowment mortgages 122–3
  fixed-rate mortgages 22, 119–20, 125, 127, 138
  flexible mortgages 127–8
  interest-only mortgages 120, 121–4
  ISA mortgages 120, 124
  mix-and-match deals 127
  penalty-free deals 127
  pension mortgages 123–4
  repayment mortgages 120–1, 124
  self-certification mortgage 115, 130
mortgagee 113
mortgagor 113
moveables (Scotland) 75
moving
  effect on lifestyle and outgoings 15–16
  expenses checklist 28–9
  help with expenses 26–7
  organised approach to 18–19
  paperwork, organising 18, 231
  reasons for 10–14
  timetable and checklist 193–5
  to the country 11–13
  to larger accommodation 14–15
  to a town or city 13–14
moving day 226–8
  at the new home 228–9
  cash supply 227
  final checks 227
  handover of keys 228
  last-minute jobs 226
  removal firm 227–9
  scale plans of new rooms 211
moving in
  first day 228–9
  home security 230–1
  placing furniture 228–9
  safety checklist 231
moving out 196–228
  with children 219, 221, 223

d-i-y removals 200, 207–10
keys, sorting and labelling
217–18
long-distance removals 196–7
packing 214–17
pets 223–5
preliminary sorting 211
preparations 211–28
putting furniture into store
197–9
removal firms 200–7
survival kit 221, 222, 226
unwanted possessions 211–14
weekday, choice of 196
multiple occupation, houses in 50

National Debtline 142
National Federation of Builders
(NFB) 103
National Homelink Service 43–4
National Land Information Service
(NLIS) 234, 238
negative equity 142–3, 252
neighbours 16, 63–4
newly built houses 30–40
advantages/disadvantages 33–4
builder bankruptcy 31, 34, 37
completion date 34, 40, 197
conveyancing 241
defects 31, 32, 89–90, 254
deposits 31, 33
drains 37
drawings and site plans 36
estate roads 34, 37
gardens 34
incentives to buy 38–9
legal completion 40
'long stop' completion date 34
looking for 34–6, 40–8
mains supplies 188
monitoring progress 38, 39–40
mortgages on 30, 33, 34, 37, 39,
139
NHBC (National House Building
Council) Buildmark Warranty
31, 33, 89–90, 254
part-exchange schemes 38
particulars and specifications 36–7

points to look for 36–7
prices 38
self-build projects 31
show houses 36
stage payments 34, 39
supervision of the works 33
timber frame houses 35–6
varying the features 33, 36
Zurich Insurance Building
Warranty 32, 33, 90, 254
newspaper advertising 35, 48,
155–6, 212, 278
NHBC (National House Building
Council) 30–2, 69
NHBC (National House Building
Council) Buildmark Scheme 31,
33, 89–90, 254

offer, making an 80–4
bargaining factors 81
contract race 10, 57, 92–3
gazumping/gazundering 93–5
pre-offer checks and
investigations 72–80
the price 81–2
process 91–2
subject to contract and survey
80–1, 91, 92
oil-fired heating systems 65
old houses
ancient or unusual properties
51–2
house improvement grants 49–50
listed buildings consent 51
listed buildings and conservation
areas 51
renovation 49–52
see also building work
'o.n.o' 46
open-plan houses 59
outhouses and greenhouses 70, 76

packing 214–17
by removal firm 202, 205, 206
labelling containers 217
lifting and carrying 215–16
packing containers 203, 216
paperwork, organising 18

parking restrictions 71
part-exchange schemes 38
particulars 45–7, 75, 151–3
    misrepresentation 46, 151, 153
    photographs 152–3
party walls 64
pension mortgages 123–4
pets, moving 26, 223–5
    caged birds 224–5
    cats 224
    dogs 223–4
    fish 225
    small pets 225
piano, moving 203
pipework 69
planning permission 49, 50–1, 73,
    97–100
planning zones 74
playgroups and nurseries 187
plumbing 26, 87, 108
pointing 68, 106
pre-contract deposit agreements
    94
prefabricated reinforced concrete
    (PRC) houses 69
preliminary enquiries 248
professional indemnity insurance
    102
property information form 247
Property Misdescriptions Act 1991
    46
property shops/centres 41, 278–9
public sector workers, housing and
    8
pubs, redundant 52

railway property, redundant 52
redecoration 67, 110, 147
registered land 241–3, 245, 246,
    250, 264
registered social landlords see
    housing associations
relocation services 44–5
removal firms
    access problems 204
    arranging date with 196, 197, 205
    charges 25, 201
    claims against 230

discharge document 229
estimates 200–1, 204
insurance for the move 205–7
long-distance removals 196–7
moving day 227–9
packing service 202, 205, 206
payment terms 205
range of services 202
removal men 205, 229
special handling and packing
    procedures 202–4
terms and conditions 204–5
tipping 229
travel boxes 203, 216
removals see moving day; moving in;
    moving out; removal firms;
    removals (d-i-y)
removals (d-i-y) 200, 207–10
    advantages/disadvantages 200,
        207
    costs 209–10
    loading the van 210
    van hire 208–10
    van plus driver hire 208
rendering 69
repayment mortgages 120–1, 124
repossession 141–2
    avoiding 142
    repossessed houses, buying 56–7
residents' parking schemes 71
retired and elderly people 11, 12,
    13, 15
'right to buy' 52–3, 129
    resales 53
    right to buy companies 53–4
rights of way 73, 239
rising damp 90
roads
    estate roads 37
    improvement proposals 74
    private roads 72
    traffic noise and inconvenience
        64–5
roofs 68, 87
    flat roofs 68
    repairs 68, 106
Royal Institute of British Architects
    (RIBA) 101

Royal Institute of Chartered
    Surveyors (RICS) 85, 102, 162
Royal Town Planning Institute
    (RTPI) 98
rubbish disposal 26, 213–14

satellite dishes 77
savings and investments 21
schoolhouses 52
schools 186–7
Scotland 274–93
    building regulations 99
    burdens 275–6
    buying a house 277–88
    co-owners 285
    consent to sale 288–9
    costs of buying and selling 286–7,
        289, 290
    date of entry 282–3
    estate agents 279–80, 290
    feudal tenure 275, 276
    feuduties 275
    feuing conditions 275
    flats 276
    house hunting 278–80
    insurance 284–5
    items included in price 283
    local authority searches 23
    missives 284–5, 292–3
    mortgages 280–1, 285–6
    offers to buy 282–3, 291–2
    property prices 274
    selling your house 288–93
    solicitors 274, 276–7, 286–7, 289
    succession (inheritance law)
        287–8
    surveys 281–2
    title 285
    upset price 277, 282
searches 23–4, 173, 247, 250
second-hand shops and dealers
    212–13
self-employed people and mortgages
    114–15, 130, 135
seller's market 19, 41
sellers' pack 144
selling your house 144–76
    advertising 153–7

agreeing terms 172
answering enquiries 158–9
bargaining 149–50, 171–2
buyers, assessing 170–1
chain-linking schemes 174
contract race 92–3, 174
costs 22–3
empty house 168–9
fixtures and fittings 150
handover of keys 175–6
information kit 159
items included in sale 150
maintaining insurance on 175,
    179, 180
misrepresentation 151, 153
offers 169–70, 173
paying off the mortgage 174–5
preparing the house for sale
    145–8
price 148–9, 150
sale by auction 270–3
sale by tender 270
sale negotiations 169–76
sale particulars 45–7, 75, 151–3
in Scotland 288–93
security factors 160, 167
sellers' pack 144
surveys 168
through an estate agent 144,
    161–9, 173–4
'under offer' 92, 174
viewers 159–61, 167
without an agent 144, 148–61,
    169–70
see also conveyancing
septic tanks and cesspools 66, 159
settlement (structural) 67, 68
shelving 76
show houses 36
sitting tenants 74–5
situation and location 62–4
skip hire 214
Social Security benefits and
    mortgage payments 140–1
Society for the Protection of
    Ancient Buildings (SPAB) 51–2,
    100
socket outlets 107, 190

sole agency 165–6
solicitors 17–18, 236–40
  acting for the developer 38–9,
    238
  acting for the lender 24, 138,
    192
  choosing 237–8
  complaints against 254–5
  completion statement 251
  fees 22, 24, 138, 250
  legal jargon 17–18
  and property centres 41, 155,
    278–9
  Scotland 274, 276–7, 286–7,
    289
  working with 239–40
solid fuel heating systems 65
specialist treatments 88–9
staircases 61
stamp duty land tax 23, 82, 192
  exemption 23, 82
Starter Home Initiative (SHI) 54
storage space 60
storing furniture 197–9
  container storage 198
  costs 197–8
  getting goods out 199
  insurance cover 198–9
  inventories 198, 199
  loose storage 198
  self-access facilities 199
stress of moving house 9
structural condition 66–9
  ceilings 67
  doors and windows 69, 87
  roof 68, 87
  seller's obligations to disclose 67
  structural surveys 24–5, 84, 85–9,
    168
  walls 67, 68–9, 87
  woodwork and floors 67–8, 87
subject to contract 80–1
surveyors 171
  building surveyors 100–1, 102
  compulsory arbitration scheme
    89–90
  preparing the house for 168
  professional associations 85

suing for negligence 89
surveys 84–9
  costs 24–5, 86
  and the home information pack
    85
  house buyer's report 24, 85
  reports 87–8
  Scotland 281–2
  specialist tests 25, 88–9
  structural surveys 24–5, 84, 85–9,
    168
  valuation for mortgage purposes
    24, 83–4, 136, 168

tax
  capital gains tax (CGT) 255–6
  inheritance tax 256
tea chests 203, 216
telegraphic transfer 193
telephone 109, 187–8
  extra sockets 109
  giving up your existing telephone
    187–8
  new installation 25, 188
  taking over an existing line 25,
    188
telephone bills 16
  outgoing calls barred 112
television aerials 66, 77, 184
television hire 183
television licences 184
tenancy in common 243
tenanted property 74–5
tender, sale by 270
thatched houses 15
'tied' accommodation 11
timber-frame houses 35–6, 96
timing the operation 18–19
title deeds 193
tool kit, emergency 219
top-up loans 24, 138
towns and cities, moving to 13–14
traffic noise and inconvenience 64–5
TransAction Protocol 77, 175, 179,
  244, 246, 247
transfer document 250
tree preservation orders 70
tree roots 70

'under offer' 92, 174
under-bidders 95–6
unlicensed conveyancers 258
unoccupied properties *see* empty
    houses
unregistered land 193, 243, 246,
    250
unwanted possessions 211–14
    advertising for sale 212
    auction sales 212
    charity shops and jumble sales
        213
    rubbish, disposal of 213–14
    second-hand shops and dealers
        212–13
    selling to new owner 211
utility rooms 61

vacant possession 74–5
valuable items 219
valuations
    by the estate agent 149, 164
    fees 24, 83
    low valuations 83–4
    for mortgage purposes 24, 83–4,
        136, 168
video film of your home 157–8
viewing houses 57–71, 159–61, 167
    accommodation and layout 60–2
    appointments 57–8
    checklist 58

first viewing 58–9
garaging 71
gardens 63, 69–70
heating and other services 65–6
neighbours 63–4
points to consider 59–60
potential problems, identifying
    64–5
situation and location 62–4
structural condition 66–9

walls
    boundary walls 70, 244–5
    external 68–9, 87
    internal 67, 87
    party walls 64
    wall ties 89
warehouses 52
washing machines 220–1
Water Regulations 108
water searches 247–8
water and sewerage charges 16, 74,
    182
water supply 66
waterproofing contractors 89
wills 255
woodwork 67, 87
woodworm 88, 89, 90, 106

Zurich Insurance Building Warranty
    32, 90, 254